Does Aid Work in India?

Does Aid Work in India?

A country study of the impact of official development assistance

Michael Lipton
and
John Toye

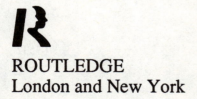

ROUTLEDGE
London and New York

First published 1990
by Routledge
11 New Fetter Lane, London EC4P 4EE
29 West 35th Street, New York, NY 10001

Typeset by LaserScript Limited, Mitcham, Surrey
Printed and bound in Great Britain by
MacKays of Chatham PLC, Chatham, Kent

British Library Cataloguing in Publication Data

Lipton, Michael, *1937–*
    Does aid work in India? : a country study of the impact of official
    development assistance
    1. India (Republic). Economic development. Foreign assistance
    I. Title II. Toye, John, *1942–*
    338.91'0954

    ISBN 0-415-01096-9

Library of Congress Cataloging in Publication Data

Lipton, Michael.
    Does aid work in India? : a country study of the impact of official
    development assistance / Michael Lipton and John Toye.
    p. cm.
    Includes index.
    ISBN 0-415-01096-9
    1. Economic assistance—India—Evaluation. I. Toye, J.F.J.
    II. Does aid work? III. Title.
    HC435.2L58 1989
    338.91'0954—dc19

                                        89-3532
                                        CIP

Contents

Tables

Preface

Since 1974, the World Bank and the International Monetary Fund have had a joint committee, called informally the Development Committee, which advises both institutions on the broad issues involved with resource transfers to developing countries. In 1982, the Bank/Fund Development Committee appointed a Task Force on Concessional Flows, whose membership consisted of nine representatives of developed countries and nine from developing countries. Their task was to report on 'problems affecting the volume and quality and effective use of concessional flows of financial aid both in the shorter and in the longer term'.

As a result of the activities of the Development Committee's Task Force, several documents have already been published. On behalf of the Development Committee, in December 1985 the World Bank issued the Report of the Task Force as Development Committee Pamphlet No.7 whose twenty-six pages provide the essential findings in a form suitable for widespread dissemination. The Bank also prepared a companion volume of 135 pages (Development Committee Pamphlet No.8) composed of supporting materials which help to explain and substantiate the essential findings of the Report.

So far so good. In carrying out its remit, the Task Force also engaged a group of twenty-three consultants, headed by Professor Robert Cassen then of IDS, Sussex, but now Director of Queen Elizabeth House, Oxford. The work of the Task Force's consultants under Robert Cassen, was published in 1986 by the Clarendon Press as *Does Aid Work? Report to an Intergovernmental Task Force* by Robert Cassen and Associates. *Does Aid Work?* was based on, among other things, a set of seven country case studies: Bangladesh, Colombia, India, Kenya, Malawi, Mali and South Korea.

The present authors were among the consultants to the Task Force and co-authored the country case study of India. This was a two- volume mimeograph document which is cited in *Does Aid Work?* as 'Lipton, M. and J. Toye with R.H. Cassen, 1984, *Aid Effectiveness: India*'. This

viii

document is the starting point of the present book. Since the general conclusions which emerge from the Cassen volume in part rest on the findings of the country case studies, and since at present none of these is available except in very limited quantities and impermanent form, it seemed to us desirable at least to publish the India study.

Since it was completed in 1984, it needed up-dating and revision. This task took us longer than we had initially expected. One reason was that the aid debate has dramatically revived since 1984, with important contributions such as Roger Riddell's *Foreign Aid Reconsidered* (London, James Currey) and Paul Mosley's *Overseas Aid: Its Defence and Reform* (Brighton, Wheatsheaf) making their appearance, as well as much specific material on aid to India. Another reason is the usual one of a variety of competing projects and activities to which both authors were committed. The effect is cumulative: the longer the delay, the more radical are the revisions which are required by unfolding events. Even now, we do not claim that we have incorporated everything of relevance to our subject which has appeared since 1984, although we have looked at a great deal of new material.

The division of labour has been that Michael Lipton originally wrote Chapters 2, 3, and 5 and John Toye wrote Chapters 1, 4, 6, and 7. However, the end product is much more of a joint effort than such a split would imply. Each author read and commented extensively on the other's chapters through several drafts, and we have both tried to follow a principle of excluding statements with which our co-author strongly disagreed. No doubt we have not achieved a uniform style of presentation, nor is each author equally knowledgeable on all topics covered by the book. But it does represent a consensus between us on what might be sensibly concluded about the impact of aid on India.

In writing this book, many debts have been incurred, which it is a pleasure now to acknowledge publicly. Our first debt is to Robert Cassen for interesting us in this project and for co-ordinating the work on the original consultants' report *Aid-Effectiveness: India*. Robert Cassen also contributed an 'Overview' to the original report which is not reproduced in this book although it served a valuable integrating purpose at the stage before the authors had had time to develop the joint approach mentioned above. During the preparation of the original report, we benefited from many interviews and conversations with officials of donor governments, aid agencies and international financial institutions, as well as with past and present representatives of the Government of India. We have followed a rule of preserving the anonymity of our informants unless they have already put their views in the public domain. We are extremely grateful for all the assistance generously given to us by these informants.

In the process of revision, we have drawn on the work of several research assistants, Olive Hamilton, Jonathon Perraton and Herman Prieto, all of whom discharged their tasks with accuracy , thoroughness, and speed, much to their credit. Many hands have helped in word-processing. Michael Lipton wished to salute the prodigious efforts of Ann Watson and John Toye is grateful to Hazel Lewis, Jo Stannard, Marion Huxley, Rosalyn Skilton, and Francine Spencer for their invaluable contributions to the production of the final typescript.

Brighton   Michael Lipton
May 1988   John Toye

Glossary

AICC	All India Congress Committee
ARDC	Agricultural Refinance and Development Corporation
ATP	Aid and Trade Provision (UK)
BDO	block development officers
BMWZ	Bundesministerium für Wirtschaftliche Zusammenarbeit (German aid ministry)
CD	community development
CDC	Commonwealth Development Corporation (UK)
CENTO	Central Treaty Organization
CGIAR	Consultative Group for International Agricultural Research
DAC	Development Assistance Committee (OECD)
DEA	Department of Economic Affairs (GoI)
DPAPs	drought prone area programmes
EFF	extended financing facility (IMF)
EGS	employment guarantee scheme
EROR	economic rate of return
EV	evaluation report (UK)
FAO	Food and Agriculture Organization (UN)
FY	financial year
GoI	Government of India
HYVs	high-yielding varieties (of cereals)
IADP	Intensive Agricultural District Programme
IAS	Indian Administrative Service
IBRD	International Bank for Reconstruction and Development ('Hard' loan section of World Bank)
ICB	international competitive bidding
ICICI	Industrial Credit and Investment Corporation of India
ICOR	incremental capital-output ratio
IDA	International Development Agency ('Soft' loan section of World Bank)
IDS	Institute of Development Studies (Brighton)
IEL	Indian Explosives Ltd
IFAD	International Fund for Agricultural Development (UNO)
IFFCO	Indian Farmers' Fertilizer Company

Glossary

IFPRI	International Food Policy Research Institute (Washington DC)
IFS	Indian Forestry Service
IIT	Indian Institutes of Technology
IMDP	Indian Manpower Programme
IRDP	Integrated Rural Development Programme
ISICO	Iron and Steel Company of India
ITDG	Intermediate Technology Development Group
LDB	land development bank
LDCs	less developed countries
LICs	low-income countries
MLD	medium- and long-term debt
MRTP	Monopolies and Restrictive Trade Practices Act (India)
NABARD	National Bank for Agriculture and Rural Development (formerly ARDC) (India)
NDDB	National Dairy Development Board (India)
NGO	non-governmental organizations
ODA/ODM	Overseas Development Administration (formerly Ministry), UK
OECD	Organization for Economic Cooperation and Development
OED	Operations Evaluation Department (World Bank)
OF	Operation Flood (EEC Indian Dairy aid project)
OOF	other official flows
PCRs	project completion reports (of World Bank)
PFI	private foreign investment
PLDB	primary land development bank
PPAs	project performance audits (of World Bank)
RBI	Reserve Bank of India
RTA	Retrospective Terms Adjustment (UK)
SAL	structural adjustment loan (World Bank)
SF	school feeding
SIDA	Swedish International Development Agency
SNAB	Swedish National Audit Bureau
SROR	social rate of return
SSA	sub-Saharan Africa
STEPs	short-term expert pools
T and V	training and visit (system of agricultural extension)
TC	technical co-operation
TISCO	Tata Iron and Steel Company (India)
USAID	US Agency for International Development
VLW	village level workers
WFP	World Food Programme

Introduction

In the 1980s, official development assistance, or 'aid' for short, has been in the doldrums. After a generation of aid-giving, politicians and the public in donor countries had become somewhat weary with it, and cynical about what aid had achieved, or could achieve. Enthusiasm for aid-giving had flagged, and the voices of those who opposed the whole enterprise – from left and right of the political spectrum, but mainly from the right – became increasingly influential. Giving foreign exchange to the governments of poor countries where economic infrastructure is weak and public administration is fragile is self-evidently a risky undertaking. It was therefore not a task of great difficulty to find colourful evidence of waste, corruption, and disastrous outcomes on at least some aid projects, nor to discover contradictions or anomalies in the aid policies of donors which could serve as grist to the anti-aid mill.

Aid-weariness also came at a convenient time for the donors. The recession of the early 1980s was accompanied by powerful pressures to cut public spending and the aid budget was often a soft target for cuts. The first half of the 1980s witnessed a steady decline in the real value of the UK's aid programme. But a recession is an extraordinarily bad time, from the point of view of poor countries in receipt of aid, for aid flows to fall. This simply adds to the misery caused by dramatic falls in the prices of primary commodity exports, and the return to positive real interest rates on debt.

The question of the effectiveness of aid arose out of this contradiction. It was hoped either that developing countries could be shown a way to get more benefits from less aid, or that by shifting aid money towards more effective uses, the political support for aid in developed countries could be revived and aid-cynicism dispelled.

India was in many ways an obvious choice of country to turn to, in order to examine in empirical depth the question of aid-effectiveness. India had a long history of receiving aid, which had progressed through a number of quite distinct phases. India had also been in receipt of large absolute amounts of aid (although, because of her huge population,

1

these translated to small amounts per head). India had been singled out in the debate on development strategy as the archetype of the country which had adopted the wrong development strategy – rapid industrialization on the basis of import substitution: this raised the question of the role of aid in the formation of economic policy and development strategy. India also appeared likely to suffer from a redistribution of aid towards sub-Saharan Africa: this raised the questions of whether India would not then be 'punished' by the aid donors for a relatively good aid performance and whether elements of India's experiences with aid management could not be transferred to the African situation, so that an India-to-Africa redistribution of aid did not result in a lowering of its overall effectiveness.

This then is the general background to the writing of this book, and some indication of the kind of questions which it addressed. The general conclusions which the original study arrived at are set out in the Appendix, and they remain broadly the conclusions which the book in its revised form points to.

Two more preliminary remarks are necessary. One is to emphasize the limits of the scope of this enquiry, which confines itself to 'official development assistance'. It does not encompass non-governmental flows of aid to India, through Oxfam, Save the Children Fund and the many, many other charities and agencies which operate there. Within official aid, we also say very little about the smallish amounts given for immediate disaster relief. The other remark is to point to a limitation of form. We have adhered closely to the format of Cassen's *Does Aid Work?* This has led us to exclude some questions which could be discussed under our general title. But it should be helpful to those who want to see clearly how much of the findings of the Cassen study rely on our interpretation of the Indian experience of aid.

Chapter 1

India's Aid Resources in Macroeconomic Context

Introduction

India is a very big country, with 765 million people in 1985 inhabiting an area of over three million square kilometres - 233 persons per square kilometre, compared with 52 for all developing countries and only 19 for sub-Saharan Africa (World Bank, 1987, 202). The sheer size of India has conditioned the relationship between aid resources and the Indian economy as a whole. In absolute terms, India has always been one of the three largest recipients of net economic aid.[1] From the major western donors in OECD – who in 1985 disbursed US$29.4bn of net economic aid to developing countries (bilaterally and via multilateral agencies), of which US$25.6bn could be clearly allocated to particular countries – India received US$1.5bn in 1985, as against US$1.8bn for Egypt (population fifty million) and US$2.0 billion for Israel (population four million). Net aid from other donors in 1985 provided a further US$7.6bn for developing countries, but almost nothing for India, since a net inflow of about US$100m from Comecon was offset by a US$91m net outflow to OPEC (i.e. capital repayments of past aid loans outweighed new aid receipts) (World Bank, 1987, 242–5; OECD, 1986, 77–82, 258, 284). These same figures show that aid donors have never been willing to provide the massive absolute sums of money required to render India's aid, per person or as a proportion of GNP, comparable with that of other low income countries. In 1985 aid constituted 0.7 per cent of India's GNP as compared with 7.8 per cent for low-income countries other than India and China; per capita aid was US$1.9 for India compared with US$16.2 for other low-income countries excluding China (World Bank, 1987, 244). This 'large-country effect' results partly from the geo-political motivation behind aid-giving. Most donors wish to appear generous in as many different countries as possible; and can win friends in twenty medium-sized poor countries, each with 35–40million people, by economizing on aid to one large country like India.

Apart from this 'large-country effect', the amount of aid that India has received has depended on the state of its bilateral relations with

3

major donors. Among western donors, which have provided the bulk of aid to India, India's relations with the United States – at least from 1960 to 1972 – were a major determinant of the size of her aid flows (Chapter 3). India's aid flows remain small compared with those of neighbouring (and similarly poor) Pakistan, reflecting both India's greater size and its more distanced, and at times turbulent political relations with the United States.

Thus, in a macroeconomic context, aid resources have always played a much smaller part in India than in Asian countries like Korea and Taiwan in the 1950s and 1960s, or in most African countries in the 1970s and early 1980s.[2] Yet the macroeconomic effects of aid on India have not been negligible. To explain these effects some preliminary problems have to be tackled.

Solutions must be found for various problems of measurement of aid resource flows;

The size of these flows over time to India must then be presented, so that trends, fluctuations and turning points can be identified;

Aid resources must then be seen relative to key macroeconomic variables such as imports, government expenditure categories, and domestic investment; such ratios provide indicators of the dynamic role of aid in financing development (its static contribution to potential welfare, in a given year, being crudely approximated by its ratio to GNP);

The econometric evidence on the link between aid resources and economic performance should be examined to see whether it suggests any conclusions on the nature of this link;

Any additional aspects of aid's contribution to the macroeconomic performance of India must be specified and evaluated.

The remainder of this chapter addresses each of these tasks and draws a set of conclusions on the impact of aid on India at the aggregate level. In the light of these conclusions, a final section also looks at one important question for future financial policy: should India continue to expand its borrowings from commercial banks and progressively reduce its absorption of concessional flows of aid?

Measurement of aid flows

International financial flows may be classified as follows:

Aid:
Multilateral aid
Bilateral aid

Other concessional finance:
Multilateral loans on 'hard' terms (IBRD and IMF loans)
Official export credits
Officially guaranteed suppliers' credits
Non-concessional finance
Loans from the Eurocurrency market
Other commercial bank lending

The definition of aid used here follows that of the OECD's Development Assistance Committee's definition of Official Development Assistance: i.e. official flows of finance for development purposes containing a grant element of at least 25 per cent. Among 'other concessional finance', multilateral loans contain a grant element of less than 25 per cent; official export credits and officially guaranteed suppliers' credits contain varying grant elements, which are offset by their being tied to specific sources at prices above the cheapest available on the world market – typically by about a fifth (Riddell, 1987, 209).

The giving of Western foreign aid to India follows a regular set of procedures. Donors meet together with Government of India officials at regular intervals, in a 'Consortium' organized by the World Bank, in order to discuss the current state of the Indian economy and the government's plans and projects for future development. There are four distinct stages in the aid process. First, at these meetings, the donors make 'pledges', that is, promises of amounts of aid to be given within a specified time period. Second, these pledges must be ratified in the donor countries. From this follows, thirdly, specific action by donors to make the resources available – the stage of aid authorization or 'commitment'. Not all available aid resources are used up straight away, however. Only when they are drawn down, to pay for components in an actual project or programme, do we reach the fourth stage: 'disbursement' or utilization. Aid flows through an invisible bureaucratic pipeline, part foreign and part national, from pledge to final utilization. This has a political pay-off for donors, incidentally. They can be thanked for the same unit of aid several times over as it makes its way along the invisible pipeline. However, the longer the gaps between stages the more the value of donors' commitments is eroded by inflation.

Flows of aid can be measured at a number of points in this pipeline. Both the OECD and the Indian Government publish figures for both aid authorizations and aid utilization. This book concentrates on utilizations; authorizations represent specific resources available from a donor but such commitments are not always embodied in formal agreements. Note that the ratio of authorization to utilization, in a sector or area, can measure the recipient government's progress in implementing aid-financed activities there; and declining or rising authorizations can show declining or rising concern, by one or all donors, for a particular country or sector. However, a historical study or a study from a macroeconomic perspective should focus on the actual transfer of resources: the aid utilization figures. Since much aid is in the form of loans, which entail repayment of principal and interest, it is helpful to show gross utilized aid alongside figures of debt service payments on concessional loans. Net aid is: gross utilized aid minus capital repayments of past aid loans; net transfers are: net aid minus interest payments on past aid loans. Such net calculations are feasible only for total aid to India, with which we are concerned here. It is not possible to show aid figures net of debt service payments at the sectoral level, only gross aid flows to a sector – because debt service repayments are a central government responsibility. Figures of gross and net utilized aid, and net transfers, to India are given in Table 1.1.

Size of aid flows to India

Absolute flows

The figures in Table 1.1 are given in Indian rupees. This does not indicate the changes due to aid in India's purchasing power over imports. Yet it is this purchasing power and its fluctuations which mainly interest us, if we want to know how much help the resources have been to the Indian economy. This is because, at least until the mid-1970s, the great bulk of aid resources were then spent on the purchase of imports. From the mid-1970s onwards, restrictions on using aid to meet locally incurred, rupee-denominated costs were somewhat relaxed, thus complicating the question of estimating the purchasing power of aid.

To estimate the changing impact of aid inflows on India's access, each year, to imported goods and services, we must adjust the rupee figures of aid to allow for:

(a) Changes in the exchange rate of the rupee;
(b) Differences in the inflation rate between India and the countries from which she imports, unless offset by exchange rate changes;
(c) Changes in the extent of aid-tying – i.e. restrictions on possible suppliers of the desired imports, which will alter the difference between the world price of the goods to be imported and the actual price that India has to pay.

As for (a), the rate of exchange between the rupee and foreign currencies has altered during the thirty-year period with which we are concerned. Until May 1966, a fixed rate of US$1 = R 4.76 was maintained. Then the rupee underwent a major devaluation to US$1 = R 7.50, which lasted until December 1971. At that point, the rupee was pegged to sterling and the nominal exchange rate remained constant until 1975, when the rupee was pegged to a basket of different foreign currencies important in India's pattern of trade, combined together by an unannounced weighting system. The margin of variation permitted around this peg was initially 2.5 per cent but this was widened to 5 per cent in January 1979 (Joshi and Little, 1986, 35).

As for (b), India's policy preference for maintaining a relatively fixed or only gradually changing nominal exchange rate (apart from the big devaluation of 1966) has meant that changes in its effective exchange rate, i.e. in the quantum of imports that can be purchased with one rupee, have depended largely on the differences between India's domestic inflation rate and the world rate of inflation. In 1973–83, India's inflation rate was lower than those of most export competitors and import suppliers. It was 7.7 per cent per year, compared with 13.8 per cent for other low-income countries (excluding China), 8.0 per cent for industrial market economies, and 29.3 per cent for middle-income countries (World Bank, 1985, 174). As a result, India's effective exchange rate fell by 23 per cent between 1974 and 1979, both stimulating exports and making imports much more costly in terms of rupees. Between 1979–83, moreover, the industrial market economies' inflation rate fell sharply, eroding India's export advantage and reducing the rupee cost of imports (Joshi and Little, 1986, 36).

As for (c), the third element which affects the purchasing power of aid resources is the stringency of donor restrictions on import procurement. Procurement-tying of aid raises the costs of associated imports because the aid recipient cannot shop around for the best buy but must purchase from the donor only. The effect on import prices – i.e. the cut in the value of aid – depends on the size, competitiveness and exchange-rate policy of the donor, but has been consistently estimated as averaging around 20 per cent (Bhagwati, 1970; Chaudhuri, 1978, 103). But the effects are hard to pin down. Table 1.2, which shows untied aid as a percentage of gross aid loans (but gives no indication of the extent of tying among grants), suggests that tying fell to historically low levels in the early and middle 1970s, but rose towards the end of the 1970s.

Taken together, these three influences on the purchasing power of aid make it very difficult to estimate the 'real value' to India of the nominal flows, or how much it changed over nearly thirty years of aid. We can, however, take into account exchange-rate fluctuation and express aid flows in US dollars (Table 1.3). These data for 1958–9 to 1971–2 (Chaudhuri, 1978)[3] indicate that, before the oil shock and floating

7

Table 1.1 External assistance to India 1966–85 (Rupees crores)[a]

	Loans	Grants	Total	Rupees	PL480/665 [b] Convertible	Gross aid	Debt service	Net aid transfer
To end Third Plan	2,388.7	336.9	2,725.6	1,403.2	–	4,128.8	685.8	3,443.0
1966–7	648.9	97.1	746.0	359.6	–	1,105.6	274.6	831.0
1967–8	759.2	60.7	819.9	310.9	30.8	1,161.6	333.0	828.6
1968–9	649.3	65.2	714.5	84.5	73.1	872.1	375.0	497.1
1969–70	628.6	26.1	654.7	107.5	62.0	824.2	412.5	411.7
1970–1	617.2	43.5	660.7	37.7	51.3	749.7	450.0	299.7
1971–2	642.6	50.5	693.1	8.8	103.1	805.0	479.3	325.7
1972–3	615.0	12.0	627.0	–	4.3	631.3	507.4	123.9
1973–4	987.9	20.7	1,008.6	–	–	1,008.6	595.8	412.8
1974–5	1,185.2	93.9	1,279.1	–	–	1,279.1	626.0	653.1
1975–6	1,429.1	283.3	1,712.4	–	92.3	1,804.7	686.9	1,117.8
1976–7	1,216.4	245.8	1,462.2	–	67.8	1,530.0	754.7	775.3
1977–8	877.2	260.6	1,137.8	–	21.9	1,159.7	820.7	339.0
1978–9	792.9	273.3	1,066.2	–	–	1,066.2	796.0	270.2
1979–80	927.8	304.4	1,232.2	–	–	1,232.2	800.7	431.5
1980–1	1,089.0	396.4	1,485.4	–	–	1,485.4	803.9	681.5

Year							
1981–2	1,142,4	350.6	1,493.0	—	—	1,493.0	849.1	643.9
1982–3	1,623.5	339.4	1,962.9	—	—	1,962.9	947.5	1,015.4
1983–4	1,478.5	303.4	1,781.9	—	—	1,781.9	1,032.5	749.4
1984–5	1,619.3	390.4	2,009.7	—	—	2,009.7	1,176.2	833.5
	21,318.7	3,954.2	25,272.9	2,312.2	506.6	28,091.7	13,407.6	14,684.1

Source Government of India, Economic Survey 1985–6, Table 7.1 (172) and Table 7.4 (179).

Notes a Conversions in rupees are at the pre-devaluation rate of exchange (US$1=R4.7619) up to the end of the Third Plan and at the post-devaluation rate of exchange (US$1=R7.50) for the subsequent years up to 1970–1. For the year 1971–2, pre-May 1971 exchange rates have been retained for conversion into rupees. For 1972–3, the rupee figures have been derived on the basis of the central rates which prevailed following the currency realignment of December 1971. From 1973–4, the quarterly average of the exchange rate of the rupee with individual donor currency has been applied to the corresponding quarterly data in respect of utilization for arriving at the equivalent rupee figure. For 1974–5, utilization figures have been worked out at current rates, which is the monthly average exchange rate of the rupee with individual donor currency. Utilization figures for 1975–6, 1976–7 and 1977–8 are based on actual daily rates of the rupee with the donor currency on the respective dates.

b PL480/665 is aid given by the USA under US Public Laws Nos 480 and 665. It has two different forms; one which generates counterpart funds in rupees; the other is 'convertible', and carries repayment obligations in hard currency.

c Crore = 10 million.

d Figures for external assistance are minus loans from the IBRD and IMF.

Table 1.2 Untied credits as a percentage of gross aid to India, 1965–82

To end Third Plan	33.4
1966–7	14.2
1967–8	18.9
1968–9	14.4
1969–70	19.9
1970–1	15.9
1971–2	18.5
1972–3	38.4
1973–4	42.0
1974–5	47.9
1975–6	45.4
1976–7	53.4
1977–8	13.6
1978–9	14.7
1979–80	13.8
1980–1	16.0
1981–2	13.4

Source Government of India, Economic Survey, 1982–3, Table 7.4
Note Figures recalculated net of IBRD loans.

Table 1.3 Average external assistance to India, 1958–72 (US$m)

	3-year average 1958–9 to 1961–2	5-year average 1961–2 to 1965–6	5-year average 1966–7 to 1970–1	1971–2
Gross aid	733	1,208	1,330	1,123
Debt service	73	232	492	626
Net aid	660	976	838	497

Source Chaudhuri (1978), Table 32, 99

exchange rates, net aid utilizations in current US dollars peaked during the Third Five Year Plan period (i.e. 1960–1 to 1965–6) and went into a marked decline thereafter.

Since the 1973 oil shock, roughly comparable data are available from the World Bank, which follows the OECD definition of aid. Table 1.4 shows India's loan disbursements and debt service repayments (of both principal and interest), distinguishing between concessional (i.e. 'aid') loans and non-concessional loans. Table 1.5 shows India's receipts of outright grants (also 'aid') by main donor source. The net transfer from the concessional loans is then aggregated with grants, where the netting off procedure does not apply, in Table 1.6. This indicates the aid transfers, in millions of current US dollars, for 1975–6 to 1985–6 – and confirms (together with Table 1.2) that, after the major peak in net aid

Table 1.4 India's loan disbursements and debt service, 1975–6 to 1985–6 (US$m)

Loan disbursements	75–6	76–7	77–8	78–9	79–80	80–1	81–2	82–3	83–4	84–5	85–6
Concessional	1,603	1,370	991	921	1,017	2,022	1,281	1,640	1,348	1,306	1,647
IDA	491	533	333	327	546	652	786	1,109	874	823	1,047
Bilateral loans	1,112	837	636	580	443	652	471	476	457	453	572
Multilateral loans			22	14	28	718	24	55	17	30	28
Non-concessional	200	168	266	254	265	462	739	775	1,189	1,546	1,804
IBRD	39	76	155	180	149	174	421	288	470	291	329
Bilateral loans	51	33	21	14	37	36	7	14	11	185	296
Commercial loans	110	59	90	60	79	252	311	473	708	1,070	1,179
Total publicly guaranteed	1,803	1,538	1,257	1,175	1,282	2,484	2,020	2,415	2,537	2,852	3,451
Private non-guaranteed	112	61	91	61	79	285	422	585	639	835	1,135
Total medium and long-term loans (excluding IMF)	1,915	1,599	1,348	1,236	1,361	2,769	2,442	3,000	3,176	3,687	4,586
Debt service payments											
Concessional	494	502	550	675	738	758	753	756	751	676	750
IDA	24	30	35	38	43	50	60	72	91	109	124
Bilateral loans	470	472	515	637	695	707	689	679	653	559	592
Multilateral loans						1	4	5	7	8	34
Non-concessional	258	255	260	285	274	279	257	379	528	782	1,131
IBRD	90	88	107	127	130	141	138	176	244	274	325
Bilateral loans	92	81	76	62	51	48	35	29	24	34	66
Commercial loans	76	86	77	96	93	90	84	174	260	474	740
Total publicly guaranteed	752	757	810	960	1,012	1,037	1,010	1,135	1,279	1,458	1,881
Private non-guaranteed	78	81	80	95	93	121	122	355	461	533	918
Total medium and long-term loan (excluding IMF)	830	838	890	1,055	1,105	1,158	1,132	1,490	1,740	1,991	2,799

Source World Bank

Table 1.5 India's grant disbursements, 1975–6 to 1985–6 (US$m)

	1975–6	1976–7	1977–8	1978–9	1979–80	1980–1	1981–2	1982–3	1983–4	1984–5	1985–6
Bilateral consortium	413.1	394.8	406.4	506.9	632.0	632.0	464.4	448.9	403.8	399.7	397.8
Austria	0.7	–	–	–	–	–	–	–	–	–	–
Belgium	–	–	–	–	–	–	–	–	–	–	–
Canada	65.4	62.3	22.4	5.8	18.4	3.3	7.6	10.7	14.1	15.8	12.3
Denmark a	5.1	10.0	4.9	14.2	15.2	19.6	10.0	16.7	16.0	17.2	11.2
France	4.3	–	–	–	–	–	–	–	–	–	–
W. Germany	12.1	4.2	–	6.3	1.3	7.8	0.8	1.9	0.1	0.3	1.4
Italy a	–	–	–	–	–	–	–	0.4	0.2	4.2	5.9
Japan	–	–	–	–	27.2	35.7	5.2	14.7	9.7	13.6	11.8
Netherlands a	19.8	15.1	6.5	5.1	30.4	28.7	23.6	50.2	29.8	36.8	40.9
Norway a	9.0	9.6	15.2	21.2	22.1	22.4	19.7	20.9	20.4	19.9	23.0
Sweden b	58.2	41.9	67.3	57.0	52.6	64.9	49.1	56.9	53.1	35.1	43.0
Switzerland a	2.9	2.5	2.9	6.0	16.8	17.1	5.3	18.8	22.3	21.7	11.9
UK	81.4	120.9	175.6	258.3	282.7	307.7	199.1	164.5	128.4	132.5	151.9
USA	154.3	128.2	111.1	133.1	165.3	124.9	143.9	93.2	109.7	102.6	84.4
Multilateral consortium	112.9	60.0	117.8	135.3	164.2	184.3	206.0	233.0	182.1	143.6	166.4
EEC a	52.9	60.0	32.8	21.3	54.4	80.9	94.0	122.6	65.7	42.1	58.4
UN a	60.0	–	85.0	114.0	109.8	103.4	112.0	110.4	116.4	101.5	108.0
IFAD	–	–	–	–	–	–	–	–	–	–	–
Total consortium	526.0	454.8	524.2	642.3	796.3	816.3	670.4	681.9	585.9	543.3	564.2
Others	15.3	7.5	–	–	1.4	5.7	–	–	–	–	–
Grand total	541.3	462.3	524.2	642.3	797.7	822.0	670.4	681.9	585.9	543.3	564.2

Source World Bank
Notes
a Relates to calender years; e.g. the figures for 1980–1 relate to calender year 1980, and so on.
b Relates to the year July–June; e.g. the figures for 1980–1 relates to period July 1980–June 1981, and so on.

Table 1.6 India's net transfer of concessional finance, 1975–6 to 1985–6 (US$m)

	1975–6	1976–7	1977–8	1978–9	1979–80	1980–1	1981–2	1982–3	1983–4	1984–5	1985–6
Concessional loan disbursements	1,603	1,370	991	921	1,017	2,022	1,281	1,640	1,348	1,306	1,647
of which debt service	494	502	550	675	738	758	753	756	751	676	750
Net position on loans	1,109	868	441	246	273	1,264	528	884	597	630	897
Total grant disbursement	541	462	524	642	798	822	670	682	586	543	564
Net position on loans and grants	1,650	1,330	965	888	1,071	2,086	1,198	1,566	1,183	1,173	1,461

Source Tables 1.3 and 1.4

flows during the Third Five Year Plan, two further peaks occurred. One was during the 1975–6 'Emergency', the other in 1980–1. Both, as we shall see, were reflected in 'real' peaks, though more modestly.

The 'Emergency' aid peak (1975–7) was a lagged response to India's severe balance-of-payments difficulties in 1972–5.[4] It was not a response of western aid donors to the declaration of a State of Emergency in India in mid-1975, as some people suspected at the time. The Aid-India Consortium did meet very soon after the Emergency was declared, and the UK raised the question of whether aid flows should be cut in response to the political changes of June 1975, but this suggestion was not acted on.

The second minor peak of the early 1980s in aid transfers to India was a response to the serious deterioration of India's economic performance in 1979–80.[5] After the return to power of a Congress (I) government in 1980, it was decided both to go to the IMF for a large medium-term loan, and to seek greater aid financing. In November 1981, a standby agreement was reached with the IMF for aid credits totalling US$5.8bn over the years 1981–2 to 1984–5. In the end only 534 rupees crores (about US$650m) were actually utilized (Government of India *Economic Survey*, 1986, 175).[6] Simultaneously, aid loans from IDA and other multilateral sources were increased from 1980–1, and sustained through 1981–2 and 1982–3. At this point, India turned, much more than ever before, toward commercial loans for balance-of-payments support.

How much could India purchase with these aid flows of nominal dollars? That depended on the fluctuating purchasing power of the dollar. The current-dollar figures should ideally be deflated by dividing, in each year, the ratio of a dollar price index of Indian imports in that year to the same price index in the base year.[7] This would give the trend in the purchasing power of aid to India. Not much work has been done in this area. Table 1.7 lists OECD estimates of net aid flows (i.e. net only of capital repaid) to India, including estimates for flows from OPEC and Comecon countries. These net flows are deflated by the US producer price index as a proxy for import inflation facing India. These figures suggest that the nominal aid peaks discussed above were reflected in real aid peaks around 1974–6 and 1980, the latter peak being smaller and shorter. Another estimate (Rubin, 1982) for real non-food aid produced broadly similar results. He took his calculations back to 1950, and concluded that in real terms 1963–6 experienced the highest ever aid inflows.

Table 1.7 Official development assistance disbursements to India, 1971–85 (US $m)

	Gross ODA	Nett ODA	Net ODA (1970 US$m)
1971	1,083.1	1,002.8	972.1
1972	728.6	614.0	569.6
1973	1,009.0	779.5	638.2
1974	1,568.4	1,365.6	941.7
1975	2,004.6	1,708.4	1,078.6
1976	2,056.8	1,820.6	1,098.8
1977	1,348.9	1,078.3	613.0
1978	1,749.8	1,338.6	796.2
1979	1,755.0	1,370.1	643.6
1980	2,664.0	2,256.2	927.3
1981	2,389.0	1,920.4	722.8
1982	2,022.0	1,545.1	570.1
1983	2,203.2	1,742.8	635.0
1984	2,022.1	1,542.1	548.7
1985	1,946.0	1,469.7	525.3

Source OECD, *Geographical Distribution of Financial Flows to Developing Countries: Disbursements and Commitments*, 1971–7, 1978–81, 1982–5.
Note Calculated using US producer price index as deflator.

Aid relative to macroeconomic categories

Although, for reasons already explained, India receives only small amounts of aid relative to its area and its population, the macroeconomic impact may still be significant. Aid can be seen as supplementing a constrained supply of foreign exchange and/or adding to total domestic investment. In this connection, one would be interested in the size of aid relative to the level of imports and the balance of payments and/or domestic savings and investment.

The role of aid in permitting India to grow relatively unconstrained by deficits on the balance of payments in the years 1956–70 is hinted at in Table 1.8 (derived from Goldsmith, 1983). This shows that, between 1956 and 1970, India's deficit on trade in goods and services (falling from three to two per cent of GNP) was largely financed by a surplus of just less than two per cent of GNP on central government capital account. This surplus does not, of course, include only aid inflows; some of it comprises non-concessional borrowing by the central government.

However, this was relatively small; so the surplus on 'capital, central' is not merely a maximum estimate, but in fact a good proxy, for the true contribution of net aid to India's balance of payments.

Table 1.8 India's balance of payments 1948–70 (as a percentage of GNP)

	1948–50	1951–5	1956–60	1961–5	1966–70
Commodity trade	–1.33	–1.04	–2.52	–1.81	–0.97
Imports [a]		8.32	9.29	7.21	6.61
Services	0.08	0.37	–0.43	–0.79	–0.89
Transfers, private	0.32	0.38	0.38	0.16	0.35
Transfers, government	0.00	0.21	0.23	0.28	0.13
Capital, private	–0.21	–0.04	0.07	0.02	–0.02
Capital, central	–1.03	0.08	1.43	1.96	1.86
Monetary authorities	2.13	0.25	0.98	0.19	–0.33
Miscellaneous [b]	–	–	0.03	0.00	0.01
Net errors and omissions	0.04	–0.21	–0.17	–0.06	–0.15

Source Goldsmith (1983), Table 3.16, 162
Notes
a Calculated from: United Nations, *Yearbook of National Accounts Statistics*, 1957–75; Government of India, *Economic Survey*, various issues
b 'Miscellaneous' includes deposit money banks and allocations of SDRs

In the second half of the 1960s, when aid inflows were at the height of their importance relative to key macroeconomic variables, aid was financing about a third of India's imports of goods and services. By the mid-1980s, the aid/imports ratio had fallen to 5 per cent (Table 1.9). The aid peak of 1975–6 financed less than 25 per cent of imports in that year, while the 1980–1 peak financed only 5 per cent. The falling aid/import ratio partly reflects the fact that imports rose from less than 7 per cent of GNP in the late 1960s to over 8 per cent in the late 1970s and over 10 per cent in the early 1980s (Tables 1.8, 1.10). By 1980–1, India had to face an import bill which suddenly had jumped by almost half while exports remained stagnant due to the rising real exchange rate. Aid was no longer available to India in sufficient quantities to cope with all her external finance requirements, and from this point both non-concessional public lending and commercial loans entered significantly for the first time into India's external financing package.

This picture is further illustrated by Table 1.10. This uses World Bank figures of India's balance of payments in a form which compares the situation in 1975–85 as closely as possible with Goldsmith's estimates in Table 1.8 for the period up to 1970. A strong positive factor in the balance of payments in the middle and late 1970s had been the inflow of private remittances from abroad. In 1975–80, current transfers to India (net of transfers out) exceeded one per cent of national income for the first time. This was partly as a result of increased labour migration to West Asia to supply labour shortages in new-rich OPEC countries, and partly a response to a government decision in November 1975 to allow non-resident Indians to open interest-bearing accounts of foreign exchange in India. These rapidly rising remittances tended to divert attention from the slowdown in export growth, and a sense of balance-of-payments security was built up as the foreign exchange reserves accumulated – from two months' worth of imports in 1974–5 to nine months' worth in 1978–9.

Table 1.9 Ratios of aid utilizations to imports in India, 1966–84

Year	Aid utilizations	Imports	Ratio
1966–7	831.0	2,194.5	37.9
1967–8	828.6	2,135.7	38.8
1968–9	497.1	1,858.4	26.7
1969–70	411.7	1,677.1	24.5
1970–1	299.7	1,770.3	16.9
1971–2	325.7	2,002.2	16.3
1972–3	123.9	2,146.6	5.8
1973–4	412.8	2,729.3	15.1
1974–5	653.1	4,156.9	15.7
1975–6	1,117.8	4,744.1	23.6
1976–7	775.3	4,816.9	16.1
1977–8	339.0	5,541.0	6.1
1978–9	270.2	7,397.5	3.7
1979–80	431.5	9,575.7	4.5
1980–1	681.5	12,543.6	5.4
1981–2	643.9	13,886.5	4.6
1982–3	1,015.4	14,913.2	6.8
1983–4	749.3	16,039.3	4.7

Source Table 1.1; and Government of India, *Economic survey*, various issues.

The vulnerability of India's balance of payments was, however, cruelly exposed when the second oil shock of 1979 was followed by the severe drought of 1979–80. The response of aid inflows in this crisis was far too weak to finance India's unprecedented deficit on commodity trade (almost 4 per cent of GDP in 1980–5). Aid in the form of grants remained constant in nominal dollar terms, and fell as a proportion of nominal GDP. Aid in the form of loans at concessional rates rose quite sharply in nominal dollars, and probably also as a proportion of nominal GDP. But even so, in order to finance the deficit of the early 1980s, India had to tap other sources. These were medium- and long-term public loans (less concessional than aid); commercial loans (by definition at full market rates); its facilities with the IMF; and its own foreign exchange reserves. Although aid still finances a significant proportion of India's imports, particularly those directly accessible to the public sector, its lower level than during the 1970s – and perhaps its reduced responsiveness to crises – now render aid insufficient as India's main instrument for coping with balance-of-payments crises.

Table 1.10 India's balance of payments, 1975–6 to 1984–5 (as a percentage of GDP at factor cost)

	1975–6 to 1979–80	*1980–1 to 1984–5*
Commodity trade	−1.44	−3.97
Imports	8.68	10.95
Services (non-factor)	+0.66	+0.70
Factor incomes (net)	−0.04	−0.13
Current transfers (net)	+1.10	+1.63
Capital, private	+0.00	+0.02
Capital, central	+1.23	+1.39
of which:		
official grant aid	+0.34	+0.24
medium and long loans (net)	+0.89	+1.15
Net credit from IMF	−0.12	+0.56
Capital flows NEI	−0.13	−0.24
Errors and omissions	+0.02	n.a
Changes in reserves	−1.29	+0.14

Source Author's calculation based on World Bank figures
Note A minus sign indicates increases in the reserves

Aid is said to be important not only as a supplement to scarce foreign exchange, but also as a means of permitting the recipient country to invest (i.e. add to physical capital) more that it can finance out of domestic saving.[8] In particular aid permits governments to finance higher levels of investment than can be financed out of the current surplus of taxation over public current outlays or from borrowing from the private sector. What then has been the statistical record on aid flows to India relative to its investment? Many of the available data on saving and investment are over-aggregated, and include some non-aid foreign inflows.[9] Only in special conditions can one regard such inflows from the 'rest of the world' (ROW) as a good proxy for the contribution of aid. They are when the non-aid elements in the ROW surplus are very small, as they were in India for most of the period until the mid-1970s.

Table 1.11 Sectoral financial surplus/deficits in India, 1951–75 (Rbn and percentages of GNP)

	1951–5	1956–60	1961–5	1966–70	1971–5	1951–75
	Absolute figures (Rbn)					
Financial institutions	0.41	0.94	2.79	3.50	12.78	20.42
Private corporations	–4.16	–8.24	–15.96	–18.07	–29.73	–76.16
Government	–8.82	–28.81	–44.26	–70.18	–123.86	–275.93
Households	8.81	18.49	33.07	45.63	130.74	236.34
Rest of the world	1.40	17.19	20.32	29.02	5.45	73.39
All sectors; absolute	23.60	73.67	116.40	166.40	307.57	682.24
	Distribution (per cent)					
Financial institutions	1.7	1.3	2.4	2.1	4.2	3.0
Private corporations	–17.6	–11.2	–13.7	–10.9	–9.8	–11.2
Government	–37.4	–39.1	–38.0	–42.2	–40.9	–40.4
Households	37.4	25.1	28.4	27.4	43.2	34.6
Rest of the world	5.9	23.3	17.5	17.4	1.8	10.8
All sectors; absolute	100.0	100.0	100.0	100.0	100.0	100.0
	Relation to gross national product (per cent)					
Financial institutions	0.08	0.14	0.28	0.21	0.44	0.30
Private corporations	–0.78	–1.25	–1.60	–1.07	–1.02	–1.22
Government	–1.69	–4.35	–4.45	–4.15	–4.24	–4.07
Households	1.69	2.81	3.32	2.70	4.47	3.48
Rest of the world	0.27	2.61	2.04	1.71	0.19	1.08
All sectors; absolute	4.51	11.81	11.67	9.83	10.35	10.15

Source Goldsmith, 1983, Table 3.15, 161

Historical figures (Goldsmith, 1983) for 1950–75 are set out in Table 1.11. Of course, for India as a whole, investment in any year must be equal to (i.e. precisely financed by) savings in that year, but there can be surpluses or deficits for each major sector's saving over its investment. Private corporations and the government have consistently invested more than they saved, while financial institutions, households and the rest of the world have consistently saved more than they have invested.[10] Between 1951 and 1975, the rest of the world supplied 20 per cent of the combined deficits of the government and private corporations, or 25 per cent of the government's deficit on its own. Dependence on a foreign surplus was heaviest during the Second Plan, when it supplied just under half of the combined government and private corporate deficits. From 1961 onwards, corporate and public deficits came progressively to depend, for finance, less on foreign inflows and more on domestic private savings,[11] as the household sector's surplus steadily increased. This increase itself represents partly the growth of household financial assets associated with increases in the scope and sophistication of financial intermediaries and, after 1975, interest-bearing foreign exchange accounts of non-resident Indians. It may also partly reflect the improved accounting of household savings.

Table 1.12 Ratios of gross aid utilizations to saving and investment in India, *1975–86* (Rupees crores)

	1 Aid Utilizations	2 Domestic Savings	3 1 as % of 2	4 Domestic investment	5 1 as % of 4
1975–6	1,804.7	16,362	11.0	16,418	11.0
1076–7	1,536.0	18,845	8.1	17,705	8.6
1977–8	1,159.7	19,935	5.8	18,621	6.2
1978–9	1,066.2	22,709	4.7	22,984	4.6
1979–80	1,232.2	25,372	4.9	26,143	4.7
1980–1	1,485.4	29,239	5.1	31,457	4.7
1981–2	1,493.0	33,411	4.5	36,229	4.1
1982–3	1,962.9	37,730	5.2	40,476	4.8
1983–4	1,781.9	44,559	4.0	47,255	3.8
1984–5	2,009.7	50,365	4.0	53,844	3.7
1985–6	—	56,682	—	61,518	—

Sources Column 1 from Table 1.1; columns 2 and 3 from World Bank figures.

From 1975–6 to 1978–9, foreign savings made a negligible, or even negative, contribution to India's disposable income (Table 1.12, column 4 minus column 2). (The negative contribution arises because repayments of interest on part-aid loans and negative non-aid foreign savings outweighed net-aid utilizations, which remained positive though small). It is in 1980 that the role of foreign savings changed dramatically. In the early 1980s foreign savings climbed back to about 1.4 per cent of disposable income (Table 1.10), within sight of the 2 per cent peak of the early 1960s. However, aid contributes much less to foreign savings in the 1980s than it did in the 1960s; much more is contributed by the swelling proportions of remittances, non-aid multilateral loans, and commercial borrowings.

To sum up: as a result of the rise in domestic saving and investment relative to sluggish aid, domestic capital formation depends much less on aid in the 1980s than under the Third Plan. Table 1.12 confirms the dwindling size of aid utilizations in relation to domestic savings and investment, even between 1975 and 1985; both ratios fell from about 11 per cent to about 4 per cent. The recent diversification of foreign finance, and the longer-term rise in domestic savings and investment, have greatly eroded the contribution of aid to India's accumulation process, since the heyday of post-Independence development planning.

The role of aid in financing government development expenditure exhibits a similar pattern, as indicated in Table 1.13.[12] Aid utilizations as a percentage of public-sector development outlays fell from around one-third in the mid-1960s to less than 5 per cent in the mid-1980s. The ratio of aid utilization to gross capital formation out of central government budgetary resources (which includes finance for capital formation elsewhere in the economy) also fell (Table 1.13), from almost 70 per cent in 1967–8 to just above 10 per cent in the mid-1980s. As with the ratio to development outlays, the decline is marked after the end of the mid-1970s aid peak. However, some gross public-sector capital formation – now probably at least close to one-half – is not normally eligible for aid.[13] Of 'new gross public development investment', we judge that utilized aid still comprises about a fifth.

Impact of aid on economic growth

As we have seen, because of statistical difficulties, it is a complex task even to set out the historical record on aid flows to India. Additional problems arise in assessing whether, let alone how, economic performance has been determined by aid. First, good (or bad) performance can cause changes in the level of aid: to reward success (or compensate for failure). Second, even if this can be allowed for, as in 'simultaneous' econometric models where growth[14] can be represented as part cause and part effect of aid (Mosley, 1987), aid levels are only one of many things that may determine growth. The macroeconomist cannot, unfortunately, hold constant all the other variables, apart from aid, that are relevant to economic performance – nor is it clear that one should, since some such variables may themselves be affected by aid.[15] One cannot inspect changes in economic growth, compare them with earlier changes in the inflows of aid, and draw simple causal conclusions, on the assumption that one variable must be influencing the other because nothing else has changed. Everything else is changing at the same time: sometimes erratically (weather, power supply);

Table 1.13 Ratios of gross aid utilizations to government expenditure categories in India 1966–85 (Rupees crores)

	Gross aid utilizations	Development outlays	Ratio (per cent)	Gross capital formation out of central government budgetary resources	Ratio (per cent)
1966-7	1,105.6	3,416	32.4	1,793	61.7
1967-8	1,161.6	3,645	31.9	1,675	69.3
1968-9	872.1	3,937	22.2	1,660	52.5
1969-70	824.2	4,166	19.8	1,612	51.1
1970-1	749.7	4,858	15.4	1,917	39.1
1971-2	805.0	5,405	14.9	2,217	36.3
1972-3	631.3	6,550	9.6	2,628	24.0
1973-4	1,008.6	6,864	14.7	2,665	37.8
1974-5	1,279.1	9,403	13.6	3,677	34.8
1975-6	1,804.7	11,574	15.6	4,663	38.7
1976-7	1,530.0	13,134	11.6	4,991	30.7
1977-8	1,159.7	15,005	7.7	5,899	19.7
1978-9	1,066.2	17,994	5.9	6,913	15.4
1979-80	1,232.2	20,298	6.1	7,229	17.0
1980-1	1,485.4	24,426	6.1	9,012	16.5
1981-2	1,493.0	28,653	5.2	10,799	13.8
1982-3	1,962.9	33,591	5.8	12,404	15.8
1983-4	1,781.9	39,274	4.5	14,702	12.1
1984-5	2,009.7	48,003	4.2	17,872	11.2

Source Government of India, *Economic Survey*, 1968–9 to 1985–6.

sometimes as a cause or effect of past aid or growth themselves. Although econometric models can cope with some of this – and do provide some indications of aid-growth relationships – any attempt to distil the impact of aid in such a multiplex scene must be more a matter of judgement than a matter of precise calculation. This is not only because of the under-development of econometrics (Leamer, 1982) and the complexities of reciprocal or of exogenous causation. It is also because of the difficulty of judging what the Indian Government, households, firms, and trading and lending partners would have done – and with what impact on growth – if aid levels had been substantially different, or had sharply changed (not the same thing).

Before considering the aid-growth link, we furnish some indicators of India's growth (Table 1.14). Over 1950–75, GNP grew at over 3 per cent a year which, with population growth of 2 per cent a year, allowed income-per-person to rise by an average 1 per cent a year. Although this represents a much better performance than was achieved in pre-Independence India (Heston, 1982), it is nevertheless modest when compared with the absolutely low starting level of income, with the plans of the government and with the experience of many other poor countries in Asia. (It should be noted that the growth rates in the 1960s are misleading: 1965–6 and 1966–7 were years of disastrous drought – the worst years for agriculture in the whole period. This leads to an understatement of the agricultural growth achieved from 1960–1 to 1965–6, and a corresponding overstatement of growth in the subsequent five-year period – in fact 1965–7 saw the beginning of the 'green revolution' in Punjab, Haryana, and Western Uttar Pradesh.) Economic growth in 1971–5, however, was clearly lower than the 1950–75 average rates. This lends some plausibility to the hypothesis of secularly slackening growth between 1950 and 1975. However, this result is very sensitive to the precise periods chosen. Further, growth over 1976–85 appears to be significantly higher than the 1950–75 average.[16] Juxtaposing Table 1.14 with Tables 1.7 and 1.3, we might conclude that growth seems to have been highest when real aid utilizations were lowest! Of course, this does not establish a causal association; high aid might be a response to growth difficulties; or rapid growth could even be a lagged response to aid flows in earlier periods.[17]

The heart of the matter is the question of the dynamic of growth. This dynamic is still heavily influenced by the performance of agriculture, although statically this might seem to be less important today; after all, agriculture's share of total output fell, from 45 per cent in 1960–4 to 41 per cent in 1975–6, and to 31 per cent in 1985–6. Nevertheless, it is still not easy for the economy's overall growth rate to exceed greatly the rate of growth of agriculture.

Table 1.14 Key growth rates of the Indian economy, 1951–85 (per cent per annum)

		1951–5	1956–60	1961–5	1966–70	1971–5	1951–75	1976–85
1.	Real GNP							
	a. Total	3.45	4.03	2.90	4.82	3.00	3.63	4.21
	b. Per head	1.87	1.89	0.60	2.40	0.89	1.53	1.91
2.	Population	1.53	2.10	2.39	2.23	2.10	2.07	2.30
3.	Agricultural production	4.22	3.80	-1.39	6.65	2.39	3.10	1.84
4.	Industrial production	8.00	7.16	9.06	3.43	3.60	6.22	5.07
5.	Labour force	1.21	1.51	1.97	2.40	–	1.78[a]	n.a
6.	Capital stock		3.70[b]	5.77			4.93[c]	n.a
7.	Area under cultivation	2.74	1.12	0.30	1.24	0.60	1.20	0.09[d]

Source Goldsmith (1983), Table 3.1, 139; and World Bank figures.
Notes a 1951–70
  b 1950–60
  c 1950–70
  d Applies to major crops only, 1977–86

Two in three Indians depend on agriculture for income. It is these Indians who, being for the most part relatively poor, are likely to spend (rather than save) extra income. If agriculture does not grow, there may be inadequate demand for the products of growth in other sectors. In particular, Indian workers - if in the poor half of India's population - spend over two-thirds of extra income on food. If food production does not grow, then rising output and income involving many workers - e.g. in parts of the service sector - becomes a source of unsustainable inflationary pressure. (There is some evidence that the latter is happening in the India of the 1980s.) If agriculture constrains growth, there is a further problem. Since the new possibilities for extending the area of cultivation, e.g. by irrigation, are constantly shrinking or becoming more costly, the growth rate of agriculture itself depends on continuously finding new methods to raise the productivity of land. Such methods must be profitable for farmers if they are to be adopted. But falling world and Indian agricultural prices undermine the potential for profitable innovation. The falling prices themselves are due in part to subsidization of food production in the EEC, Japan and the USA; in part to India's own past adoption of improved methods; but mostly to the concentration of the gains from growth in India on richer people, who have a low income-elasticity of demand for food. India's industry, for both reasons, is still influenced strongly by the performance of agriculture: through its supply of food as an urban wage-good, its supply of raw materials, and its major role as a source of demand for industrial consumer goods. A strangely steady 70 per cent of India's workforce is engaged in agriculture (World Bank, 1987, 264); that proportion usually drops with growth, but not in India. One possible 'escape route with growth' would be to encourage labour intensive small industry, which would reduce this proportion. However, centrally-run or – influenced projects – private or public, aid-financed or not – have so far made little contribution to rural non-farm activity.[18]

Apart from this, growth is influenced through a variety of mechanisms which determine whether the total productivity of the resources invested in industry rises or falls. This can be viewed in terms of the familiar Harrod-Domar identity: the rate of growth equals the savings ratio divided by the incremental capital-output ratio, which in turn is the sum of the sectoral ICORs weighted by sectoral shares in output. As the share of manufacturing in GNP rises with development, its ICOR becomes increasingly important. In India it appears to have suffered a twenty-year increase (1960–80) across the board, not related to compositional changes in the structure of manufacturing (Ahluwalia, 1985, 132), nor to particular industries which are especially capital-intensive in their operating technology (Ahluwalia, 1985, 141). The fairly stable growth of GNP in 1950–80 reflects the fact that though the savings ratio doubled, the incremental capital-output ratio almost doubled too. These findings have raised a number of crucial policy questions,[19] some specifically related to aid. It almost certainly raised the savings ratio; did it also reduce capacity utilization, or the efficiency with which utilized capital produced output, thus raising the ICOR? Aid – through its effects on the level of demand; by selection of sectors; or by choosing simple or troublesome technologies – can affect the level of capacity utilization. Perhaps most importantly, the allocation of aid resources – both between and within sectors – may concentrate them unduly on activities with high capital-intensity and low labour share. This would lead to slower and less equitable growth, both by raising the capital-output ratio, and by placing extra income in the hands of persons relatively less likely to spend it on extra Indian production.

We calculated comparable figures to Goldsmith's for 1950–75 from World Bank data for 1976–85, and added them as a final column in Table 1.14. What do they tell us of India's recent economic performance? The dominance of agriculture continues to be eroded, and economic growth is less tightly tied to agriculture's own growth performance. Although the figures indicate indifferent agricultural growth from 1976 to 1985, this is critically dependent on the years chosen. A collection of detailed studies of Indian agriculture in 1951–81 (Jakhade, 1983) rejected the hypothesis of secular deceleration; since 1981 (except in the disastrous 1987 drought) there has, if anything, been acceleration. Overall, India's total real GNP grew faster in 1976–85 than in the relatively buoyant 1950s, and certainly much faster than during the long years of slowdown and stagnation from 1960–75. The hypothesis of secularly slackening growth seems implausible with respect to the last ten years. The medium-term growth of real per capita product was also faster than in any comparable period since Independence, despite an apparent upturn – already being reversed[20] – in the rate of population growth. Year-to-year growth, however, was still significantly influenced by the state of the harvest; possibly the variability of food (and farm) output, though not its worst-case levels per person, had deteriorated after 1960 or so (Lipton with Longhurst, 1985, discussing work by Hazell and others). Cycles with troughs in the drought years of 1979–80 and 1982–3 are evident when the decade's growth rates are disaggregated by sector. The industrial growth rate overall recovered from the previous period of stagnation, but not dramatically. Services have been the fastest growing of the sectors, which must raise some questions about how robust recent growth will prove to be, particularly with respect to the growth of government services. The sedate pace of industrial growth was disappointing, especially given the rise in the investment rate from 22 per cent in 1975–6 to 25 per cent in 1985–6.

So much for major indicators of India's macroeconomic performance. What of the impact of aid upon it? Although economic growth was fastest in 1955–70, when aid made its greatest relative contribution to the balance of payments and to the financial deficits of the government and corporate sectors, aid was falling relative to these aggregates throughout this period. The peak in aid around 1980, when there may have been some acceleration in the underlying growth rate, was nevertheless low relative to macroeconomic aggregates by historical standards. The associations cannot by themselves be regarded as conclusive evidence of an aid/growth link. Economists have applied econometric tests to the aid and growth data, seeking more rigorous evidence for or against a link. Predictably, with different researchers testing differently specified equations with different data sets, the results have appeared to be contradictory.

One might have thought that econometric studies of the aid/growth link would have taken changes in national income as the dependent variable and aid utilizations (net of repayments with a balance of payments constraint, gross with a savings constraint: Lipton, 1972), along with domestic saving and non-concessional foreign finance, as the independent variables, thus linking the three main sources of investment funds with output changes in a simple Harrod-Domar type of formulation. This has been attempted in cross-section studies, which generally show some positive effect of aid on growth (Mosley, 1987, especially 130). Econometric studies of aid to India, however, take a different tack, using investment as the dependent variable and aid (along with various government budget indicators and sometimes the level of national income itself) as the independent variable. For example, Chaudhuri (1978; 107–8) tested an equation of the form:

$$I_t = a + bY_t + cA_t$$

where I is investment, Y is net national product and A is gross utilized aid (including a small but unspecified amount of concessional finance with a grant element too low to constitute aid) minus food aid. Food aid was excluded on the grounds that it was not intended to finance public investment.[21] The following result was obtained:

$$I = 11449.908 - 0.007Y + 3.149A$$
$$(4.22) \quad (-0.22) \quad (3.08)$$
$$R^2 = 0.937 \quad \text{D.W.} = 1.47$$

This result had encouragingly high values of the correlation coefficient and the t-statistic on the A variable, while the Durbin-Watson statistic is sufficiently near to 2 that autocorrelation of the Y and A variables need not be a serious worry. The analysis thus suggests that aid had a fairly strong positive effect on the level of investment.

Other analysts relying on econometric studies have not been in agreement. A Task Force of the Asian Development Bank used time-series data for India, Malaysia, Sri Lanka, and Thailand to examine whether foreign aid added to gross government investment (ADB, 1977, 305–6). Government capital formation was regressed on two different measures of foreign aid, plus the government budget deficit, the size of government domestic borrowing and two measures of the foreign exchange gap. The conclusion was that foreign savings added to government capital formation in only one of the four countries - Sri Lanka. This result seems odd, for it has hardly ever been seriously questioned that aid raises government investment; the debate has been over whether aid 'crowds out' private investment.

Not unexpectedly, with such radically differing results, research has continued in an attempt to resolve the conflict. The most elaborate recent attempt is by Rubin (1982). He regressed Indian public sector gross fixed capital formation on foreign aid inflows and an array of other variables - government consumption, agricultural output and domestic and foreign inflation. His definition of aid was similar to Chaudhuri's, in that it excluded food aid, but his figures were net, rather than gross, of repayments and deflated (by the US producer price index) to a 1970 price base. His initial finding concurred with that of the ADB study quoted above - that foreign aid had 'no significant effect on public investment in India' (Rubin, 127). However, when the flow of foreign aid was added to the stock of foreign exchange reserves, the combined variable - admittedly a bastardized one called 'foreign resources' - did have a significant explanatory effect (25 per cent of the change in government capital formation) with an R^2 of 0.88. This result was interpreted as follows:

> Aid does not simply 'finance' projects, in the sense that it provides for expenditures that would not have been undertaken otherwise ... Foreign aid appears to be as much a subsidy to maintain reserves as a way of financing new spending

> (Rubin, 1982, 129–30)

However, this conclusion can just as well be interpreted to mean that – given the permissible depletion of reserves – new aid meant new public investment. Any excess of investment over saving is financed by aid, other foreign inflows, or depletions of foreign-exchange reserves.

These and similar econometric studies may be too narrowly focused. In the first place, as the above quotation suggests, the effectiveness of aid in changing economic performance must judged against some set of assumed objectives – including permissible levels of reserves – which policy-makers are trying to achieve. Looking only at the impact of aid on investment tends to suggest that policy-makers are (or should be) trying to maximise the amount of investment; it is far from obvious that they do, or should. We need to know whether aid-financed projects have increased or reduced the return to investment. Secondly, to look at investment as a single category is too aggregative. Aid may stimulate different categories of investment differently. Also the marginal productivity of investment will not (unless we assume an economy free of all types of distortion) be equal in different sectors. In such conditions, one needs a much more elaborately specified model of the 'pathways of aid effectiveness' (e.g. Mosley, 1987, 142–8) before econometric techniques are able to yield much insight. Some would go further than this to argue that the impacts of aid are so sector-selective that, in principle, econometric methods applied at the macroeconomic level are inappropriate to capture them. We do not go deeper into that question here.

However, as one illustration of some of the difficulties involved in tracing aid impacts, it is worth noting the relationship between growth and aid in the form of emergency food imports to India. If the government – absent such emergency aid – would not have acquired commercial food imports, the extra food aid does not directly influence investment, but boosts consumption. This helps to break important bottlenecks in productive activity and adds substantially to the productivity of existing resources, including labour. Certainly food aid, which was excluded from most of the econometric studies, at one time played this role in the Indian economy. Sen has pointed out that, since Independence in India, it has become almost impossible for a famine to take place:

> No matter how and where famine threatens – whether with a flood or a drought, whether in Bihar in 1967–8, in Maharashtra in 1971–3, or in West Bengal in 1978 – an obligatory policy response prevents the famine actually occurring.
>
> (Sen, 1983, 757)

This excellent record of swift public action to avert famine must have been facilitated to some degree by authorised foreign aid funds, which could be utilized at critical moments (with donor agreement) to pay for additional imports of food for the public distribution system. If one argues that, without aid, the Government of India would have had to pay for such food imports itself, then this kind of food aid can be credited with relaxing the foreign-exchange constraint on investment which existed until the mid-1970s – a role increasingly played, as food aid dwindled and releasable public-sector food stocks grew, by depletions of such food stocks. Food aid, in either case, maintains both working capacity and mass demand for non-food products.

In India, success in averting acute hunger co-exists with the ability to tolerate endemic malnutrition (Sen, 1983). If emergency food imports financed by aid contributed to the former, can one argue that recurrent food imports, for example under US Public Law 480, contributed to the latter, by blunting the incentives of domestic food producers? Before 1965, when PL 480 wheat imports were available against rupee rather than foreign exchange payments, it seems likely that such aid did indeed have some effect in depressing supplies from domestic wheat producers. The required calculation is the net effect of the increase in supply due to aid minus the loss in supply due to depressed domestic prices. The most reliable estimate of this net effect (see p. 51) is that every ton of food aid added five-sixths of a ton to total Indian supplies of grain. This is simply a supply-side calculation and neglects the demand shifts resulting from subsidization. In any case, it has been argued that the depressive effect on supply arose not from food aid as such, but from the system of urban food distribution at subsidized prices (Chaudhuri, 1978, 102–3). The criticism applies not to food aid *per se* but to food aid when channelled through the particular Indian environment of distributional controls. In this sense, it is analogous to Kidron's criticisms of the effects of private foreign investment in India (see Chapter 7). Thus recurrent food aid, like emergency aid-financed food imports, had, on balance, beneficial effects. But the real point of the food aid illustration is that these effects would not show up at all in the results of the kinds of econometric investigation of the aid/growth link which have been commonest in the literature on India.

India's future capital inflows: aid or commercial lending?

So far we have said little about sources of finance for capital formation, other than aid and domestic savings. Is there no non-aid foreign inflow which could offer an alternative to aid? Indeed, throughout the 1960s and 1970s:

> Without doing much violence to reality, the role of foreign capital
> in resource mobilisation can be discussed in the form of the role of
> foreign aid in Indian economic development.
>
> (Chaudhuri, 1978, 95)

That is to say, non-aid sources of external finance, such as private foreign investment, other concessional finance, and commercial lending to government or public sector organizations, were relatively insignificant. The flow of private foreign investment (PFI) had always been small since Independence. This was understandable given the Indian Government's policy towards PFI, which varied from deep suspicion to merely moderate suspicion. Private foreign investors were faced by the Indian Government with a large and fluctuating apparatus of official controls, including the Foreign Exchange Regulation Act, over their activities, which most found discouraging. The result was a flow of PFI which was, in net terms, probably negative (Chaudhuri, 1978, 170–2) as pre-Independence foreign assets were gradually repatriated. At the same time, until the second oil price shock of 1979-80, the Government of India, unlike many other developing countries in the mid-1970s, did not take on large quantities of commercial debt. This again seems to have been a conscious policy decision. As a result, India's ratio of debt service payments (capital and interest) to export receipts fell through the 1970s, from 28 per cent (1971–2) to 12 per cent (1978–9) (Patel, 1986, 59).

By 1980, however, India's position changed abruptly. The combination of the second oil shock with the drought-affected harvest of the previous year led India to seek a substantial IMF stand-by facility to help to finance a period of structural adjustment. The US$5.8bn from the IMF's Extended Fund Facility, only a fraction of which was used, covered the period 1981–2 to 1984–5. A major purpose was to tide over a transition to lesser dependence on imported oil by means of greater exploitation of domestic sources of oil, natural gas, and coal. Given the deterioration of India's terms of trade, volumes of agricultural exports had to grow rapidly as, in the longer run, did exports of manufactured goods. All of these changes needed to be accompanied by considerable improvements in India's economic infrastructure (roads, ports, railways, and power supply) and changes in institutions and economic policies. Apart from the IMF facility designed to underwrite the costs of these structural adjustments, India had to tap commercial sources of borrowing much more extensively than it ever had to do in the past. India was relatively well placed for this. It was not, like many other developing countries, already enmeshed in the gathering debt crisis with the commercial banks. Indeed, as the net outflows of commercial bank funds from Latin America and sub-Saharan Africa in the 1980s shows, such banks were looking for safer places to put their funds – and recession-hit developed countries were unpromising, leaving India quite attractive. It had already secured the support of key agencies such as the IMF and the World Bank for its policy of structural adjustment. This meant that India was relatively credit-worthy in the eyes of the commercial banks. To some extent it was also well placed because the foreign trade sector is small in relation to the rest of the economy. Thus, a small fall in the proportion of resources servicing the domestic sector – being large relative to exports – can have a large impact on the resources gap and on the ability to service foreign debt incurred partially to cover that gap. However, precisely because the foreign trade sector is relatively small, a fairly low debt:GNP ratio can give rise to a high debt:exports ratio. The ability to prevent or rectify this depends on the ease of movements of resources from the domestic to the foreign trade sector.

India began to tap the international credit market in a serious way in 1980–1. For the public sector, large-scale Eurocurrency financing was arranged for the National Aluminium Company's projects (R544 crores) and for the Oil and Natural Gas Corporation (R160 crores). Private-sector companies were selectively permitted to sell bonds abroad through the International Finance Corporation to finance approved projects. Oil-exporting developing countries have been encouraged both to advance loans and to make equity investments. During 1981–2, according to the *Economic Survey 1982–3*, the total commitment of commercial borrowings was R1,204 crores. This was equivalent to about US$1.5bn, which was in line with India's undertaking to the IMF at the time of the Extended Fund Facility loan agreement. These signs of increased reliance on foreign commercial borrowing were not much publicized. But should India, with its good credit rating, resort increasingly to commercial borrowing from the international capital markets? Most shrewd judges are inclined to give a qualified 'yes' to this question, for example, Patel (1986, 59). The qualification is that caution has to be exercised in borrowing commercially because a high credit rating crumbles rapidly as soon as a developing country deviates from its planned trajectory of growth and debt repayment. Problems can occur with 'blips' in repayment which can suddenly boost debt service ratios; if the 'blip' coincides with domestic problems, confidence may collapse. Aid is probably still necessary both as a safeguard and attractor of commercial loans, rather than as an alternative. The relative shift from aid to less concessional finance and commercial loans, and from longer-term to shorter-term loans, has profound implications for India which are considered below.

Any likely future Indian level of foreign commercial borrowing will represent a balance between the forces creating the demand for such credit and the forces creating the supply. On the demand side, the major influences are:

India's demand for foreign exchange to buy imports, given assumptions about (i) the likely rate of growth of Indian GNP; (ii) the ratio of extra imports to extra GNP (at various price levels); (iii) exchange rates; (iv) import prices relative to prices in India; and (v) India's import controls.

The availability of foreign exchange from India's exports and inward remittances, given assumptions about (i) the rest of the world's demand schedule for India's goods and services (including the services of Indian emigrant labour); (ii) India's ability to supply them at various prices; (iii) exchange rates; (iv) India's inflation relative to that of its customers abroad; and (v) their import controls.

The projected difference between India's foreign-exchange demands for imported goods and services, and its foreign-exchange availability from exports, gives the projected deficit on the current account of the balance of payments. This can be financed by, for example, a run-down of gold and foreign exchange reserves. India's projected demand for aid, other concessional finance and foreign commercial credit will thus depend on (i) the current-account balance-of-payments deficit, and (ii) the difference between the existing and the desired level of gold and foreign-exchange reserves.

The major influences on the supply schedule of commercial credit to India are the price and quantity available of competing non-commercial credit, i.e. various kinds of concessional flows – and the 'confidence' of commercial investors in India's ability and willingness to meet her commercial obligations. Obviously the supply of concessional flows affects India's demand for the commercial flows. In the case of concessional flows, aid as a source of finance has proved highly resistant to any significant expansion in the 1980s (save perhaps in once-for-all response to drought, as in 1987). But commercial credit can have a highly unpleasant 'whiplash effect', whereby yesterday one was expansively encouraged to borrow, today one hits a minor economic hazard and tomorrow one's creditworthiness has vanished.

Trying to place precise numbers on the above determinants of India's future level of commercial borrowing is extremely hazardous. Some years ago, a careful attempt was made by the World Bank (1981b). It examined various alternative blends of aid, other concessional finance, and non-concessional finance (the Bank's own blends reviewed were the existing blend; 80 per cent IDA/20 per cent IBRD; an intermediate blend 50 per cent IDA/50 per cent IBRD; and a hard blend 25 per cent IDA/75 per cent IBRD). These were juxtaposed with alternative assumptions about India's future size of resources gap (i.e. the annual deficits on the current balance of payments). Each case would imply various levels of the balance-of-payments deficit and of the debt service ratio. The main or central projection was made on the assumptions that the overall growth rate would be 4 to 5 per cent per annum (i.e. somewhat above its long-term historical rate of 3 per cent p.a); that import volumes would grow at about the same rate as GNP, and export volumes at about their 1970s rate of 7 per cent p.a.; and that foreign exchange reserves were required to cover 3 months' worth of imports. On these assumptions - and given plausible changes in prices - India's current-account deficit on the balance of payments could be kept down to 'manageable' proportions, defined as being less than 2 per cent of GNP. It was then judged likely (World Bank, 1981b) that India would be regarded by foreign lenders as credit-worthy for the absolutely large sums that would be required to cover about half this deficit by the end of the 1980s. In other words, by the World Bank's calculations, India's new commercial loans abroad would then be as large, each year, as those from IDA and IBRD taken together.

Whether a switch towards commercial borrowing of this magnitude really is feasible – i.e. whether India can reduce its reliance on aid in line with falling relative disbursements and maintain growth - depends on whether the above assumptions are realistic. The most doubtful may prove to be an export volume growth rate of at least 7 per cent a year through the 1980s. That rate was achieved in 1970–1 to 1978–9, but even by 1981 it was clear that this fact should not breed excessive optimism. The world trading environment suffered a general recession in the early 1980s and an increase in specific measures of protection against Third World imports; the halting recovery of the western economies in 1985–7 did little to improve these matters; and the liquidity crises of late 1987 posed renewed threats. Moreover, India's export performance in the latter half of the 1970s reflected its relatively low inflation *vis-à-vis* its developing-country competitors and the developed countries. Its exports suffered in the first half of the 1980s when global inflation rates, especially in developed countries, fell sharply while India's was stable or slightly higher (see p.9). Much depends on India's ability to continue a rapid change in the structure of its exports away from staple primary exports and towards manufactured goods. There have been some hopeful early signs of this in chemicals and engineering, but the growth of iron and steel exports has been disappointing. If the required dynamism in exports cannot be achieved, the balance of payments deficit can in principle be contained by reducing the overall growth rate and thus the growth rate of imports. But since the improvement of infrastructure itself requires imports, this would inevitably lengthen the time during which structural adjustment takes place and that, in turn, may have a deleterious effect on foreign lenders' confidence. In brief, the less well India's exports perform, the greater the deficit, and hence the need to supplement concessional with commercial inflows; but the less the readiness of commercial lenders to supply such inflows, and hence the higher the interest-rate supplements that India will have to pay. These supplements, in turn, would burden the future balance of payments, impeding both creditworthiness and growth in the long-term.

Since the World Bank's 1981 projections mentioned above were made, the other key supply side factor – the availability and terms of aid and other concessional finance – has changed for the worse. The 1986–7 decisions to replenish IDA less generously than had been sought by the World Bank – despite the Bank's prior concurrence with the largest donor to IDA (the USA) that India's share in IDA lending had to fall sharply – must raise the volume of required commercial borrowing by India.

There are thus reasons for suggesting that the Bank's projections may have been somewhat optimistic. Much thus rests on the amounts and terms offered by bilateral aid donors and by the commercial banks themselves and by suppliers of non-aid (but still slightly concessional) finance, mainly the IBRD; and by commercial banks.[22] IBRD money seems unlikely to compensate for the loss of IDA money at an appropriate substitution ratio (see p.36). Nor is it yet clear whether bilateral aid donors will take a lead from the Bank in hardening their terms to India. Such uncertainties compound those affecting India's ability to make her exports grow strongly. India herself is reluctant to go so rapidly as envisaged by the Bank in the direction of private commercial borrowing. The considerations here are more political than economic: the government believes that it will encounter less political pressure by relying on multilateral lending. It fears to accumulate a heavy bank debt, because it fears that in the event of, say, two successive bad harvests, it would be seriously exposed to political pressures on its economic policy as a price for receiving a financial package to bail it out. Drought still arrives in India unpredictably, but seldom less than once a decade. The failure of the 1987 monsoon means that a second successive year of drought in 1988 would place the country in a most vulnerable position, that could be used, as it was after 1965–6, to try and force the government's hand on the nature and speed of economic liberalization. What has been painfully learned through the aid policy dialogue (see Chapter 3) might not be heeded when worried commercial bankers get together with their Foreign Offices.

As indicated in the earlier sections, Measurement of aid flows (pp. 4–6) and Size of aid flows to India (absolute flows) (pp. 6–14), no single statistic can summarize the value of aid, or of total concessional finance, relative to non-concessional finance. Thus there can be no single numerical answer to the question: 'What volume of non-concessional finance would balance, in its value to the Indian economy, a given volume of concessional finance?' The primary measure of the value of aid relative to non-concessional finance is the size of the grant element (see note 1), but the costs of tying must also be taken into account. Apart from tying, loans have other hidden costs which affect their value to the recipients: most notably, the costs of negotiating the loan, of fees, of meeting any special requirements of the lender, and of delay, i.e. of reduction in the present value of returns to an investment because it has to be held up until the loan is finally authorized. Just as the costs of tying vary as between different types of aid, so these costs of negotiation and delay vary between other types of finance. Eurocurrency loans are usually less costly, in this respect, than IBRD loans (Harvey, 1983, 25), though of course the formal interest rate is higher. Finally one has to note that the rate of interest payable on loans from the Eurocurrency markets, since 1985 from the IBRD, and frequently from private banks, is not fixed. Thus one does not know *ex ante* what such a loan will cost over its term, although the initial rate of interest is, of course, known. This is an element of uncertainty, rather than a calculable risk. The future course of interest rates is extremely difficult to predict, and an over-optimistic prediction leads to short-term debt service problems.[23]

When these complications do not apply, the problem becomes more tractable. When we are comparing two different types of loan which have a common term and whose interest rates, though different, are fixed over the life of the loan, the size of the grant element in the loan can be related to the 'substitution ratio' of the loans. 'Substitution ratio' here means that number by which the volume of the concessional loans must be multiplied to give the volume of non-concessional finance which is of equivalent value. As the grant element ranges from zero to 100 per cent, so the substitution ratio varies from one to infinity.[24] In the Indian case, the substitution ratio lies somewhere between two and three, if we are thinking of the substitution of loans on 'hard terms' loans from IBRD for loans on 'soft terms' from IDA.

A switch towards commercial borrowing by India raises several problems (Anagol, 1987). The commercial terms imply higher borrowing for the same level of effective resources at higher interest rates, raising both the debt and debt service ratios. Further the loan terms are usually shorter than with various forms of concessional finance (with IDA terms longer than IBRD ones), again raising the debt service ratio. Not only are interest rates variable, but so far in the 1980s they have been very high in real terms (by historical standards). The level and speed of returns to projects must therefore be assessed carefully in determining what level of commercial borrowing India can safely undertake. One estimate (Anagol, 1987, 31) suggests a level of US$1–2bn per annum, roughly comparable to current gross aid utilizations. This is close to the World Bank's conclusion in 1981 (see p.34). Of course, the export growth rate may itself partly depend on the level of finance – and may substantially affect the readiness of commercial lenders to provide new cash (p. 34). More past lending and disappointing current exports both would imply rising debt service ratios alongside falling credit ratings. The dangers of this 'Latin

American scenario', especially if the economy deviates from its growth path, are such that it would be reckless to project expansion of commercial loans, in the late 1980s and early 1990s, on a scale sufficient to replace aid to India; they can, however, be an increasingly valuable complement to such aid.

Indeed, India's requirement for concessional finance – to safeguard and 'soften' the total debt position created by the growing IBRD and commercial elements – has for several years been stressed by the World Bank. David Hopper, then Vice-President for South Asia, told the 1984 All-India Consortium meeting:

> As the composition of capital flows to India hardens, the risk of severe deterioration in the external economic environment and the impact that this could have on the debt service burden are and will remain sources of deep concern to the Government of India .... [T]o minimise these risks, India needs our more active participation through the provision of more aid on the best possible terms.
>
> (Badhwar, 1984, 22)

As will be shown in Chapter 7, this macroeconomic judgement is reinforced by microeconomic considerations. Resource allocation throughout the economy is still distorted by India's pervasive 'control syndrome'. India has begun to tackle this, but such policy reforms create some losers. Some of these people – particularly if they are poor - need to be cushioned by the continued availability (if required) of aid. Otherwise the reform process will prove politically unsustainable and will be reversed, again damaging exports and eroding India's credit-worthiness. This is yet another way in which access to aid is a complement, not an alternative, to commercial borrowing by India.

Conclusions

Our conclusions on the scale, role, and impact of the aid inflow to India over the last thirty years may be summarized as follows.

Scale

1. Although India's aid receipts are the third largest in the world, she receives 11.6 per cent of the global net disbursements of aid to low-income countries (yet contains 31.4 per cent of their population), and only 5.7 per cent of total disbursements to all developing countries (for 20.8 per cent of population) (World Bank, 1987, 202–3, 244–5).[26]
2. In current rupees, India by the mid-1980s had utilized nearly R150bn of foreign aid, net of debt service and repayments. The peak occurred in

1961–6 (during the Third Five Year Plan), with smaller peaks in 1975–6 and around 1980 (Table 1.1).

3. Figures in current US dollars for the period since 1971 (Table 1.6) indicate that aid net of repayments peaked in 1974–6 and again around 1980.

4. None of these figures reveals the purchasing power of these concessional flows. That would require (i) an estimate of the inflation of prices of goods purchased with aid; and (ii) the level of aid-tying, and changes in that level over time. Allowing for the inflation factor only, we confirm that aid flows under the Third Plan represented the greatest annual transfer of purchasing power; the minor peaks also survive; but the 1984 and 1985 purchasing power of India's net aid disbursements appear to be barely half the levels of 1974–6 (Table 1.6), for a recipient population over 20 per cent higher.

Role

5. Figures for the central government capital account items in the balance of payments indicate the maximum contribution which aid could have made to closing the current–account gap. This gap reached nearly 2 per cent of GNP in 1961–5 – mostly covered by net aid. From 1975–6 until 1980, aid flows (although reduced) were greater than required to cover the much smaller current-account deficit, and permitted the building up of foreign-exchange reserves to levels unprecedented for India since 1958. Since 1980, aid flows have been insufficient to cover the greatly increased current-account deficit, and have had to be supplemented by non-concessional flows and a rundown of reserves.

6. Figures of foreign savings show the maximum contribution of aid flows to the deficit of Indian investment over Indian saving. Between 1951 and 1975, there were few other foreign inflows; aid – roughly speaking, foreign savings – amounted to one-quarter of the deficits of the government and the private corporate sector. Aid then played an important role in permitting public and corporate investment to be undertaken well ahead of the development of the household sector's propensity to save. Since 1980, however, non-aid foreign savings have dramatically increased their contribution to India's total savings. The average contribution of total foreign savings in the 1980s has been around 7 per cent, although the aid element in foreign savings has sharply declined: aid's average contribution to India's total saving in the early 1980s was less than 4 per cent, half the proportion of the mid-1970s (Table 1.12). Aid's contribution to government investment fell from over 50 per cent in the late 1960s to just above 10 per cent in the mid-1980s (though its contribution to 'aidable' public investment is

probably around a fifth). Meanwhile, commercial loans and official non-aid finance have played an ever-increasing role.

Impact

7. India's economic growth had a good start in the 1950s; perhaps slowed a little from the early 1960s to the mid-1970s; and achieved a more dynamic tempo - through still not as rapid as in some other Asian economies (including China) - in the 1980s. Agriculture is still the dominant cause of fluctuations in growth; its share in GNP, i.e. its statistical dominance of the overall growth rate, is being increasingly eroded, but not so its demand and supply roles in constraining that rate.
8. The attempts to find the link between aid and economic performance by econometric methods have been diverse and have produced conflicting results. Several look for the impact of aid on aggregate investment without considering the objectives of Indian policy-makers, without disaggregating investment (or aid) by type and sector, and without focusing on the indirect effects of aid on productivity via extra food consumption. Food aid to India is often ignored, although in the 1960s and 1970s it was probably helpful in relaxing the foreign exchange constraint. As a whole, aid almost certainly raised India's ratio of total savings (domestic and foreign) to GNP – i.e. aid did little to counter the steady rise in India's domestic savings ratio (and much to add foreign savings). Alongside this rise, India suffered an almost offsetting fall in the utilization and/or productivity of capital (so its growth rate shows little or no secular rise). The concentration of aid in the 1960s on steel, heavy electricals, etc. certainly contributed to this, but the less capital-intensive and more rural emphases of aid in 1973–81 may have reversed the trend. However, it may well be that aid now being channelled to new industrial investment will be less effective because of the pervasive inefficiencies which some have detected in Indian public sector industry (e.g. Weiner, 1986, 609: cf. Chakravarty, 1987).

References

Ahluwalia, I.J. (1985) *Industrial Growth in India: Stagnation since the Mid-Sixties*, Delhi, Oxford University Press.

Anagol, M. (1987) 'Implications of commercial borrowing for India', *International Journal of Development Banking*, 5: 1, January.

Asian Development Bank (1977) *Rural Asia: Challenge and Opportunity*, New York and London, Praeger Publishers.

Badhwar, I. (1984) 'Letter from Washington', *India Today*, 15 August.

Bhagwati, J. N. (1970) 'The tying of aid', in J. N. Bhagwati and R. Eckaus (eds), *Foreign Aid*, Harmondsworth, Penguin.

Chakravarthy, S. (1987) *Development Planning: the Indian Experience*, Oxford, Clarendon Press.

Chaudhuri, P.K. (1978) *The Indian Economy: Poverty and Development*, London, Crosby Lockwood Staples.

Goldsmith, R.W. (1983) *The Financial Development of India 1860-1977*, London and New Haven, Yale University Press.

Government of India (1983, 1986) *Economic Survey 1982-3 and 1985-6*, New Delhi, Government of India Press.

Hamilton, C. (1983), 'Capitalist industrialization in East Asia's Four Little Tigers', *Journal of Contemporary Asia*, 13: 1.

Harvey, C. (1983) *Analysis of Project Finance in Developing Countries*, London, Heinemann Educational Books.

Heston, A. (1982) 'National Income', in D. Kumar (ed.) *Cambridge Economic History of India*, vol.2.

Jakhade, V. (ed.) (1983) Special Issue of the *Indian Journal of Agricultural Economics*, 38: 4, December.

Joshi, V. and Little, I.M.D. (1986) 'Indian macroeconomic policies', Oxford (mimeo).

Leamer, H., (1982) 'Let's take the con out of econometrics', *American Economic Review*.

Lipton, M. (1972) 'Aid allocation where aid is inadequate', in T. Byres (ed.) *Foreign Resources and Economic Development*, London, Frank Cass.

Lipton, M. with Longhurst, R. (1985) *Modern Varieties, International Agricultural Research and the Poor*, Study Paper 2, Consultative Group on International Agricultural Research, World Bank, Washington DC.

Mosley, P. (1987) *Overseas Aid: its Defence and Reform*, Brighton, Wheatsheaf Books.

OECD (1980 et seq.) *Geographical Distribution of Financial Flows to Developing Countries*, Paris.

OECD (1986) *Development Co-operation*, Paris.

Patel, I.G. (1986) *Essays in Economic Policy and Economic Growth*, Basingstoke, Macmillan.

Riddell, R. (1987) *Foreign Aid Reconsidered*, Baltimore, Johns Hopkins University Press.

Rubin, B.R. (1982) *Private Power and Public Investment in India*, University of Chicago, unpublished PhD thesis.

Sen, A.K. (1983) 'Development – which way now?', *Economic Journal, 93: 372, December*.

Weiner, M. (1986) 'The Political Economy of Industrial Growth in India' *World Politics* 38: 4, July.

World Bank (1980, 1985 and 1987) *World Development Report*, New York, Oxford University Press.

World Bank (1981a) *Accelerated Development in sub-Saharan Africa*, Washington DC.

World Bank (1981b) 'India's Balance of Payments Prospects: Resource Requirements and Creditworthiness', unpublished memorandum.

World Bank (1984) *Situation and Prospects of the indian Economy – A Medium Term Perspective*, Report 4962-IN (3 vols) for official use only.

World Bank (1986) *India: Economic Situation and Development Prospects*, Report 6690-IN (2 vols).

Chapter 2

Aid and Poverty in India

Dilemmas in using policy against poverty

Problems and performance

In assessing the effects of aid on India's performance in reducing poverty, we face several problems.

(i) The performance has not been very good. Between the late 1950s and the mid-1980s, the absolute number of Indians below a (fixed and harsh) poverty line has increased sharply. There has been at best a very small decline – masked by major fluctuations – in the proportion of the (growing) population below this line. There has been little or no easing in the intensity of their poverty. This is despite growth, rapid by historical standards, in GNP per person.

(ii) Aid to India was not obviously relevant. Until the late 1960s, it was concentrated on activities – or on types of aid flow – not very likely to affect poverty directly. Since then, aid has been small relative to Indian investment. Aid is therefore not likely to have had much direct impact on poverty in India.

(iii) However, it would be mistaken to 'blame' aid for India's unsatisfactory performance in poverty alleviation. The smallness of the aid/investment ratio, and the nature of India's planning procedure, ensure that many aid-financed activities would have happened anyway. (Even if all would, this does not, as will be shown, mean that aid makes no difference). But for aid, poverty might have got worse. The most important example is that, beyond reasonable doubt, Indian poverty would have been much worse without the spread of the high-yielding cereal varieties. This is indirectly linked to aid, both for Indian agriculture in particular and for tropical agricultural research more generally.

(iv) Owing to (i) and (ii) above, assessment of the aid-poverty nexus must concentrate on specifics; there is little point in testing aggregate relationships 'linking' small or possibly irrelevant aid to very slow progress in reducing poverty.

With the labour force growing at over 2 per cent annually in 1951–81 – so that its bargaining power becomes weaker as more workers compete for jobs – such progress, in a deeply unequal society, is likely to be slow. Yet in India a wide range of activities and organizational forms – public and voluntary, central and local – is nominally directed at the reduction of poverty. Despite the numerous evaluation efforts, little is really known about which efforts have succeeded, let alone which can be supported by aid. Such support could make a real difference, either if aid added to the volume of government (or Indian private) anti-poverty outlays, rather than merely releasing them for other uses; or if aid accompanied technical inflows, or a joint learning process between Indian and donor agencies, that increased the efficiency of anti-poverty activity, and/or the extent to which the benefits of such activity reached the poorest. Conversely, inappropriate aid could damage some poor groups or places.

There are three main ways for aid to a project or programme to benefit poor people. First, aid may benefit them as producers, by helping to provide the poor with land, credit, capital, or jobs. Second, aid may – by increasing the volume, accessibility, or quality of poor people's health or education – raise their productive performance (World Bank, 1980; Jamison and Lau, 1982; Chaudhri, 1979) or their general well-being. Third, aid may benefit the poor as consumers, either by raising their direct access to consumption benefits from public goods, or by lowering the price (or raising the secure availability) of what they buy – mainly, in India, cheap food: over 70 per cent of spending by the poorer half of India's households is on food, and over 50 per cent on cereals and pulses alone.

Overwhelmingly the main contribution of aid to poverty reduction in India has been in the third area: through the indirect contribution of aid-supported agricultural research, in conjunction with aid-supported farm inputs (especially irrigation and extension), in helping to increase the availability of low-cost calories. However this contribution has been largely offset by two problems, one of policy and one of politics, which aid can to some extent help to resolve. The policy problem arises if, as food production per person rises, real income-per-head of poor people – largely determining their 'exchange entitlements' to food (Sen, 1981) – does not. Since only poor people spend a lot of extra income on food, where is the extra demand to come from? Initially, the Indian Government used extra 'green revolution' food production to replace imports, a process from which poor food consumers gained little. Since the mid-1970s, extra wheat output has been used to build up public stocks to unprecedented levels of 20-30 million tons. Up to a point (say 10-12 million tons) such stocks are needed to increase the safety of the poor. However, the expense of tying up savings in grain stocks, at the cost of devoting them to real investment, is large. Another option – followed for rice and sorghum – is simply to let the extra 'green revolution' output restrain the price of grains. Poor consumers benefit; but many of the very poorest depend for income on landless labour to produce these food items. If prices of these grains fall, their production (and hence employment) are discouraged. The apparent solution to the policy problem is to raise the purchasing, as well as the producing, power of the poor, who are net food buyers. But that brings us to the political problem of poverty alleviation. Discussion of this, and of aid's role in alleviating it, is deferred to p. 47, after our review of what has happened to poverty in India.

Trends in poverty in India: a political dilemma?

The detailed analysis of poverty in India is fraught with controversies. These have led people to lose sight of the four key facts described below, which are hardly in dispute. Large and detailed surveys, notably the Indian National Sample Survey, provide pretty reliable results about the key trends.

First, the proportion of Indians in poverty, and the average severity of that poverty, have not changed much since Independence. On nationwide data the proportion below a fairly rigorously defined poverty line – while fluctuating – can be shown from many data sets not to have changed systematically, probably since the mid-1950s, almost certainly since the early 1960s (Kumar, 1974, 35; on the rural data summaries, see Ahluwalia, 1978, 302; 1986; and Saith, 1981, 197–201). The rural incidence fluctuates between 40 and 55 per cent, mainly depending on whether food is cheap, and on whether farm output is high enough to provide ample work (Ahluwalia, 1986; Minhas *et al.*, 1987). Of the Indian poor, about one-third (15–20 per cent of Indians) are at serious risk of eating too few calories (Sukhatme, 1978; Lipton, 1983). Since the ultra-poor families contain a much larger proportion of children, the proportion of under-fives affected by nutritionally dangerous poverty is even higher than that of adults. In the poorest one-fifth of Indian households there are twice as many children per adult as in the best-off one-fifth, and their risk of death is probably about double. About one-third of these infant deaths are due to the interactions of hunger and infection (Mitra, 1978; Lipton, 1983; and 1983a, 43–5).

The life of a typical poor Indian has certainly improved – and lengthened – since Independence, even though his or her real private consumption has not increased in an average year. Better public health, together with public works and food distribution to anticipate famine, have brought age-specific death rates steadily down. Nevertheless, the proportion of Indians unable to afford the basic minimum package of privately purchased consumer goods – to buy enough to eat, even if they spend only the meagre 20–30 per cent of outlay on non-foods typical of their income and household composition – was not much different in 1986 from 1960, when average real income in India was 50 per cent lower.

All this relates to incidence of poverty – proportions of Indians below an inevitably arbitrary poverty line. Recently much work has been done on intensity of poverty – the gap between the poverty line and the outlay, income, or calorie intake of the average poor person – and on the distribution of income among poor persons (Sen, 1981). Since about 1960, intensity and distribution of poverty show no clear trend. This, therefore, must be said of the 'severity of poverty' also – since severity is the resultant of intensity, incidence, and distribution among the poor.

One major bright spot is that extreme fluctuations in poverty have been reduced. This is probably not the result of reduced variability in foodgrain output; modern varieties of cereals are nowadays usually safer than the varieties they displace, but they do tend to 'concentrate' production in areas subject to similar weather shocks, and population growth has pushed grain production out towards riskier lands. But, in the 1960s and early 1970s, grain stocks supported by food aid reduced the damage done by bad seasons and years. Since the mid-1970s, huge (and costly) grain stocks were increasingly accumulated without net imports, as the supply of food from the new cereal varieties outpaced demand from the near-stagnant incomes of the poor; such stocks were ready to be mobilized for times and places of food crisis. Rural foodgrain distribution via fair-price grain shops has lagged behind urban, but state schemes have lately offset this, by providing public employment or school food as an emergency reserve. Thus since 1943 India, unlike China, has avoided massive famine deaths due to the sharpening of already severe poverty in below-average years (Sen, 1983). A consequence is that the linkage of extreme poverty, as such, to very high death-rates has been weakened. This is partly due to aid, both to build food reserves in the 1960s, and to develop agriculture and irrigation in the 1970s; but the vast bulk of the efforts have been Indian.

Nevertheless, poor people's purchasing power in normal times shows no clear uptrend since Independence. A second undisputed fact is that this was accompanied by steady growth in real GNP per person. Although slow, and although interrupted by occasional bad harvests, this growth has been about 1.5 per cent per head per year ever since the early 1950s. Since the 1973 oil crisis, and especially since 1980, the performance has improved somewhat.

So India has experienced just over 80 per cent growth of real GDP per person since Independence (1.5 per cent compound for forty years); probably, no significant improvement in the average annual real private income (and hence nutrition) of the 'poorer half'; and major improvement in its access to publicly provided services, many of them – above all health, and access to emergency famine prevention – improving the efficiency with which nutrition is converted into welfare, especially in bad times.

The third undisputed fact is that India's poverty-reducing performance shows marked variation among different parts of India (Ahluwalia, 1978, 305-6, 314; Rao, 1985). Trends in real wage-rates suggest significant improvements for the rural and urban poor in the 'green revolution' heartland states, Punjab and Haryana (Bhalla, 1979). In some other states, especially Kerala, overall policies – on land reform, labour legislation, health and education – kept the levels of poverty and under-nutrition much lower than state income-per-person would suggest; elsewhere, rural employment guarantees (Maharashtra) or free school meals (Tamil Nadu) had some impact. Conversely, the parts of India untouched by either major agricultural innovation or systematic redistribution – most of South Bihar, Orissa, Madhya Pradesh – must have experienced major worsening of poverty during 1960–88, since other areas improved yet the national average did not. Even there, fluctuations were softened; there was not a massive Bihar famine in 1967. But high infant and child mortality – and lethargy due to adult poverty and hunger – plague much of Bihar every year.

The fourth fact is that this bad performance in reducing poverty has persisted despite a rather favourable policy environment. Huge sums have been spent on poverty programmes. If a large part of the money has gone to the non-poor, or to administration, or to purely temporary respite for the poor, the question is why this was not prevented by democratic procedures and pressures. These, alongside growing literacy, should have led to much more, and more effective, political organization of poor people than has been witnessed. As for governmental attitudes, the First Plan (1951–2 to 1956–7) was the first major Third World planning document explicitly to stress employment and poverty-reduction even if there were a cost in foregone growth. The slogans of *garibi hatao* ('banish poverty'), from all political quarters, have been backed with overt, costly actions through a whole series of official programmes. In the Seventh Five Year Plan for 1985–90 (vol. 1, 1985, pp 27–9), of the R1,800bn of allocated public outlays, R35bn are for the Integrated Rural Development Programme (IRDP, distributing non-farm assets to the rural poor); R47bn for rural employment schemes; R31bn for 'special area programmes' in impoverished regions; R25bn for welfare of scheduled castes and tribes; and R17bn for nutrition programmes – apart from major poverty-directed components in the plans for housing and urban development (R43bn), family welfare (R33bn), and water and sanitation (R65bn). Each such programme generates a career-structure that rewards success in reaching the poor. In the past, each has registered some real achievements, and some failures. Most programmes have passed on, absorbed in a new programme or fashion. Why has the poverty outcome not been better?

Two main sorts of explanations are offered, with different policy implications. India's political parties have been generally unsuccessful in organising the rural poor; for example, fewer than 5 per cent of all rural Indians are members of any political organization or peasant movement, even on very generous definitions (Alexander, 1981). One explanation claims that India's social structure creates a 'dilemma of politics' for any group that undertakes actions to advance the poor.

Before explaining this dilemma, we look at an alternative demographic explanation. It is India's poorest couples who have the largest, fastest-growing families, with the highest proportion of children too young to work. Each such couple finds that it pays to produce many children, as a low-cost source of future income (Becker, 1981, ch. 5). However, when these children do join the labour force, their increasing numbers mean that they compete ever more fiercely for scarce jobs, or for scarce land to work. Yet among the owners of capital, and of farmland (for hire or for working), population grows more slowly (Lipton, 1983a). Employers – owners of land and capital – thus become fewer and more concentrated, relative to poor workers in the labour market. Labour becomes more plentiful, and hence weaker, relative to employers. Yet the poor rely increasingly on labour income, not owned land; and the real wage and the volume of available work per person are both depressed by demographic pressures. Anti-poverty schemes (and 'green revolutions') can at best offset this baleful trend. Thus, for example, in its first six years of life IRDP, according to its severest and most articulate critic (Rath, 1985), pulled about 3 per cent of India's rural poor above the poverty line – yet the proportion of India's rural people in poverty by 1983 did not appear to be significantly lower than in 1960. Does this alternative, non-political explanation account for the persistence of poverty in India alongside growth? The policy responses of the Government of India and donors do not suggest they believe so.

The short-run policy suggested by the demographic explanation involves concentration on labour-intensive activities, so as to strengthen the employment position of the growing numbers of poor. Despite intermittent efforts, however, aid projects, especially outside agriculture, have generally been less labour-intensive than other projects. The Indian Government, whose procedures allow it considerable choice among projects for limited aid support, has increasingly preferred aid to go to projects that are heavy on technology and capital, where it sees donors as having most to contribute. In the long run the demographic explanation also suggests efforts in family planning. India's First Plan carried one of the developing world's earliest commitments to it, and there has been a major learning process subsequently (Cassen, 1978, 146). Massive, well-funded, and partly successful GoI efforts have received some aid support. For every thousand Indians, there were 45 births in 1963, but 'only' 33 in 1985. In 1970, one in eight married couples used contraception; by 1984 it was one in three (World Bank, 1987, 256). However, family planning efforts cannot succeed unless they are overwhelmingly Indian, and for political reasons, only small parts of family planning programmes in India can be supported by aid. Nor is it automatic that family planning affects mainly the poor rather than the accessible urban non-poor.

The demographic 'explanation', anyway, cannot explain much of the growth-with-poverty paradox. Real wage-rate averages across India – being close to subsistence – have no down-trend. In any event, there is no obvious relationship, across Indian regions, between population pressure and failure to reduce poverty. (If anything, the evidence (Repetto, 1979) suggests that, as in Kerala, better distribution of the gains from growth brings down fertility.) So one turns to another explanation: to what, we have suggested, is a political dilemma. This dilemma is as follows. A 'pro-poor' agency of the state may either enlist or exclude powerful groups from its anti-poverty efforts. Enlistment risks subversion; exclusion risks blocking.

It is regularly observed that the better-off are able to obtain benefits of schemes labelled 'For the Poor': subsidized credit and fertilizers; 'low-cost' urban housing; food rations; even about one-third of the small-scale assets distributed in IRDP (Rath, 1985). The dilemma of politics, that has severely limited India's poverty-reducing efforts, is this. Assume that a disinterested, or career-orientated, part of the state genuinely seeks to implement a law or policy aimed at helping some weak, disorganized, inarticulate people. Such actions are likely to harm some strong groupings. Should the 'pro-poor' part of the state, then, work with or against such groups? If enlisted to support its policy against poverty, they will seek to subvert that policy – either by emasculation (e.g. by writing loopholes into land reform legislation) or by capturing the benefits (e.g. by obtaining the credit allegedly subsidized 'to help the poor'). If excluded from anti-poverty policy, the privileged (in the absence of powerful and articulate pressure from below) can often block the anti-poverty policy – e.g. by using the courts against genuine land reform; or by insisting on central actions to impede radical reforms by state governments. Rath (1985) recognizes an economic counterpart to this dilemma; he seeks to escape it by arguing that the better-off should be included in programmes to develop a poor region as a whole, and that 'assets for the poor' are foredoomed without overall market development – an argument also implicit in the 'linkages' approach (Mellor, 1976; Hazell and Roell, 1983). But the central dilemma is political: economic 'solutions' that incorporate the rich may achieve little for the poor if they do not first gain some power.

Of course the state – even a more or less independent anti-poverty agency of the state – is not simply a neutral, passive agent. If its officials ally themselves with the powerful (or the poor), the problem of subversion (or blocking) of pro-poor actions becomes even worse. Such an account could well be accepted both by advocates of free-market styles of development, and by centralizers. The former see the state as the main source of privilege; the latter indict private power and ownership; but both blame the interaction of state rent-creating activity (including poverty programmes) with unequal power-balances (the rich being strong in seeking rents, the poor inarticulate or weak in doing so) for the imperfect performance of India's anti-poverty programmes despite growth. Nevertheless, aid donors must conduct a 'policy dialogue' with those in power: officials of the Indian state. These, in turn, can move the pro-poor inputs – cash, food, or whatever – only through channels substantially influenced by existing power structures. Aid may ultimately reach semi-independent (e.g. parastatal) public agencies, or voluntary organizations, or the private sector; but the state is the first recipient.

However, this is far too gloomy a view, for three reasons. First, a genuinely federal, multi-ministerial democracy like India has numerous and varied power-holding agencies. Many important ones include direct incentives to get benefits to poor constituents. Aid donors can, to some extent, steer resources to agencies of this type.

Second, many sorts of producer and consumer assets are relatively likely to be used by the poor. Wealthy people will seldom want to eat broken rice or sorghum, for example. The better-off already take for granted such facilities as primary schooling or basic health care; providing more of them, especially with a subsidy, is likely to reach mainly the poor. Even such facilities as site-and-service housing or small-scale rural credit – in principle, readily diverted to the non-poor, or blocked by competing private suppliers – are in practice 'aidable' in most societies in ways that reach mainly the poor. Hence it is not credible – even in India, where aid is a small and tightly-programmed part of public expenditure – that aid is wholly fungible, and can do nothing to help the parts of the Indian State who wish to increase the share of its outlays (however financed) that reaches the poor.

Third, the vigour and openness of debate in India overstates the failures of each anti-poverty programme in turn. All pro-poor programmes, given the 'dilemma' and the demography, have limits and leakages, but also many beneficiaries. Aid can support some of these programmes. Indeed – though the main determinants of progress out of poverty are internal in almost every country – if aid cannot provide some net gains to the poor in India's relatively open and pluralist society, it has little chance of doing so anywhere.

Scale and structure of aid: impact on poverty

Smallness of aid

The evidence of Chapter 1 might suggest that aid to India is, relative to population and GNP, just too small to affect poverty. At such low levels, extra aid for a specific purpose, e.g. a new anti-poverty project, does seem likely in part to be used for the relief of GoI domestic funds. However, gross project aid is about 15 to 20 per cent of public sector project investment; and donors retain considerable leverage through selection of which agencies or locations to help (see Chapter 5).

However, declining real aid ever since the late 1960s probably does mean declining capacity by donors to support (or influence) Indian policies against poverty. The big cuts in food aid in the 1970s did not specially harm poor food consumers – it was low income, not low food availability, that denied them claims over India's food stockpiles. However, donor support for Indian anti-poverty actions declined because dwindling food aid was not replaced by other forms of aid. When, as in India, aid in real terms is small and declining, both the difficulty and the importance of focusing it on poverty are likely to increase.

Recency of sectoral anti-poverty emphasis

The sectoral composition of Indian aid receipts has substantially shifted towards activities more likely to reduce poverty. Unfortunately, however, this improvement took place during the very period – from about 1971–2 – when downward pressures on total Indian net aid were most severe. Until the end of the Third Plan (1965–6), aid to industrial development alone, excluding steel aid, comprised 59.8 per cent of authorized and sectorally allocable aid (i.e. excluding the 2 to 3 per cent of 'debt relief and miscellaneous'), and 57.5 per cent of aid utilized. In 1966–74, the respective proportions were 65.1 per cent and 68.4 per cent; by the period 1974–5 to 1978–9 they had fallen to 29.5 per cent and 40.8 per cent respectively, and by the period 1980–1 to 1984–5 to 28.2 per cent and 31.6 per cent (RBI, 1984–5, statement III).

'Industrial development' means overwhelmingly – especially for aid donors, who have been unable to steer much support to small-scale or rural industry – a form of investment that, whatever its virtues, produces rather few jobs, and rather low values of mass consumption goods, per rupee of investment.[1] The same applies to aid for transport and communications, power and iron and steel. With other industrial development, these comprised 96.2 per cent of sectorally allocable aid authorization (and 98.4 per cent of utilizations) in the first three Plans, i.e. prior to 1965–6. In 1966–74 the proportions were 73.7 per cent of aid authorized (81.3 per cent of aid utilized); in the period 1974–5 to 1978–9, 58.6 per cent (66.6 per cent); and in 1980–1 to 1984–5, 52.7 per cent (61.7 per cent). Authorizations to the 'heavy' sectors turned up sharply after 1982–3, and for the three most recent years with available data stood at well over 73 per cent of all aid authorized (RBI, 1984–5, statement III). Although poverty impact monitoring in the World Bank group is beginning to cover these 'heavy' sectors more fully, they remain relatively little poverty-focused. Donors' involvement with poverty alleviation in India is likely to have been much more, at project level, in 1975–82 than before or since, on these data. The 'non-heavy' forms of 'sectoral aid' - those with the greatest potential to benefit poor people - are probably food aid and aid to agriculture. (Other areas where aid has had a significant poverty impact are examined on pp. 71–3.)

Food aid

Food aid was barely 3 per cent of total aid during the first three Plans. In 1966-74 it comprised almost 9 per cent – still mainly wheat. Its importance dwindled with the US withdrawal from the Indian aid scene (1972-8), and with the attainment by India of virtual food self-sufficiency, albeit at low levels of nutrition. In recent years EC skimmed-milk powder has been given to the GoI for sale to provide counterpart funds in support of dairy development through 'Operation Flood' (RBI, 1984–5, statement III). Has all this helped the poor?

(i) There is no doubt that the short-run effects of cereal aid, in years when India combined bad harvests with foreign-exchange crisis (notably 1965-6 and 1966-7), saved the lives of many thousands of poor people. Nor is there much doubt that, in the early years of food aid, the long-run effects of food aid on poor people were bad – the discouragement of some domestic food production and employment.

(ii) Until the late 1960s, India's food aid managers were learning by their mistakes. Rural areas, especially remote ones, contained few fair-price shops and therefore received relatively little consumption support from food aid. Yet these areas suffered from glutted markets and price disincentives.

(iii) The best estimate of the 'disincentive effect' of an extra ton of food aid per year, via extra food supply and lower farm-gate prices, upon Indian farmers' output remains one made in 1977: that every ton of sustained annual cereals aid reduced Indian annual grain output by about one-sixth of a ton (Plocki and Blandford, 1977).

(iv) This does not allow for the further depression of farm-gate prices by food aid on the demand side – by the consumers switching from market purchases of food to subsidized food aid in fair price shops. However, since such consumers are likely to be very poor, this effect is small: they enjoy extra real income (i.e. via subsidized, aid-backed food) mainly as extra food consumption, and do not much reduce market demand for home-grown food. If we allow for this small extra cut in price incentives, it might be reasonable to suppose that each ton of food aid reduced domestic cereals output in India by 0.2 tons.

(v) The main cost to the poor was via employment. If the 0.2 tons of 'lost' domestic cereals output corresponded to land taken out of production, it meant some four to eight days of extra unemployment; if to land switched to other (usually less labour-intensive) crops, some two to four days; and if to lower inputs into cereals production and hence lower yields, some one and a half-to-two days.

(vi) Apart from employment effects, there were consumption effects. If each extra ton of food aid indeed meant 0.2 tons of lost domestic output this still left 0.8 tons as a favourable balance.[2] The poorest half of Indians spend well over 70 per cent of income on food, mostly on cereals; the richest fifth spend well below 40 per cent. Actions to stabilize food availability and to prevent consumer price upsurges, therefore, are bound to help the poor as consumers. Also, the use of food aid as wage goods, in support of agriculture-linked public works – and the learning of lessons about the need to stabilize, not depress, producer prices through cereal aid releases – improved the impact on poor producers.

With India at least 'self-sufficient' in foodgrains in normal years, and with EEC's wish both to remedy its past relative neglect of India[3] and to dispose of its dairy surpluses, food aid to India has shifted towards powdered milk and butteroil. First around Anand in Kaira district, Gujarat, and recently elsewhere, 'Operation Flood' (OF) has sought to follow up the apparent success of Indian dairy development programmes. In Kaira at least, such programmes do seem to have reached many poor, even landless, owners of one-to-three milch buffaloes or cattle, and to have provided them with reliable and competitively-priced marketing and processing facilities. 'OF' involves the sale of EEC milk products, mainly in cities, and the use of counterpart funds to support such dairy development. Unfortunately, the project is surrounded by intemperate attacks and excessive claims. Certainly, few projects have got gains to the landless, and this one has. But glutting markets with subsidized dairy-product aid, to raise counterpart funds, is an odd means to finance dairy-producer expansion. Milk producers in areas not benefited by Operation Flood suffer twice, as prices are reduced by EEC milk powder and by dairy products from OF areas. And one is worried about diverting increasingly scarce land from grains to dairy products, which (even if employment-intensive in production) remain too costly to be important in poor people's diets. Most serious is the lack of genuinely independent evaluation of the poverty impact, or cost-effectiveness, of these large and controversial projects.[4] We discuss the issues further in the context of project aid (Chapter 5).

Volume of aid to agriculture

But the main development since about 1970, affecting India's poor via aid has not been in the sphere of food aid, but in crop production. Increasingly, donors came in the 1970s to believe that aid must attack the syndrome of 'growth without poverty reduction' by increasing the productivity of the poor (rather than by welfare schemes), and that expanded smallholder food production was the best path. Until the end of the Third Plan, agriculture had received only 1.8 per cent of sectorally allocable aid authorized for India (and 1.0 per cent of aid utilized). Even in 1966–74, the period of the big (and aid-backed) breakthroughs with new wheat varieties and of India's main thrust to foodgrain self-sufficiency and stockbuilding, the proportion was only 9.0 per cent (4.6 per cent). In 1974–5 to 1978–9, it leapt to 29.6 per cent (19.7 per cent) (RBI, 1984–5, statement III). Meanwhile, the gap between the proportion of aid authorized and utilized for agriculture was steadily shrinking, due largely to gradually improving implementation of irrigation plans. By 1980–1 to 1984–5, indeed, agriculture's share in authorized aid funds (29.4 per cent) was below its share of utilization (39.3 per cent). However, new authorized aid to agriculture, in real terms, was edging down again, to about 22 per cent of total aid authorized in 1982–5. This is partly because of a sense among donors that low world commodity prices are reducing returns to agricultural aid, and partly because GoI increasingly sees aid donors' comparative advantage in high-technology sectors and investments.

Aid to agriculture: poverty-oriented?

Aid to agriculture in India has been substantially, and increasingly, for irrigation, credit, extension, and other inputs in support of high-yielding variety (HYV) cereal production.[5] Probably, a substantial rise in the share of Indian resources used in that way is necessary to raise the level of living of India's hungry poor, but it is not sufficient. First, such aid might benefit mainly big farmers. Second, to the extent that it does reach smallholders, it might displace, not increase, Indian Government resource allocations to smallholder food production. Third, aid to smallholder food production might be inefficiently applied. Finally, it might leave untouched major or growing proportions of poor Indians, perhaps including most of the poorest – largely landless farm labourers, their jobs perhaps threatened by aid-linked mechanization of ploughing or post-harvest processing. Overarching all these problems is the fact that donors have overstressed the somewhat vulgar-Malthusian perspective that poverty and hunger are due mainly to inadequate *available* food per head of (growing) populations. Add the misperception that India's growing numbers of hungry people are mainly 'small farmers' and one readily gets stuck with the perspective (Ford Foundation, 1959) that 'more food from progressive smallholders' holds the key to the reduction of poverty. In much of Africa and parts of India, this is valid; increasingly, however, poverty reduction (especially in Eastern India) depends on increased employment, and hence more real income – leading to extra exchange *entitlements* to food (Sen, 1981, 1986) – for near-landless workers. Agriculture is crucial here too, and aid can help; but the formulations and formulae of the early 1960s are no longer quite right.

'Green Revolution' and aid

Before assessing the required changes, we must sketch the content of aid to Indian agricultural production. The most dramatic and cost-effective component was the support of research into HYV wheats, and recently other cereals. Even when based in India, such research was substantially helped by aid to international centres under the auspices of the Consultative Group for International Agricultural Research, CGIAR. Also, significant aid supported some of the bases of domestic Indian research and extension, including US support for India's network of agricultural universities, and World Bank support for the 'training and visit' extension system. Yet the development, application, and extension of fertilizer-responsive wheat and rice HYVs did not absorb even 2 per cent of India's aid, and 2 to 3 per cent of world aid. Without such HYVs Indian cereal output, now typically enough for low-level self-sufficiency, would be 15 to 20 per cent less. This does not, however, 'prove' that the remaining 97.5 per cent of aid is unacceptably unproductive. First, research (and therefore research aid) inevitably seeks an adequate average return by mixing extremely successful activities with failures, and one obviously cannot predict exactly which will be which. Second, aid to agriculture also falls into this category to some extent; average rates of return are somewhat higher on Bank projects in this sector than in others, but so is the proportion of projects (and to a lesser extent, of money) with very bad returns (Lipton, 1987, 5–6). Third, many agricultural-sector investments – aided or not – showed decent but unsensational returns prior to HYVs, which themselves did very well partly because such prior projects, e.g. tubewells in Western Uttar Pradesh, already existed.

The outstanding returns to and for research on HYVs, then, does not prove that all aid can achieve similar returns, nor that returns on most aid are too low. However, such research is indeed a powerful example of the cost-effectiveness, both in growing more food and (we shall argue below) in reducing poverty, of aid for research-based, food-linked biological inputs. But four cautionary notes must be added.

(i) This dramatic success in parts of India – as in parts of several other Asian and Latin American countries – depended on a long-standing domestic network of agricultural research. There is statistical evidence that national research capacity[6] determines the usefulness, for a developing country, of inputs from the (largely aid-financed) international research system (Evenson and Kislev, 1985).

(ii) The anti-poverty success of the high-yielding varieties was due partly to the economic attractiveness of their product types for consumers and smallholders. In the early stages of the green revolution, this attractiveness was largely fortuitous. It certainly cannot be assumed for other countries or future developments.

(iii) The high returns to small outlays of aid for agricultural research would have been impossible without large prior outlays (partly aid-backed) for other agricultural investments. Such outlays, especially on irrigation, prior to HYVs produced decent but seldom sensational returns.

(iv) The early successes of HYVs, on reliably watered rice and wheat, have proved harder to achieve elsewhere.

The green-revolution inputs were developed to meet a problem described in the following terms by the Ford Foundation (1959). Until the early 1960s, modest yield increases could suffice to keep food production slightly ahead of population, because the cropped area could still increase. After about 1963, as was clear well beforehand, almost all economically arable land would be in use. To feed India's growing population at existing levels of demand – let alone those generated by growth of income-per-head – would increasingly use up foreign exchange, thus impeding imports seen to be needed for industrialization. Food aid was not reliable in bad years, and might in any case depress local food output. Thus it was the perceived foreign-exchange consequences of area exhaustion alongside population growth, not considerations of poverty, that drove the yield-oriented green revolution strategy, and especially donor support for it.

Nevertheless, contrary to much ill-informed discussion, the HYV technologies were oriented towards inputs and effects that – perhaps more by luck than judgement – were, in their techno-economic nature and potential, dramatically pro-poor, even apart from their main effect in raising food availability (Lipton, 1978; Lipton with Longhurst, 1989). On the side of production, the HYVs – being short-strawed, fertilizer-responsive and high-yielding – greatly[7] increased demand for labour; thus both the small farmer (with ready access to family labour) and the hired worker benefited. On the consumption side, the breeding of varieties for high grain weight not only raised grain supply and hence restrained price, but produced types of grain that were mainly 'inferior goods', standing at a 10 to 20 per cent price discount below the generally finer traditional varieties, and thus being especially attractive to poor buyers and to producers who aimed mainly at low-cost, household-level consumption. For both production and consumption, the HYVs reduced risk: for consumers, by enabling a build-up of grain stocks, and by concentrating output growth in relatively low-risk and water-controlled regions; for producers, by a steady stream of varietal adaptations to reduce crop vulnerability.

All these pro-poor elements were, more or less, undermined by the dilemma outlined on p.47, as applied to HYV-based agricultural policy in India. Urban elites and the larger farmers who supplied food to the cities were largely able to divert many of its gains to themselves. The production benefits of increased yield for farm labourers have been greatly reduced as 'bigger' farmers (not huge kulaks, but operators of 10 to 25 acres) lobbied successfully for subsidies for tractors and other machinery (and fuel for them), so as to replace workers as they became costlier. (Higher yields made it feasible to pay for such new inputs even with quite small subsidies.) There is nothing about the HYVs that requires labour-replacing complementary inputs[8] but the political process – weakly organized rural workers in growing numbers; and larger farmers on whom governments depended for urbanized surpluses of production and savings – has linked the two. Aid donors have often been insufficiently careful – as late as 1973, World Bank-supported combine harvesters, presumably supplied to India on IDA terms, were on sale in Ludhiana – and may sometimes have made things worse. Such processes were at work all over Asia; by the mid-1980s, each 10 per cent yield increase due to HYVs brought only a 1 to 1.5 per cent rise in labour use, as against the 4 per cent typical of the late 1960s (Jayasuriya and Shand, 1986).

But the real lesson, for governments and donors alike, is that the potential 'pro-poor' effects of HYVs via extra demand for labour are safe only if (i) the great majority of poor farm workers are self-employed most of the time, or if (ii) (near-) landless farm employees take most of the gains from increased labour demand as higher levels of employment rather than as higher wage-rates. These, plus big-farmer political lobbying mean labour displacement, partly or wholly offsetting the initial gains to poor workers from higher demand for labour. If there are to be subsidies, perhaps they should be to labour migration, not to labour-displacing inputs or the credit to buy them.

As regards reduced risk and instability, the favourable effect on the poor of HYVs (and aid to support them) has been undermined by their extreme regional concentration upon areas providing surpluses – of food and savings – for urban use. Thus a small shortfall of rain (or a pest problem) in a few critical – and co-variant – irrigated districts now makes a disproportionate difference to grain output, and even more to marketed surplus and hence urban food supply, at all-India level. Thus, despite the fact that there is usually a reduction in output instability for each individual farmer who adopts up-to-date, more robust seeds, the heavy concentration of such seeds in a few areas, in order to provide a more easily procured surplus, has probably increased co-variance among farmers, and the instability of total output (Hazell, 1982). This can destabilize consumption (i) if stocks do not vary much, and if urban availability is no longer so much affected by import levels;[9] (ii) if, as is likely, cutbacks in output mean even bigger proportionate cutbacks in employment. Better-off middle farmers, when harvests are bad, increase the proportion of farmwork performed by family labour; thus the (poorer) labourers face reduced job prospects just when food prices are pulled upwards.

Cereal imports – in the context of the strategic food problem, as seen by donors and planners alike in a period when economists concentrated more on import constraints and macro-policy than on poverty reduction or micro-markets – are also critical in determining the consumption benefits from HYV cereals. The very large production increases from biochemical innovation have been used almost entirely to replace foodgrain imports, and to build central grain stocks and replace deterioration in them. Hence calorie availability per person is not significantly higher in India today than in 1950–3 (FAO, Food Balance Sheets, and 1984, 179). Calories per consumer unit among the poor have probably not declined or increased much – though there have been offsetting regional trends, themselves reflecting the patchy spread of HYVs (see Subbarao, 1987, 4).

This very pattern suggests that without the biochemical strategy, and especially the new cereal varieties, many more poor people in India in the 1970s would have died. Given oil price rises, the stresses affecting Indian imports would, in the absence of cereal HYVs, have worsened poor people's consumption levels, probably substantially. But HYVs did not suffice, in face of demographic and politico-allocative pressures, actually to raise most poor people's food consumption levels.

However, even if the extra yield had added to cereal imports rather than displaced them, without structural change to raise demand for grains, prices of cereals to producers would have fallen. Suppose the price of aggregate farm output (in terms of farmers' total purchases) had fallen 20 per cent; probably that output would have fallen by about 3 to 4 per cent, and farm income by about 23 per cent. Employment in rural areas would have fallen – perhaps half as fast on the farms as output, but also off the farms, as declining farmers' income reduced their local expenditure. Given the distributional factors that allocated the fruits of the HYVs to the not-so-poor, such innovations – even though potentially pro-poor – had to fail the poor, either on the side of production (if imports were maintained, and farm prices and hence output and jobs were thereby restrained), or on the side of consumption (if imports fell, and food availability per head was therefore not pushed up by the HYVs). Crudely, the former was the effect of the policy for rice, the latter for wheat. Sorghum and finger millet HYVs did better for the poor.

Hence the GoI and aid donors, if they were to embody HYVs in projects providing long term gains for the rural poor, had to select paths of growth that steered assets or jobs to them. Otherwise, the poor could not afford more food, even if it were produced; and maintenance of producers' incentives would depend on the use of any extra food to displace imports.[10] However, donors have not 'grasped the nettle' of how aid to India might be used to get assets or jobs directly to the rural poor. Indirect means have been preferred, principally through support of irrigation, credit, and extension; these have indeed complemented HYVs, and have thereby helped to prevent absolute falls in food availability for the poor. However, such indirect methods have not avoided the biases that, in any highly unequal system, tend to steer the gains largely to the rich. The lesson of donor involvement in Indian irrigation, credit and extension is that 'focus on poverty' depends, not only on sectoral involvement in producing poor people's foods, but on explicit action to strengthen poor people's asset base or job opportunities, and thus their bargaining power. Such action is mainly the responsibility of governments in developing countries, not of aid donors. However, within a large and democratic federal polity such as India, there are usually many instruments and intermediaries that donors – if they wish – can select to get assets to the poor.

Irrigation

Aid flow data do not show irrigation separately; however, it was a large component of aid flows. The World Bank and other donors showed insight within the irrigation 'policy dialogue' (see Chapters 3 and 5), but the genuine and important process of mutual learning, while it improved system efficiency, has failed the poor in several ways. First, the evidence that simple wells (not tubewells) had much the best income-distribution effects (Narain and Roy, 1980) was not translated into aid. Second, main-system design has until recently understressed both technical devices and irrigation-management choices that might improve crop mixes, reduce corruption (and overuse by persons nearer the source), and hence improve the access by poor users, especially tail-enders (Wade and Chambers, 1980); donors spent much energy in persuading water-users to co-operate, but too little, until recently, in creating main systems that made co-operation attractive. Third, some donors' bias in favour of major new structures has slighted not only local construction methods, but, more important, water management and maintenance. Fourth, big irrigation has often driven out small. Deep tubewells in Northwest India lower the water-table and poor people's shallow wells run dry. Some donors are correcting these errors, which led to equity losses and gross under-performance of irrigation systems (Chambers, 1988).

Despite the failures of irrigation expansion to reach the poorer regions, or even many poorer farmers in richer regions – and despite shortfalls in actual behind stated, and stated behind planned, irrigated area – irrigation expansion, especially of groundwater, has been essen-tial to attain the huge expansion of grain output associated with the HYVs.

It is impossible to say how much of the new irrigation capital paid for out of aid would have happened anyway, using GoI money, without aid, but some would not. Indian total investment was constrained by shortages of foreign exchange for most of the 1960s and 1970s. Moreover, in India – unlike sub-Saharan Africa (FAO, 1978, 1979) – the expansion of aid to agriculture since the mid-1970s has not been offset by a corresponding fall in the sector's share in domestically financed investment, in which irrigation plays the major role.

Rural credit

Donors have provided substantial support for institutional rural credit expansion in India (OED, 1981) – both in the 'co-operative period' and in the more recent period of commercial-bank emphasis. Many donor inputs have flowed through apex bodies like the Agricultural Refinance Corporation and its successor, the National Bank for Agriculture and Rural Development (NABARD). The growing emphasis of the USA and other donors upon the role of private enterprise in economic development should make them even more favourably disposed to aid rural credit (which each farmer applies to support his own productive activities) rather than state investment. Yet aid for rural credit is a major source of controversy in regard to overall usefulness, as well as to effectiveness in reaching the poor. The controversy centres on two issues.

First, primary organizations (village-level co-operative societies, branch banks) generally show dismal, non-improving repayment and default records. The appearance is somewhat excessive; e.g. in Southern Tamil Nadu, where 40 per cent of loans are recorded as overdue, only 4 per cent of lending is seriously enough in default to warrant court action or writing off. The rest may be no more than the results of delayed repayment. Yet default is reflected in growing government subsidies, largely as *de facto* grants or write-offs to allow apex organizations (such as NABARD) – themselves apparently very efficient – to make up loans not repaid by farmers to local branches, and hence by branches, via national bodies like commercial banks, to the apex. Such chronic deficits, apart from impairing financial management and diverting public savings away from planned investment uses, help mainly non-poor farmers. Yet, despite the bad financial and social record, the economic performance of lending in support of rural credit in India – as reflected, for example, in the economic rate of return recorded in World Bank post-evaluations – generally looks much better than that of either farm or non-farm projects as a whole (Lipton, 1987a, 15; OED, 1981). This is perhaps due in part to the attribution to private investment out of rural credit of some benefits in fact accruing because of public investments; but, even when this is allowed for, the economic performance of aid to rural credit in India looks good. Yet the financial performance does not; institutional lenders, such as rural branch banks, have great difficulty in recovering their loans, especially from powerful large farmers. This remains the case even when we allow for the fact that much alleged 'default' is merely roll-over from one year to the next.

Second, major efforts are made, in some aid-financed credit schemes, to provide low-interest loans confined to poorer farmers and areas; or to link credit to the purchase of assets in small amounts by poor households, as with IRDP. Yet substantial parts of such subsidized institutional credit are collared by influential, articulate, and normally richer farmers. This is not only an inequitable use of aid; the cheaper credit also encourages the non-poor rural recipients to adopt longer-maturing, i.e. more capital-intensive, sets of inputs and outputs. Credit projects are analysed in Chapter 5; here we address the issue of whether aid to rural credit can help the poor.

Donors' growing scepticism about aid for rural credit has been fuelled mainly by experience of Latin American rural banks and co-operatives, which – first at branch level, eventually at the centre – have been bankrupted by subsidizing on-lending and permitting defaults, while rapid inflation eroded what did get repaid.[11] Even when Indian formal rural credit depended almost entirely on co-operatives, it was never typified by such indiscipline as in much of Latin America, nor surrounded by such rapid inflation. Yet default rates were high. This led in 1982–3 to the cessation of aid to NABARD by the USAID (despite an expanding overall programme of US aid to India) and to a threat of suspension, until overdues were reduced, by the Bank group. Within this group, a major attack on subsidized credit was launched (e.g. Adams *et al.*, 1984). In 1989, the Bank group stopped new support

Such reactions are not motivated only by justified concern for financial stability – or even by less-justified doubts about economic returns to aid for rural credit – but also by concerns about equity and poverty. Since loans (for purchased inputs) form a much higher proportion of production costs among better-off farmers than among poor ones, aid for rural credit, especially but not only[12] if on-lending is subsidized, appears to involve transfer to the better off. This is even clearer when, as is usually the case, richer farmers' default/loan ratios are higher (Lipton, 1976). The effect on the poor is still worse if – as in the case of major World Bank credit projects – the credit permits the purchase of tractors, profitable allegedly because they increase output, but in reality because they displace labour.[13]

It is, nevertheless, mistaken to conclude that aid for credit does not help the poor in absolute terms (though it may raise rich people's incomes by proportionately more). In India, such aid has almost certainly raised the supply of both institutional and total rural credit (i.e. fungibility for the state, and to intermediary public-sector lenders, of aid for rural credit has been well below 100 per cent). This increased and more competitive supply of credit has reduced its price to the poor, not only to the rich who initially benefited. At farm level, certainly, some production loans have been, or have permitted farmers' own resources to be, diverted to consumption (i.e. fungibility for end-use borrowers of rural credit is significant); but such diversion is less likely for larger farmers, well below 100 per cent even for small ones, and not obviously damaging anyway.[14] Low or subsidized rural interest-rates in India did little to discourage the supply of savings, but much to raise the demand for cash to invest (Iqbal, 1983). This must have raised investment in, and hence availability and stability for poor people, of food production. Moreover, extra rural credit usually increased the use of current inputs such as fertilizers, whose expansion makes so much difference to HYVs. These inputs absorb the great bulk of credit for Indian rural production, and are highly complementary with extra work from poor hired labourers.[15] If some credit has been diverted to labour-displacing investments, the fault lies much more with overt subsidies to capital (and fuel) than with credit or credit subsidies. These, in any event, have been dwindling in India.

This does not justify complacency about the effects on poverty (or efficiency) of aid to a default-ridden, and in places still subsidized, rural credit system. However, in village economies that are credit-constrained even at existing production levels, the increases in input use needed to make high-yielding varieties profitable for farmers (and hence to achieve extra local employment and food security for the poor) depend on extra credit supply. Initially, except where there has been a really dramatic breakthrough in agricultural productivity, this may well be acceptable to poor and risk-averse farmers only at rather lower rates than the informal credit market will provide. The leakage of formal credit into 'rich farmers' subsidies' can best be tackled by a gradual shift to more realistic interest rates, firm action against defaulters, and avoidance of price or credit biases towards labour-intensive inputs. Donors increasingly find Indian credit authorities supporting such aims, albeit in the teeth of local élites and their 'official' supporters. To withdraw from aid to rural credit would be to retard, not to assist, its effective reform – and to damage the prospects of spreading, to smallholders in less promising and safe areas, capacity to buy modern inputs and hence to provide poor people, as workers and consumers, with more local work and securer food. In the longer term, however, direct producer benefits to the rural poor, linked to aid for credit, will require access to productive assets; IRDP, for all its faults, is a step in this direction, but major long-run progress is likely to require land reform.

Other agricultural aid and poverty

Despite the world-wide tendency for extension workers to reach more 'acres per day' (and to satisfy patrons) by concentrating on big farmers, the extension services also remain an important determinant of the speed at which many innovations reach poorer and less well-informed people. Major aid support – amounting to about half the total cost of extension, which was 0.22 per cent of annual GNP from Indian agriculture between 1977 to 1982 (Moore, 1984) – has gone, chiefly from the World Bank, to the 'training and visit' system of agricultural extension in India. 'T and V' may have set the scene for major improvement in Indian extension by removing from extension workers the panoply of tasks in input distribution (and paperwork) that had encumbered them. It has replaced such tasks with clear messages, initially to identified 'contact farmers'. It has defined duties, training and overview in the framework of farm needs, instead of crop-specific traditions. However, if T and V is to help poor farmers, extension workers have to be trained and motivated to this end; and critics complain that career structures of village-level workers remain largely neglected, yet that T and V has diverted key senior personnel out of the overall rural administrative system that is needed to make extension useful. As for training, by early 1983, only 11 per cent of the Indian T and V vote for training had been used. The 'contact farmer' method had degenerated, via a search for 'progressive farmers', into a widespread misperception that wealth and literacy were, as such, desirable in the initial audience for extension messages. Part of the problem may have been the familiar 'pilot illusion': the T and V 'pilot project' (Benor and Harrison, 1977) had gained greatly not only from high 'pilot' inputs, but from the progressiveness of agriculture in Chambal district, Rajasthan, and from the suitability of centralized 'fortnightly T and V messages' to a rather homogeneous canal area. As T and V was rapidly spread across successive states – partly because state governments saw it as a source of cash and jobs – it had to handle less promising, more diverse, and more polarized farming conditions. The gains from T and V (as indeed from any form of extension) in such circumstances – and especially its effects on poor, illiterate, non-contact farmers – are more dubious (Moore, 1984), though some increase in adoption of recommended practices has been demonstrated (Feder and Slade, 1986).

Such a critique, however, may be too short-term, not because the above difficulties are mere teething troubles; rather, the long-term prospects of extension – and of its orderly management via T and V – depend upon preparing farm habits for (and readying extension officers to make the best of) subsequent innovations. These may include new biological and chemical inputs that provide significantly more profitable prospects for smallholders – with expanded labour inputs – to grow more food for poor consumers. The districts that achieved the apparently cheap, dramatic green revolution breakthroughs of 1965–72 were those with substantial earlier outlays on traditional research, water control, credit, and above all conventional, in the short term not very high-yielding, extension (Evenson and Kislev, 1975). True, HYVs' potentially 'pro-poor' biases in production have been in part subverted by the 'pro-rich' biases of access: to extension information, credit and irrigation. Aid donors have shown too little response to this. However, the evidence on biological and chemical innovations is clearly that, though bigger farmers gain first and most, poor ones follow. The role of 'anti-poverty' aid to extension is to help to train workers motivated to help poor farmers to adopt swiftly – and, if reasonably profitable, labour-intensively[16] – as and when such innovations become available.

In many developing countries, donors have sought to support attempts to increase poor people's bargaining power by means of 'integrated rural development projects'.[17] Cutting across ministerial boundaries, such projects seek to tackle a whole range of interlocking barriers to poor people's advance: in agriculture, credit, health, education, etc. In practice, many such projects have depended heavily on non-replicable levels of local administrative input or, more usually, on project personnel from the aid agencies themselves. Such personnel, even if very able, are not integrated into national administrative systems. When they leave, those systems, inevitably divided into departmental areas of responsibility, must take over the project, as merely one of many responsibilities. Too often, coherence and purpose dwindle, and buildings alone remain to impress, as 'cathedrals in the desert'.[18] It must be said, however, that integrated projects in Asia, especially in Sri Lanka but also in some parts of India, have a much better record than in Africa (Lipton, 1987, 8–10). There is a compelling logic, despite its current unpopularity, in the view that a given public outlay in a rural area (or elsewhere: see p.178) will do best if divided among complementary activities – health and food production; irrigation, crop development and extension – than if concentrated on just one. The problem is: how to exploit the multi-sectoral complementarities, without risking either administrative incoherence or a sort of area-level donor neo-colonialism?

Rural assets for the poor?

Both the central and state governments have, sometimes with donor support, engaged in multi-sector activity. Comprehensive watershed management, the Drought-prone Areas Programme, and other central schemes have aroused opposition from line ministries, and have recently been played down. West Bengal's 'Comprehensive Area Development Programme' – more orientated to the village level and linked to land rights – remains a significant effort. Both centre and states, however, have largely avoided 'integrated' projects of the variety that, in the name of fighting poverty in the short run, disintegrate the long-run administrative capacity to do so. Unfortunately, donors, faced by this restriction on error, have not been presented by GoI with (and have not themselves adopted) any clear alternative anti-poverty strategy (at least rurally; urban housing aid and health aid nationwide, are partial exceptions). India's Seventh Plan, for the first time, contains such a strategy, with the 'twin pillars' of the 'integrated rural development programme (IRDP) and the rural employment programmes; but it is not a strategy for which donor inputs – increasingly focused by GoI on higher-technology activity and increasingly 'tied' by bilateral donors – are obviously appropriate, or sought; and it comes when India's real aid receipts are lower than ever, and when the salience of the Plan in government thinking (and of poverty in some donors' thinking) is not clear. Moreover, to ensure that the benefits of rural change are steered towards India's poor, those poor must gain local power, with a base in the local economy. Political power in a state capital has, on its own, severely limited scope to help the really poor, because 'poor people's parties' in India are weak; torn between hostile constituencies (Herring, 1983) and limited by the local power, over law as well as economy, of the better-off. Could the poor gain local economic power from an emerging labour shortage? The rapid growth of the Indian workforce, and the world context of technical progress that saves on high labour-costs both militate against that. The alternative is for poor people to gain more ownership, privately or jointly, of the means of production.

There is nothing statist or centralizing about this proposal. Income and asset distribution in rural India are unequal by Western (or African) standards. Yet abundant labour – and persistent scarcity of savings, domestic or foreign – should dictate labour-intensive production, such as is associated with small, fairly equal family enterprises. At issue is not 'state ownership' – indeed, the state is bound to reflect existing power – but diffusion of private control over assets.

Suppose, however, that the state reflects the dominant, asset-owning groups within existing power structures; that donors see their own interests as lying in the use of aid to help the efficient poor; and that this ultimately requires asset redistribution. The scope of aid to influence a strong, sovereign, and in India elected, state in these matters should not be exaggerated. Nevertheless, many parts of the Indian state would welcome an aid emphasis upon asset redistribution to reduce poverty. Donors have done rather little to respond with prompt offers of cash help to support the many official Indian policy statements favouring redistribution of rights in land and water. Land reform – where efficient, and where planned in conjunction with other input supplies – is formally supported, as an object of aid, not only by such countries as Sweden and Holland but by the leader of the Indian aid consortium (World Bank, 1975–82). The widespread belief that there is, in India, no land reform to support is quite wrong; not only have several million hectares been officially redistributed since 1960, but much more has been privately 'redistributed', via market sale or via transfer to poor family members, by big owners, fearful of the implementation of official land reform and its ceilings legislation (Vyas, 1979; Lipton, 1985). Despite the avowed policies of most donors and GoI in favour of land reform, aid to India has done very little of significance to assist it – not even on the modest scale achieved, in the much less auspicious political circumstances of North-East Brazil, through World Bank support.

Moreover, where land reform appears unacceptable, there are other approaches that get assets to the poor. For example, Oxfam in Western Orissa and *Proshika* in Bangladesh (Wood, 1984) both provide landless workers with sources of, and rights to, irrigation water, which is then sold to farmers. The IRDP, which is being massively expanded in India's Seventh Plan, seeks to identify the poorest households in selected villages in each block, and then to provide them with loans, tools, training, and supervisory help in the acquisition and use of income-generating non-land assets.

Assets', inputs', and HYVs' impact on the poor

Research and development of HYVs of food staples, with necessary support from expanded irrigation, credit, and extension,[19] have done much to prevent decline in the food consumption of India's growing numbers of poor. Huge public outlays have been required for that support, and significant though much smaller outlays for the HYVs themselves. Aid has helped to finance these outlays, and to provide useful, two-way policy dialogue. Aid outside India, to international research into cereals, has also made a major impact, in conjunction with sophisticated adaptive research in India, upon food availability (and emergency stocks). However, outside the green revolution lead areas, the poor as producers have gained little from aid. The success in 'holding the line' as regards poor people's consumption – perhaps a bit better in the 1980s – despite population growth, alongside the failure in most respects to strengthen them as producers, is mainly a reflection of Indian efforts, successful in growing more food, but disappointingly inequitable.

North Indian HYV wheat – and probably HYV rice in South India, and hybrid sorghum in the West-Centre – is now adopted as widely by poor farmers as by rich ones, and perhaps farmed more intensively. However, despite the pro-poor nature of the HYV-fertilizer technology and its recent spread, the gains in adopting areas have accrued mostly to the middle, not the poor, farmer; landless and near-landless labourers, who found employment rising by about 40 per cent when HYVs doubled yields (as in several districts they did in ten years), now find the employment rise barely 10–15 per cent.[20] While no state is without major HYV areas, there are huge blanks (especially in the East-Central Indian 'poverty square') where poor wheat farmers in small surplus (and their employees) have actually lost from lower prices due to HYVs. The most striking symptom of the triumph and tragedy of poverty-orientated food efforts – and aid – in India is the build-up of a 20 to 30 million ton public grain reserve, alongside an almost unaltered incidence of under-nutrition. The ultimate reason, about which aid can do little, is lack of 'poor power'. But the immediate reasons is that since the very poor are increasingly near-landless labourers (Lipton with Longhurst, 1989), the effect of agro-technical change on rural poverty depends more and more on its employment impact, not on its impact on 'big' or 'small' farmers.[21] However, farms with less land per family member are more labour-intensive than other farms; also, by absorbing the labour of their moderately poor operators, small farms keep their owners from seeking hired work, which is left to the very poor as an income source. Therefore, the growth of small farming is a crucial weapon in the struggle for high-employment agricultural growth patterns. Why, despite their potential techno-economic merits for small and labour-intensive farms, have not HYVs in India helped them more?

The first immediate reason is the adoption sequence. Whatever the objective risks,[22] a major innovation is always subjectively risky, until farmers' observation of nearby successes and techniques has created widespread confidence. Hence poor, risk-averse farmers are seldom early innovators – especially because bigger farmers have better access to early information. So the bigger farmers adopt a new HYV first, and can sell more in the early stages of its spread – before its wide-scale adoption has greatly raised the cereal's supply and brought down its relative price. Anything that helps smaller farms to adopt innovations sooner will also help them to share more in the gains – and to deliver employment benefits as a result. Such projects as the UK-aided 'fertilizer education scheme' in Orissa are clearly relevant here.

The second reason why smaller farmers do less well than the HYV technology would suggest lies in its delivery system. Timely and adequate credit tends to go to bigger farmers, often through subsidized official channels. Inputs, especially appropriate fertilizer-mixes, possess economies of scale in delivery, again favouring larger users. Yet extra inputs (and credit to buy them) are often needed to justify outlay on better seeds.

The third reason lies in regional imbalances in research and irrigation. HYVs were at first heavily concentrated in a few reliably-irrigated areas. By increasing domestic marketed surplus, this sometimes actually reduced incomes in competing areas, for example parts of Madhya Pradesh. This has happened even in well-favoured areas, to some farmers unable to secure reliable water. Of course, that is not a case for slowing down HYVs in suitable areas, or for forcing them on unsuitable ones. It does make a case for research (and sometimes irrigation) to shrink the pale of unsuitable areas – and for using some of the 'gains of the green revolution' to steer new, potentially economic, off-farm activity to poor people in those regions. Aid for research in semi-arid areas has helped with the first task; but donors have not yet contributed much support for non-farm rural activity in 'backward' areas.

Fourth, we have referred to adverse price effects on some of the rural poor. As big farmers in favoured areas, helped by early innovation, raised output, prices were pressed downwards. This reduced the value of real outputs – whether sold or eaten at home – from generally poorer farmers, from the later innovators, from those with less access to delivery systems, and from areas less responsive to HYVs. Aid, both for HYVs and for irrigation and other supportive inputs, by its regional concentration tended to increase these disparities. However, by concentrating on extra output in rural areas most readily amenable to rapid HYV-based growth, aid helped to employ the many near-landless in such areas. Such aid, by raising food supply and thus restraining food prices, also helped the urban poor. In the short term, this effect also helped the rural poorest – net buyers of food – by restraining food prices. However, the longer-term impact on these groups via rural employment, especially in some non-HYV areas, may be damaging.

Fifth, underlying all these sequences of frustration – these slips between the cup of poverty-reducing HYVs, and the parched lips of the poor – is the motivation of Indian food policy. Essentially, and despite the genuine concern (predating that of most donors) of large parts of the GoI machine to reduce poverty, the central aim of Indian food policy has been to obtain an adequate domestic supply of food, so as to ensure that no major foreign-exchange shortage would be threatened by a need to import food. Planners with this 'central aim' – however genuine their hatred of poverty – are bound to be at least half pleased when food surpluses, delivered to urban areas, surge ahead. The 'central aim' is also almost unavoidable, once GoI accepts that food output in the wake of HYVs increases much faster than poor people's purchasing power. In that case the extra output at least of the main urban grain (wheat) *must* be used, first to displace food imports, then to build up stocks – not to add massively to supply; for, if the latter happens, farm-gate prices of wheat could tumble out of control, and future investments in expanded farm output would be discouraged. This 'central aim' also explains why Indian (and donor) authorities, in large part genuinely concerned for land reform and employment-intensive technology, have – at least – tolerated dynamic damage to the rural poor, in the wake of HYVs even if not necessarily as a result of them. This dynamic damage is probably at least as important as the static maldistributions we have discussed.

First, in the Punjab and Haryana – in marked contrast to other Indian states less 'overrun' by HYVs – the process of tenancy resumption, well under way before the HYVs arrived, has accelerated in their wake. Since the early 1960s, owners of 10 to 20 acres have resumed tenancies and turned tenant farmers into landless employees, while owners of 0 to 1 acres have ceased to farm the land themselves and have rented it out to medium-to-large operators. The tiny ex-owners are probably better off as landless employees in the Punjab's post-HYV boom – certainly the incidence of poverty sharply declined in that state in the 1970s (Chadha, 1983) – but 'poor power' (and security) suffer in the process. Second, again especially in these areas but also in the HYV rice areas of Tamil Nadu and coastal Andhra, labour-replacing innovation has followed in the wake of HYVs.[23] Combined with the increasing reliance of India's rural poor – as population growth has reduced holding size – on employment for income, this too has reduced the benefits of HYVs to them.

It is demographics and politics, not technology or economics, that have shifted the benefits of HYVs – and hence of the aid that supports them – to some extent away from the poor. HYVs do not render profitable, in most cases, the tractors, weedicides, and modern rice mills that 'unemploy' poor workers, 'save' labour-costs, and add little or nothing to consumable output (Agarwal, 1980; Binswanger, 1978; Greeley, 1987). What happens is that HYVs first intensify seasonal labour peaks; then induce bigger farmers to press for subsidies to inputs that substitute for increasingly organized, or temporarily costly, labour; and finally induce urban groups to concede such subsidies. The new labour-displacing equipment is then used not only in peak seasons, but for much of the year. It displaces workers and is less costly for larger farmers. The process further concentrates HYV output (and benefits) with surplus farmers, who restrain food prices via their sales to urban groups. HYVs may well strengthen both urban food buyers and surplus farmers politically – but HYVs do not create an economic case for labour-replacing innovations, or for the exclusion of poor people from operating high-grade land. Nor, of course, do HYVs cause the steady demographic pressure that renders such innovation and exclusion so harmful to the poor.

Given the politico-demographic framework – are HYVs nevertheless a cheap way for projects (and aid donors) to benefit the poor? Certainly, with GoI cooperation and a supportive local frame of research and extension, aid to cereal production does more for employment, food-price restraint, and hence poverty alleviation, than the heavy-industry patterns of aid that prevailed before the 1970s (see p.49). Since inadequate supply of wage-goods from agriculture in the 1950s and 1960s have regularly constrained non-farm growth, but not *vice versa* – and since investment in agriculture has been regularly, and probably since HYVs increasingly, associated with much more GNP gain than equal amounts of off-farm investment (Lipton, 1968) – it is not plausible to deny the relative efficiency of farm investment and aid.[24] Moreover, there does seem to have been a (small) real rise in agriculture's share of total Indian investment since about 1970; unlike most of Africa, in India the ruralization of aid has not in practice been wholly fungible, i.e. has not led to a wholly offsetting fall in the rural share of domestic investment efforts. It is admittedly difficult to steer farm support to really small holdings; however, several states, and several national institutions of agricultural development, try hard, and with some success. Smallholder development tends to mean labour-intensive farming, and thus to encourage smallholder families to work on the home farm instead of competing with landless labourers for 'commercial' work. Also, it usually enriches people with a higher propensity to buy labour-intensive inputs and consumer-goods than does big-farm development.[25] So there is some spin-off even to the landless. This is a specific economic process, not a vague hope of 'trickle-down'. Nevertheless, the poverty of those with only labour-power to sell has, ultimately, to be tackled by off-farm employment and/or generation or distribution, of productive assets. Probably both off-farm employment and non-farm assets will not suffice; a combination of the HYV approach (spread to rain-fed areas and to 'inferior' cereals such as millets and sorghum) with land redistribution (so that extra HYV output accrues to poor growers who will eat their extra output, instead of selling to to swell central grain stocks) may well be necessary.[26]

In well-watered places, HYVs plus redistribution of access or demand or entitlements to food, can greatly ease the problems of rural poverty; and aid can help. What of the Eastern, Central and other areas of unreliable water? There has, since the mid-1970s (and due to combined efforts by Indian scientists and the aid-supported International Crops Research Institute for the Semi-arid Tropics, Hyderabad), been major progress with hybrid sorghum and finger-millet in some rain-fed areas (Rao, Rajpurohit, Sawant). However, the spread of HYVs to rain-fed areas is as yet small scale, slow, costly, and uncertain. 'Fast food' from HYVs will usually require, for many years, some degree of water assurance. But in most of India the inexpensive options in irrigation have been used up, and it is increasingly expensive as it spreads to new areas. Such rising costs – and management problems – are smaller in the case of farmer-controlled micro-irrigation, but many forms of this depend upon the costly use of fossil-fuel energy to lift water to the cropland. Also, while generally not more so than land (Narain and Roy), irrigation water can readily be maldistributed.

Nevertheless, the spread of water control to poorer farmers and regions remains a key element in their food security. Irrigation – which has been supported by major aid inputs to Indian (and other Asian) agriculture – constitutes a major element in an effective short-run attack on poverty and hunger, even if there are plenty of cereals in government stocks and the poor lack the money to buy it. Reliable irrigation can provide reliable jobs to the landless; can ease the process of agricultural diversification into labour-intensive and income-elastic crops, such as vegetables; and can stabilize food supply from poor farmers' own land. Its success in these areas depends on an outlay on well-designed irrigation; land developed per rupee spent; irrigated area as a proportion of developed land; and access of poor people to such areas or to jobs (or cheap food) from them.

(i) In discussing policy dialogue, we consider the World Bank's role, learning as much as teaching, in improvement of strategies for Indian irrigation design. (ii) However, there has been less success in improving the rate of land development per rupee spent on irrigation construction, however good its design. (iii) Despite the new concern of the agricultural and irrigation experts with inadequate 'water management', shortfalls in irrigated area per unit of land developed below design expectations have, especially in South India, massively reduced the efficiency of outlays on irrigation, not least in producing extra food or work for the poor. (iv) Finally, the choice of systems that might raise the share, in irrigated area, of tail-enders and other poor users remains neglected, especially in the bigger aided projects. Although some small-scale irrigation systems are better at blending efficiency with equity, preference at the construction stage is often given to big gravity-flow systems. Such systems 'build in' preferences for larger farmers, head-enders or co-operatives of several adjacent farmers (usually in practice dominated by larger farmers or head-enders). Poor users are often harmed by neglect of negative externalities from richer or stronger water users: upstream growers plant 'thirsty' paddy, depriving tail-enders of water for a second crop; or deep tube- wells lower the water table and render hand pumps useless (Wade and Chambers, 1980; Howes, 1982). Improved design can reach the poor only if it anticipates problems and provides technical structures and/or incentives to irrigation engineers and managers to facilitate equitable solutions.

In summary, aid has successfully supported the outlays on HYVs research, irrigation, extension, and credit in raising food output. This has prevented the rise in oil and industrial import costs (and the associated fall in food imports) from making the poor even poorer, as consumers. But such aid – despite the fact that HYVs are technically suited to employment-intensive production on small farms – must do more for the poor as producers. If poor people's access to income from production does not rise, then in the long run their food consumption cannot rise either, unless real food prices fall. Higher food supply may restrain food prices – but, with population and workforce growing, employers can respond by correspondingly restraining money wages.[27] Poor people, increasingly rural labourers rather than even 'small' farmers, did initially get much more work due to HYVs – but that gain was eroded as labour-displacing methods spread. HYVs are, as such, a 'poor-specific' technology; but they enter a power context in which their gains are largely diverted to help the rich. The answer has to be redistribution of agriculture-linked assets, and of work chances, towards the poor. Both donor and recipient rhetoric in India supports this. So do many specific, substantial outlays, actions, and agencies. But huge problems remain; and progress has so far been very modest. Since India – unlike most LDCs, and surprisingly in view of its fairly steady growth – has not significantly reduced the share of its workforce in agriculture (of about 70 per cent), it is plainly central to get assets and/or labour income to its agricultural poor. At a time and by methods agreed after consultation with the Indian Government, leading donors should clarify their readiness to lend in support of well-conceived programmes for redistributive land reform.

Aid other than to food and agriculture: poverty impact

Apart from raising private consumption of the poor via increases in food availability that restrain its price, or increasing poor people's incomes from work or assets, aid (or domestic outlays) can take a third path towards reducing poverty. Several types of product are already purchased privately by the rich, yet are normally unavailable to the poor unless supplied socially, so that any expansion of public provision is by definition poverty-focused. At least three types of such service – primary-preventive health and primary education (World Bank, 1980) and contraception (World Bank, 1984) – have high economic rates of return, and major positive externalities, even when supplied free to people who cannot afford them.

Health

Health aid comprised 8 to 10 per cent of total public health outlay, capital, and current, in the 1950s, when PL 480 counterpart funds from the US paid for most of the attempts – initially very successful – at malaria eradication and control. The proportion fell steadily to 2 to 3 per cent in the 1970s (Jeffrey, 1985). However, health aid – and technical assistance from WHO and UNICEF – proved effective in supporting the 'socio-economic' wing of the Indian medical establishment against its 'medical purist' wing. The socio-economic wing has sought to redirect effort, away from high-technology teaching hospitals, towards preventive medicine, rurally focused, and making much more use of para-medical personnel. The medical purists aimed at exemplary standards of treatment, rather than at high cost-effectiveness in use of medical resources. In the early 1970s, the socio-economic wing was in a minority, and the medical purists were dominant. By 1980, that had

71

been reversed, substantially because of policy dialogue – mutual learning and exchange of knowledge, not arm-twisting – associated with health aid.

Education

Accompanying this reversal came a shift in educational outlays towards primary schooling. Aid, since it finances almost entirely capital outlays in this sector, pays for only a small part of total public-sector educational costs, which comprise mainly teachers' salaries. However, IDA educational aid shifted heavily towards the primary sub-sector (World Bank, 1982) in India as elsewhere. This helped those forces in the Indian educational sector which sought parallel changes, shifting educational outlays towards the poor majority, who seldom proceed beyond primary school.

Family planning

In family planning, major Indian programmes began during the 1951–6 First Plan, long before any substantial donor interest. But 'new model projects' were aid-backed after 1972 – by Sweden in Uttar Pradesh, by Denmark in Tamil Nadu and Madhya Pradesh, by the UK in Orissa, by the UN Fund for Population Activities in Bihar and Rajasthan, and by USAID in five states. These projects all sought effective integration of family planning and child care. They were 'new', in that they at once sought to set contraception into the context of reducing infant and child mortality, thus persuading parents to reduce their family size norms; and sought to provide a wide range of subsidized services locally. It is poor people whose households and child/adult ratios are much the highest (Lipton, 1983a), who have least access to contraception and highest family size norms (World Bank, 1984), and who lose income if their workforces grow fast relatively to the demand for labour. Therefore, the poor gain most from aid directed towards family planning programmes. In 1951 an average Indian woman bore six children in her life; today, only four. But only Kerala – which has no special programme but has wider health access and more equal income distribution than other states, both reducing fertility – has significantly accelerated fertility decline among the poor (Zachariah and Kurup, 1984). Elsewhere fertility reduction is more successful if gains from growth are widely distributed among the poor (Repetto, 1979). Donors may need to seek out programmes that operate alongside effective action to raise the income of poor people, thus reducing their expected dependence on child labour (and on incomes from grown-up children, for security in old age).

Urban housing

Aid to urban housing has seen major reversals of donor strategy, pioneered by Canada and the Bank group. Unusually, such reversals were clearly more cause than effect of an improved poverty-focus of programmes in recipient countries. Until the mid-1970s, aid supported large, so-called 'low-cost', public housing programmes, which in fact were affordable only to the top 30 to 50 per cent of townspeople. Donors became uneasy about such patterns. The first move was towards loans to help poor people buy 'site-and-service' plots, with loans advanced to borrowers on the understanding that they would use simple materials (supplied) plus their own labour to construct owner-occupied homes. Next came a further move 'downmarket', towards loans for 'slum upgrading', again assuming owner-occupancy and dwellers' labour. Most recently, donors and lenders have shifted from prohibition to positive encouragement of hiring-in of construction labour and renting-out of parts of improved homes. World Bank (1982) and other assessments indicate that these three steps have provided progressively increasing, and recently significant, shares of benefit, as far down the per-person income-distribution as the fourth, third, and even second-poorest decile of households. While the main examples of this success are not in South Asia, Calcutta has benefited substantially (see Chapter 5).

In these urban schemes, one major drawback is the lack of opportunity provided, on most sites, for productive work and/or asset ownership. Such sources of 'poor power' are usually essential, in city as in village, if aid is to improve the sustainable growth rate of poor people's incomes. An ongoing UK-aided project in Hyderabad is one of the few to combine slum upgrading (and site-and-service building) with support for productive on-site micro-assets – repair work, family retailing, etc. Using the Hyderabad City Department of Community Development as a focus, it seeks to link urban housing, education, family industry, and housing, in a sort of Integrated Urban Development Programme, directly responsive to highly localized committees of slum dwellers – initially, perhaps, subverted or led by 'big men' or slum landlords, but often, it has been found, reverting to more genuine participation later. Whether this will prove replicable or succumb to 'pilot syndrome' remains to be seen.

Learning from India

There is now widespread concern about the falling trend of food output per person in sub-Saharan Africa. There has also been considerable redirection of aid towards SSA with the aim of remedying this.[28] Much of this extra aid has rightly gone in general balance-of-payments support; however, such support – both sectoral (and maintenance) aid and 'policy dialogue' has increasingly emphasized agriculture. African governments have undertaken some policy reforms affecting food prices and marketing (though few have shifted significant real resources towards support of food production). It is increasingly obvious in almost every country in SSA (as in South Asia) that – with 70 to 80 per cent of poor people's outlay spent on food, and 55 to 75 per cent of their working time used to produce it – 'poor people' and 'food adequacy' tend to be helped or harmed by almost identical policy sets, including aid policy sets. Food adequacy, of course, depends on entitlements to food, as well as its physical availability. However, in much of SSA most of the poor are still small farmers, and so widespread rises in food output and availability in SSA – more clearly than in India – would directly improve poor people's 'entitlements' to food (Sen, 1981) in most cases.[29] If more rapid increases in food availability via extra output from smallholders would contribute to solving a major part of SSA's poverty problem, how can aid help? In that context, India has more to teach donors about 'aid effectiveness against poverty' than to learn from them.

First, India teaches that big rises in food output are necessary but not sufficient to roll back poverty in face of a rapidly growing rural labour supply. In the sense now being given to the expression 'solving the food problem' by most African countries, and by most recommended food strategies, India has solved its food problem: it has achieved self-sufficiency in food staples, given the effective demand for them in an average year, and has accumulated enough stocks to reduce acute food insecurity greatly. Yet it has not, at national level, substantially reduced the proportionate incidence or average intensity of poverty, under-nutrition or hunger.

Aid to African agricultures could fall into a similar trap if it 'merely' helped to solve food production problems by raising output of food staples on larger farms – typically without greatly raising demand for labour. A typical producer of extra food staples under such a strategy, a big farmer or a tractor-driver, being decently fed already, would not greatly raise demand for staples as income rose. In such circumstances, either food prices fall, or extra output of food staples is offset by reduced food imports. If food prices fall, future investment in food production is discouraged, and employers can restrain poor workers' money-wages to match the restraint in living costs (because supply of unskilled labour is elastic to the real wage). If net food imports fall to offset rising domestic output, food availability does not increase. In either case, extra food output alone – unless on poor people's farms, or labour-intensive – need not create extra real incomes for the poor. Extra food supply, unless the poor also attain higher demand capacity, can leave them, as in India, almost as under-nourished as before in a normal year (though a bit safer in a bad year). Although, in most of SSA, greater access to new land enables the poor to gain more as producers from expanded food production than in most of India, the inexorably rising rural labour supply is eroding these options in more and more of Africa, as it has already done in most of Asia.

The second 'Indian lesson for SSA' is more hopeful. India, despite national failure to reduce average poverty, has – with the help of very modest aid inflows – scored two sorts of success. (i) Nationally, the extra food output, centrally stored, plus improved information and distribution, mean that the terrible downward fluctuations in poverty, the once-regular famines and mass deaths, have been largely eliminated since 1943. Even extreme climatic misfortunes (e.g. 1965 and 1966; 1987; and the long Western Indian drought of the early 1970s) were met without major rises in death-rates (Drèze, 1987). (ii) As for poverty in average years, there is a plethora of local and scheme-specific successes. Some general conclusions are already being drawn from these successes (Subbarao, 1987). The several hundred formal evaluations of micro-projects in the GoI's 'Concurrent Evaluation' of IRDP – while of mixed quality, and usually damaged by absence of proper 'before and after' comparisons or control-groups – provide much further information.

Donors should, perhaps via the Consortium, request GoI permission to finance and co-ordinate a detailed review, to be undertaken by one or more independent Indian institutions, of the national, village, and project evidence. Such a review should cover not only 'successes and failures' in cost-effectively (and apparently lastingly) raising the level or stability of poor people's productivity and/or well-being, but also the usefulness or otherwise of different sorts of aid and TC in different sorts of success. It is hard to envisage a piece of research more useful in the short-to-medium term for poverty alleviation in SSA, especially if African institutions of scholarship and administration can be involved.

For India, there has also been a chronic training problem, which – in a proper context – such a review could help to solve. After the review had helped to evaluate the successive poverty alleviation programmes (local, state, and national; public, voluntary, and private), its results should be used to train personnel to staff such programmes. A review of Indian experience (and data) on poverty alleviation programmes, apart from greatly helping donors – and African administrators – could also catalyse one of the larger Indian research centres or universities, already involved in some work of this sort, to formulate a standing programme of 'Poverty Action, Training, and Research', possibly networked across several state-level research institutions. Such a programme should help central and state governments to select, design, implement, staff, and evaluate future DPAPs, EGSs or IRDPs.[30]

Finally, although there is some conflict of evidence, we believe that most donors have not done enough to render their own procedures conducive to cost-effective anti-poverty aid.

(i) Many Indian officials believe that aid agencies' inability or reluctance to pay local or recurrent costs pushed their aid away from poverty-oriented programmes, which often have a small direct foreign-exchange content.[31] Many – indeed most – donor agency representatives, on the other hand, deny that this inability exists, or assert that it is avoidable. In respect of multilateral – or untied bilateral – aid, we see no reason why donors should refuse support of local capital costs. Recurrent costs present real problems, however. A project may die unless the aid agency takes some initial risks by supporting recurrent costs. Yet, if it is too ready to bear too many such costs for too long, the recipient government is not adequately involved in, or committed to, the project.[32]

(ii) Aid-tying – which was certainly linked to the extreme concentration of early aid to India on industry – plainly and seriously impedes poverty impact. It tends to impose capital-intensity and import-intensity, at the cost of employment. And it is difficult to identify imports to tie, in direct support of most rural poverty programmes.

(iii) Consortium procedures insufficiently review poverty alleviation, let alone to encouraging donors (or recipients) to spend on it. The Bank group, as chairman, does prepare several excellent papers on basic needs, poverty, health, etc., for Consortium meetings. These papers appear to be tabled, but not incorporated into main documents, and, according to the minutes, not discussed when pledges are being gathered (see World Bank, 1978). The decline from the mid-1970s in the regularity or care with which poverty and unemployment are tracked in India may well, in part, be a response to the weak follow-up by the international aid community of its stated concern for poverty reduction in India.

(iv) Internal relations, inside aid agencies, between central and line (project and loan) staff may militate against effective anti-poverty aid. Line staff are motivated to move money quickly, safely, and in big amounts. Poverty screening during the project cycle, however attractive to central staff responding to international pressures, is far less so to time-constrained line officials. Quick, simple, reasonably reliable guidelines are needed – even on such apparently commonsense matters as ensuring that poor persons displaced by irrigation schemes, often tribals without formalized rights, are not harmed.

References

Adams, D.W., Graham, D.H., and von Pischke, J.D.(1984) *Undermining*

Rural Development with Cheap Credit, Colorado, Westview Press.

Asian Development Bank (1977) *Asian Agricultural Survey 1976*, Manila.

Agarwal, B. (1980) 'Tractorization, productivity, and employment: a reassessment', *Journal of Development Studies* 16: 3, April.

Ahluwalia, M.S. (1978) 'Rural poverty and agricultural performance in India', *Journal of Development Studies* 14: 3, April.

Ahluwalia, M.S. (1986) 'Rural poverty, agricultural production and prices: a re-examination' in J. Mellor and G. Desai (eds) *Agricultural Change and Rural Poverty*, Delhi, Oxford University Press.

Alderman, H. and Sahn, D. (1987) 'The effects of human capital on wages and the determinants of labour supply in a developing country', *Journal of Development Economics* 29:2.

Alexander, K. (1981) *Peasant Organisation in South India*, New Delhi, Indian Social Research Institute.

Becker, G. (1981) *A Treatise on the Family*, Cambridge, Mass., Harvard University Press.

Benor, D. and Harrison, J. (1977) *Agricultural Extension: the Training and Visit System*, Washington DC, World Bank.

Bhalla, S. (1979) 'Real wage rates of agricultural labourers in the Punjab', *Economic and Political Weekly XIV*, 26, 30 June.

Binswanger, H. (1978) *The Economics of Tractorization in South Asia*, New York, Agricultural Development Council.

Cassen, R.H. (1978) *India: Population, Economy, Society*, London and Basingstoke, Macmillan.

Chadha, G.K. (1983) *Dynamics of Rural Transformation: a Study of Punjab 1950-80*, New Delhi, Jawarharlal Nehru University, Centre for Regional Development.

Chambers, R. (1988) *Managing Canal Irrigation: Practical Analysis from South Asia*, New Delhi, Oxford and IBH Publishing Co.

Chaudhri, D.P. (1979) *Education, Innovations, and Agricultural Development*, London, Croom Helm.

Dasgupta, B. (1977) *Village Society and Labour Use*, New Delhi, Oxford University Press.

Drèze, J.P. (1988) *Famine Prevention in India*, London, LSE Development Economics Research Programme 3.

Evenson, R. and Kislev, Y. (1975) *Agricultural Research and Productivity*, New Haven, Yale University Press.

FAO (1978, 1979, 1984) *State of Food and Agriculture*, Rome.

Feder, G. and Slade, R. (1986) 'A comparative analysis of some aspects of the training and visit system of agricultural extension in India', *Journal of Development Studies*, 22: 2, January.

Ford Foundation (1959) *Report on India's Foodgrain Crisis and Steps to Meet It*, New Delhi, Government of India.

Greeley, M. (1987) *Postharvest Losses, Technology and Employment: the case of rice in Bangladesh*, Boulder, Colorado, Westview Press.

Hazell, P. (1982) *Instability in Indian Foodgrain Production*, IFPRI Research Report 30, Washington DC, International Food Policy Research Institute.

Hazell, P. and Roell, A. (1983) *Rural Growth Linkages*, IFPRI Research

Report 33, Washington DC, International Food Policy Research Institute.

Herring, R. (1983) *Land to the Tiller*, New Haven, Yale University Press.

Howes, M. (1982) 'The creation and appropriation of value in irrigated agriculture' in M. Greeley and M. Howes (eds) (1982) *Rural Technology, Rural Institutions and the Rural Poorest*, Comilla, Bangladesh, CIRDAP/IDS.

Iqbal, F. (1983) 'The demand for funds by agricultural householders: evidence from rural India', *Journal of Development Studies*, 20: 1, October.

IRRI/ADC (1983) *Consequences of Small-farm Mechanization*, Los Banos, Philippines, International Rice Research Institute.

Ishikawa, S. (1978) *Labour Absorption in Asian Agriculture*, Bangkok, International Labour Organization.

Jamison, D. and Lau, L. (1982) *Farmer Education and Farm Efficiency*, Baltimore, Maryland, Johns Hopkins University Press.

Jayasuriya, S.K. and Shand, R.T. (1986) 'Technical change and labour absorption in Asian agriculture: some emerging trends', *World Development* 14: 3, March.

Jeffrey, R. (1985) *Health and the State in India*, Edinburgh, University of Edinburgh PhD thesis (unpublished).

Kumar, D. (1974) 'Changes in income distribution and poverty in India: a review of the literature', *World Development*, 2: 1, January.

Lipton, M. (1968) 'Urban bias and rural planning', in P. Streeten and M. Lipton, (eds) (1968), *The Crisis of Indian Planning*, Oxford, Oxford University Press for RIIA.

Lipton, M. (1976) 'Agricultural finance and rural credit in developing countries', *World Development* 4: 7, July.

Lipton, M. (1978) 'Interfarm, inter-regional and farm-nonfarm distribution: the impact of the new cereal varieties', *World Development*, 6: 3, March.

Lipton, M. (1983) *Poverty, Undernutrition and Hunger*, Staff Working Paper 597, Washington DC, World Bank.

Lipton, M. (1983a) *Demography and Poverty*, Staff Working Paper 623, Washington DC, World Bank.

Lipton, M. (1983b) *Labour and Poverty*, Staff Working Paper 616, Washington DC, World Bank.

Lipton, M. (1985) *Land Assets and Rural Poverty*, Staff Working Paper 744, Washington DC, World Bank.

Lipton, M. (1987) *Improving the Impact of Aid for Rural Development*, IDS Discussion Paper 233, Brighton, IDS.

Lipton, M. (1987a) *Improving Agricultural Aid Impact on Low-Income Countries*, IDS Discussion Paper 234, Brighton, Institute of Development Studies.

Lipton, M., with Longhurst, R. (1989) *New Seeds and Poor People*, London, Unwin Hyman.

Mellor, J.W. (1976) *The New Economics of Growth: a Strategy for India and the Developing World*, Ithaca, New York and London, Cornell University Press..

Minhas, B.S., Jain, L.R., Kansal, S.M. and Saluja, M.R. (1987) 'On the choice of appropriate consumer price indices and data sets for estimating the incidence of poverty in India', *Indian Economic Review*, 22:1, January-June.

Mitra, A. (1978) *India's Population: Aspects of Quality and Control*, vol. 1, New Delhi, Abhinav.

Moore, M. (1984) 'Institutional development, the World Bank, and India's new agricultural extension programme', *Journal of Development Studies*, 20: 4, July .

Narain, D. and Roy, S. (1980) *Impact of Irrigation and Labour Availability on Multiple Cropping (India)*, IFPRI Research Report 20, Washington DC, International Food Policy Research Institute.

OED (Operations Evaluation Division) (1981) *Agricultural Credit Projects: a Review of Recent Experience in India*, Report 3415, Washington DC, World Bank.

Plocki, J. and Blandford, D. (1977) *Evaluating the Disincentive Effect of PL 480 Food Aid: the Indian Case Reconsidered*, Ithaca, New York, Cornell University Press.

Rath, N. (1985) '*Garibi hatao*: can IRDP do it?', *Economic and Political Weekly* 20: 6, 9 February.

RBI (Reserve Bank of India) (various years), *Report on Currency and Finance*, Bombay.

Repetto, R. (1979) *Economic Inequality and Fertility in Developing Countries*, Baltimore, Maryland, Johns Hopkins University Press.

Saith, A, (1981) 'Production, prices and poverty in rural India', *Journal of Development Studies*, 17: 2, January.

Sen, A.K. (1981) *Poverty and Famines: an Essay on Entitlement and Deprivation*, Oxford, Clarendon Press.

Sen, A. K. (1983) 'Development: which way now?', *Economic Journal*, 93: 372 December.

Subbarao, K. (1987) 'Interventions to fill nutrition gaps at the household-level: a Review of India's experience', mimeo, Delhi, World Bank.

Sukhatme, P. (1978) 'Assessment of adequacy of diets at different income levels', *Economic and Political Weekly*, 12: 31, 3 August.

Vyas, V. (1979) 'Structural change in Indian agriculture', Indian Journal of Agricultural Economics 1.

Wade, R. and Chambers, R. (1980) 'Managing the main system: canal irrigation's blind spot', *Economic and Political Weekly* XV: 39 September.

Wood, G. (1984) 'Provision of irrigation assets by the landless: a new approach to agrarian reform', *Agricultural Administration*, October.

World Bank, (1975, 1982) *Land Reform*, (policy paper), Washington DC.

World Bank (1978) *Report on Consortia and Consultative Groups*, Washington DC.

World Bank (1980, 1984, 1985, 1987) *World Development Report*, Washington DC.

World Bank (1982) *Focus on Poverty*, Washington DC.

Zachariah, K. and Kurup, R. (1984) 'Determinants of fertility decline in Kerala' in T. Dyson and N. Crook (eds) *India's Demography: Essays on the Contemporary Population*, New Delhi, S. Asian Publishers.

Chapter 3

Policy Dialogue

Surprising facts and aid processes

The facts about aid and India's economic performance since Independence, as we have shown, are fairly clear. But they are also counter-intuitive. Most 'intelligent laymen' – even most economists not specializing in development – probably believe: (i) that aid to India has been large; (ii) that India's growth performance has been bad; (iii) that this is partly due to substantial, and rather successful, policy emphasis on equity and poverty alleviation at the cost of growth; and (iv) that aid played a major role in both the growth outcome and the equity outcome.

The truth on the first three propositions is almost exactly the opposite: (i) aid to India was smallish relative to GNP, investment, or population – especially by comparison with most other LDCs; (ii) India's growth performance, by comparison with its own past or with most other developing countries and regions, has been acceptable, consistent, and above all improving, despite the increasingly difficult circumstances of 1973–86; (iii) despite real policy efforts, however — and although equity (e.g. in access to schools or land) normally improves growth – income distribution has worsened, and poverty did not become less prevalent in 1961–86.

The truth in regard to proposition (iv) above is more complex. Aid has usually been too small and diffuse to be the main factor underlying India's growth or equity performance. Yet, as Chapter 2 suggests, its impact on policies for some sectors, and on some macro-policies also, has been crucial. While part of this impact can be related to numbers – gross aid was and is not small compared to the Indian Centre's public-sector development investment, or to its foreign-exchange requirements – most cannot. The story of the 1965 devaluation, or more happily of the policy adjustments (described on pp. 93–4) cannot be told without explaining the changing processes by which the Government of India and the donors jointly determined both the uses of aid and its policy surround.

From bilateral leverage to multilateral sector dialogue

Until the mid-1960s, the relationship between India and aid donors seemed to be smooth and successful. The Planning Commission was using a small but significant volume of aid resources, together with public savings, to negotiate, with states and ministries, more or less binding assignments of public investment. This accompanied fairly steady, albeit slow, real growth of GNP per person. India was able to run down the sterling balances, and, together with the first major expansion of aid, these cushioned the shock of the mid-term adjustment required to the Second Five Year Plan. The alleviation of poverty, already spelled out as an objective (alongside growth) in the First Plan, was not yet demonstrably under-fulfilled. With spare land to keep food output growing ahead of population, and with some reserves of foreign exchange, India's planning problems at this early stage presented an illusion of being readily manageable; bad outcomes could to some extent be blamed on bad monsoons. The model of state-led, industrializing investment was accepted by India and tolerated by the donors. They therefore saw little need to use aid flows to India to exert influence on economic policies there, either by direct leverage involving threats to withdraw aid or promises to increase it, or by give-and-take policy discussions. Moreover, while it is now unfashionable to say so, formal economic planning – which need not, though in India it increasingly did, supersede market mechanisms – played a vital role in this smooth relationship.

However, such planning was to be disrupted. This happened largely because of the increasing sharpness of inter-ministerial and inter-state conflicts about scarce foreign exchange. These conflicts exposed the lack of political clout – of interest-group base – of the Planning Commission, especially after Nehru's death in 1963 was followed by a gradual reduction of the real involvement of the prime minister (who remained, and still remains, formally the chairman). In 1960–5 the balance of payments constraint on growth was tightened by a series of events: exhaustion of the sterling balances; hostilities with China and Pakistan; drought; and the using up of spare land. Also the constraint was made more harmful, and harder to relax, by policy weaknesses, including trade policies hampering exports, and neglect of agriculture. Events plus policy weaknesses undermined the low-key approaches by donors to Indian economic policy, and also, unfortunately, their acceptance that this was made by Indians. Donors no longer had confidence that a policy régime, which they were increasingly supporting with aid, was working. Moreover, the way in which it seemed to be not working – deepening, successive foreign-exchange shortages – meant that donors ceased to be able to 'send messages' in relatively non-interventionist ways by selecting projects from the plan to support. Such plainly legitimate influence became no longer feasible because foreign-exchange (and other) constraints made the plan an increasingly unreliable predictor of what GoI would in fact be able to do, and when. A major lesson of the Indian experience is that satisfactory donor-recipient policy interchange – whether as 'policy dialogue' or as simple mutual trust – may depend on at least a medium-term public investment programme, if not necessarily on a full-blown 'Plan'. This suggests that donor pressure in Africa in the 1980s, to 'wind down' formal state activity and planning, may militate against donors' capacity to relate effectively to public policies.

It was not just India's growing balance of payments constraints that doomed the easy aid relationships of 1951-64.[1] The growing role of such aid, and the dominance of a single donor, also militated against a low profile. In 1963–4, gross aid utilized was US$1.25bn, or 29.1 per cent of gross public investment in that year (Chaudhuri, 1978, 98–9; Mellor, 1976, 152). Over half this aid, and a much larger proportion of the crucial food aid component, came from a single donor, the USA (Singh, 1973, 68). If one donor (as a source of finance or as a respected co-ordinator of other donors) becomes so dominant, it is always on the cards that it may seek to turn its views of – or perceived interests in – the recipient's economic, or foreign, policy into a major determinant of the recipient's scale or pattern of public investment. Such attempted 'leverage' was a major feature of India's aid scene from 1965 to 1971, when US bilateral aid was suspended (until 1978) following the hostilities between India and Pakistan.

India's Plans by the mid-1960s assumed smooth access to foreign exchange, and hence a smooth inflow of pledged aid,[2] especially US aid. If donors were to provide such smooth flows with minimal 'strings', they had to be confident of 'acceptable' Indian policies, foreign as well as economic. This was especially true of the US, where the Executive faced an annual, and increasingly critical, congressional process of authorization before it could release its aid. The whole process was consistent with respect for India's sovereignty only so long as the set of policies 'acceptable' to donors overlapped substantially with the set 'acceptable' to the GoI. Both Indian and donor assumptions were shattered, never fully to recover, by the events of 1965–6, and the subsequent combination of dwindling aid and increased leverage. These events showed that bilateral macro-leverage, whether desirable or not, is unlikely to prove feasible except in conditions of acute distress. Even then, the use of such leverage produces reactions and resentments that poison future aid relationships.

The experience has produced three realignments in the 1970s and 1980s. First, leverage has (supposedly) given way to policy dialogue.

Second, the pressure of a predominant single donor, the USA, has given way to the concerted action of donors and recipient together within the World Bank Consortium (often supported, as in 1974–5, by IMF approaches). Third, the emphasis by donors on macroeconomic policy has given way to concentration on particular sectors. All three changes have improved the capacity of donors to raise the benefits of aid to India, but have probably not gone far enough.

Moreover, a sectoral policy dialogue mediated by a 'key donor' such as the World Bank – while it has had major successes – is under some threat. It requires, from the key donor, deep knowledge of India; continuity of personnel both in Delhi and at the aid headquarters; and substantial decentralization of staff to local and project level. These requirements, especially the last, have not been fully achieved, even by the World Bank in India. A Consortium-based sectoral dialogue could also be subverted by the very errors that helped to destroy – in our view fortunately – the older attempts at one-donor macro-leverage: by an unduly ideological approach; by excessive rigidity; by shifting fashions; by mistaken selection of topics, or sub-sectors, for dialogue; or, above all, by failures to 'deliver the goods'. All these problems can affect either donors or recipient. They are detailed later in this chapter (p. 94 to p. 113).

Finally, donors that seek 'lessons from India' for other policy dialogues – notably with African countries – need to recall four special features of the Indian aid relationship. First, clear and project-specific GoI priorities for foreign exchange allocation – initially published in the successive Five Year Plans (Rao and Narain, 1963, 16) – provided until the mid-1960s, and to a lesser extent still provide, a framework in which, without interfering in Indian policy-making, donors could signal their own preferences and request responses. Second, India has many trained, skilled public-sector personnel at various levels, who can interact with donor personnel – teaching at least as much as learning – in sectoral policy dialogues. Third, both India and the key donor (the World Bank) have access in most activities to a supportive, open and critical network of professional and academic analysis, operational review, and basic research, both inside and outside official institutions.[3] Where these conditions are not met, even good donor procedures are unlikely to produce a genuine and sustainable policy dialogue. Creating these necessary conditions is obstructed by some of the reductions in state planning, power, and spending that in the 1980s have been called for by donors in their dealings with some African countries (World Bank, 1981). The donors' current approach to Africa – more, and more orderly, aid, to be funnelled to or by smaller and less powerful governments – risks inconsistency. Without the proper environment for aid management and policy, and specifically without the three conditions listed above, more aid to, and more effective policy dialogue with, smaller governments is certainly inconsistent, and a wrong lesson to draw from the Indian experience.

A fourth special circumstance of the Indian aid scene, affecting the scope for policy dialogue, is the sheer volume of aid. If gross aid utilization is financing very large parts of gross public investment – as in India in the mid-1960s, and even more in sub-Saharan Africa today[4] – the performance of aided projects as a whole becomes critically dependent on 'good' domestic policies.[5] Hence the inducement to donors to seek 'leverage' on macro-policies becomes extremely strong (although the responsive capacity of governments is often weakened at macro-policy level by very large aid involvements, which can involve the diversion of domestic personnel into managing aid projects) (Lele, 1979, 1987). If the proportion of gross public investment financed by gross aid utilization drops below about 25 per cent, as has been the case in recent years in India, donors lose both power over and interest in macro-policies, and must shift from macro-level policy dialogue. But to what should they shift: projects, areas, or sectors?

(i) In many countries donors have identified large 'island projects' for aid. These have been outside the purview of general administration, yet have sucked resources from it. Wisely, GoI has seldom allowed this. (ii) Also, perhaps less wisely, GoI has left little scope for donor dialogue with particular states. It has instead centralised aid negotiations at Central Government level. (iii) Thus a donor to India, seeking to concentrate policy dialogues associated with scarce aid, has had little choice but to conduct these dialogues about particular sectors. Such sector dialogue is made much easier by a fairly long-term relationship, in which mutual respect is built up between specific, experienced sector experts from the donor and the recipient sides. Where the volume of aid is large (e.g. from the Bank group), or where the donor concentrates heavily on a sub-sector and/or allies itself with other 'like-minded donors' (e.g. the Scandinavians on health aid), donors are likely to make the necessary long-term full-time appoint- ments. Such long-term personnel, especially in conjunction with corresponding Indian experts, can achieve a lot in a defined sector – but the process carries risks (see pp. 98–9).

Such sectoral concentration is a sensible outcome of the search for effective aid, and in India is almost unavoidable now that aid has shrunk, given the GoI's dislike of island or regional concentration. However, donors tend to press for macro-policy conditions if aid is large and outcomes seem unsatisfactory (see note 5). This is so especially when aid goes not to projects but to general balance of payments support. (Examples are food aid to India in 1955–70 or to much of Africa since the mid-1970s; and general-purpose, non-project aid to permit the maintenance of current imports in much of Africa since 1980). How is a donor, in these circumstances, to avoid improper – and often politically naïve – leverage, while safeguarding a proper interest in the good use of non-project aid?[6]

Unless one or two key variables are so seriously out of alignment as totally to subvert development in a sector – quite a rare occurrence[7] – sectoral dialogues are probably the most fruitful approach developmentally. In Africa, the World Bank's switch since the mid-1980s, from macro-policy conditions (in 'structural adjustment lending') towards 'sectoral adjustment loans' (Rose, 1985) renders the approach even more plausible. However, sector dialogue may be less appealing politically, especially for bilateral donors – who, after all, fund the multilateral agencies. Such donors are tempted to use aid to impose overall political ideology (e.g. market capitalism or centrally planned socialism), or to buy political or commercial favours by a high-level project presence. In the absence of 'India-style' constraints of aid size (gross aid utilization below, say, 25 per cent of public investment), will big donors yield to the temptation to switch back, from genuine economic policy dialogue, to macro-leverage with overtly politico-ideological components? In the absence of 'India-style' aid management by central Government, will donors concentrate even genuine policy dialogue not on sectors, but (perhaps less desirably) on support for large-scale 'island projects', e.g. in areas controlled by local authorities – what has been bitterly termed 'rent-a-district' – as has happened elsewhere in South Asia, and as is widespread in Africa? Before we return to the sectoral 'middle path', we review the history of the alternative approaches to aid policy dialogue in India.

Before leverage

The coming in of foreign aid has coincided with the starting of economic planning in India; and this has been most fortunate from the point of view of evolving some kind of rationality and order in formulating requests for foreign aid...the Plan provides a measure of the total foreign exchange required and the balance [needed, after expected] export earnings. And it is this gap that...determines the country's need for foreign aid.

(Rao and Narain, 1963, 16).

Each Five Year Plan lists projects, priorities, and expected foreign-exchange sources, including donors, who in some cases are yet 'to be identified' when the Plan is published. On top of this, when India was in food deficit, expected food aid inflows released GoI-controlled foreign exchange for Plan projects. Each donor country could select projects to support, and could assess how much support to give to India's total programme, by project aid or by general programme support (including food aid).

In 1963, an authoritative Indian view stated:

> there is a high degree of mutual discussion... regarding the terms of aid, including projects selected... One does not get the impression that the donor country dominates...nor does there appear to be any atmosphere of tension and strain... While all this is no doubt due in part to the good sense and goodwill of the donor countries, it is mainly due to the fact that India has a systematic and well-formulated programme of economic development through its Five-year Plans...into which fall all the projects for which foreign aid is either offered or asked... Coordination...is secured on a national basis by the Central Ministry of Finance, Department of Economic Affairs, [although] in choosing the projects which they will aid, donor countries are influenced by their own ideological or economic outlook.
>
> (Rao and Narain, 1963, 36)

A corresponding view from a donor expert[8] was equally sanguine. Rosen (1967, 262–3, 268–9), after describing the US interest in political democracy and stability in India, continues:

> The US has given the aid on the assumption that Indian planning and policies were of sufficiently high quality and were adequate for the requirements of development, and therefore American interests in the structure of the plans and in Indian policies for their implementation were relatively slight.
>
> (Rosen, 1967)

Rosen, indeed, recommended more active, though modest and diplomatic, policy involvement by the US in India.

The best testimony to the non-salience of 'leverage' and 'policy dialogue' – during the period when aid was building up to its greatest proportionate contribution to India's public expenditures (Mellor, 1976, 152; Chaudhuri, 1978, 99) – comes from Tarlok Singh (1974, 310–40). In his persuasive discussion of 'External Resources and Self-reliance', the Deputy Secretary of the Planning Commission (1950–66) and a major author of the first four Five Year Plans made no mention of leverage or policy dialogue whatever. Later he makes rather cryptic remarks about the events of 1965–6, to which we return below. But plainly the interesting fact about leverage and macro-policy conditionality, from 1960 until late 1964, as with Conan Doyle's *Silver Blaze*, is that the dog did not bark in the night. A justly proud recipient, India, and a justly concerned (and increasingly predominant) single donor, the USA, managed, in the 1950s and early 1960s, without overt and explicit policy conditions. Yet these proved deeply offensive in India after 1965 (so that explicit sectoral substitutes were evolved), and for most of Africa in the 1980s have been supposed by major donors to be almost essential. Why the peaceful times in India before 1965?

Part of the reason, as Rao and Narain state and as Rosen implies, lay in the integration of aid into a functioning series of Plans; the loss of this mechanism certainly sharpened conflicts and concerns about leverage. The formal arrangement remained – and still remains – as described by Rao and Narain (1963, 16), but the substance is much less. The Draft Fourth Plan (1968) represented an assertion of older methods and priorities against the 'deal' negotiated with the donors in 1965–6, but the Commission could not carry the chief ministers of the states. Three years of 'plan holiday' (Annual Plans) followed. The Fifth Plan was knocked sideways by the 1973 oil price explosion; the Commission's refusal to recognise the implications (more taxes or a smaller Plan) led to a public row, to the resignation from the Commission of a disinterested and perceptive economist (Dr B.S. Minhas), and to considerable loss of public confidence in the Commission. Meanwhile – although the prime minister retained the formal chairmanship – Mrs Gandhi appeared to downplay the Commission's importance, and seldom attended its meetings (as her predecessors had done frequently). Donors, too, weakened the Commission by public utterances that increasingly appeared to equate planning with misplaced economic interventionism. When, as often happened, Plans had to be pared to the core in order to meet foreign-exchange crises, that core was determined largely by pressures from chief ministers (of states), secondly by line ministries (at the centre), and least by Planning Commission priorities. During the 1970s the growth of a 'parallel economy', fuelled by money from tax evasion and other illegal activities, reduced the role of planners (Jha, 1980, 45–60). During Rajiv Gandhi's premiership, serious attempts have been made to reduce the political factors (associated with the financing of the Congress Party) leading to this last problem; however, the Commission's authority has been further damaged by the government's felt need to make large investment commitments, not included in the Plan, in public speeches not previously discussed with the Commission.

The framework of 1950–64, in which the Indian Plans enabled policy dialogue to take place as an informal and relatively uncontentious contraposition of donor preferences with a clearly stated set of GoI priorities, has therefore never been fully restored. There remained a set of projects, foreign-exchange assignments, and priorities, formulated in a Five Year Plan. But the authority of that Plan had dwindled.[9] Hence neither donors nor recipients knew whether Plan projects – to which donor money might have been assigned – would, in time of pressure, retain the support of complementary domestically-funded outlays. Since neither individual donors nor the Consortium could rely alone, or even mainly, on the Plan, a less project-related and more apparently interventionist dialogue was bound gradually to supervene, even apart from the traumatic events of 1965–71.

This suggests that formal planning has clear advantages for donors even if they are highly market-oriented. In the acrimonious debates of 1965–71, US critics were too ready to identify India's 'big' Plans, a big state, capital-intensive industrialization, inward-lookingness, a preference for 'material balances', and sympathy for Soviet-type planning. Yet all these are separable, even if they overlapped in some key Indian persons of influence. A Plan, as a modality for ordering public (and predicting prioritized private) activity, always eases the task of reconciling donor and recipient priorities. Such a Plan can involve a small or big, shrinking or growing, private sector. However, the decline of India's Plans was not the only reason why the 'golden age' of relaxed, yet clear and specific, policy dialogue gave way to the mutual abrasiveness of 1965–72. The underlying reason was that India, lacking much scope for bringing new land into cultivation, or for low-cost irrigation, was faced with severe wage-goods (food) constraints on growth,[10] and with near-crisis when, as in 1965–6 and 1966–7, monsoons were bad. On top of the growing foreign-exchange costs of food imports, India's hostilities with China (1962) and Pakistan (1965, 1971) had major foreign-exchange costs, immediate and long-term, further restraining the planned rate and path of industrial growth. Meanwhile, some of GoI's methods of licensing, allocating and rationing, especially for foreign exchange, induced inefficiencies, actual and incipient corruption, and diversion of GNP into burgeoning 'economic rents' for those lucky enough to own the capacity to make something in heavy demand but legally limited supply. This diverted GNP, from risk-takers towards possessors; business energy, from seeking profits towards obtaining licences to corner protected markets (Krueger, 1974; Papanek, 1971); and (by encouraging the production of non-tradeables, and secondly of protected industrial products) resources, away from the agricultural sector, already so crucial a constraint upon growth, and increasingly constrained by land shortage. In short, the period of cheap land, cheap post-colonial catching up, and steady growth was by 1965 over. Its ending cruelly exposed the extent to which GoI policies rationed the newly-scarce resources inefficiently. For the donors (increasingly dominated by the USA), it was less and less possible to feel that India's democracy and firm government sufficed to justify its ever-growing aid. The honeymoon period, with informal – or no – policy dialogue, was over.

Towards the crisis of bilateral macro-leverage

Early signs of danger, for an aid budget increasingly dominated by the bilateral Indio-US aid relationship, are recorded by Rao and Narain

> Since this study was completed, a series of events...between aid-giving and aid-receiving countries [created] tensions... Certain aspects of Indian action and policy... - the Goa action, the Kashmir dispute, India's defence expenditure, the [purchase of Mig fighters from the USSR, and statements by Foreign Minister] Krishna Menon... - led to some strong speeches in the [US] legislature which appear to encroach on India's sovereignty and freedom of action...the Senate Foreign Relations Committee voted a specific cut in the proposed US aid to India... [Although] the Kennedy administration eventually succeeded in getting...the bulk of what it had [requested for India], initial reactions were somewhat intemperate in character. [But] subsequent action both in the US and in India showed considerable maturity which nipped in the bud the growth...of the tension.
>
> (Rao and Narain, 1963, Epilogue, 97)

Unfortunately, a better and gloomier guide to the future of the Indo-US aid relationship (and of bilateral macro-dialogue in aid generally?) was Eugene Black's farewell speech as President of the World Bank (cited in Rao and Narain, 1963, 98): 'Aid which is at the mercy of the variable winds of diplomacy offers a poor basis for the rational programming of economic development'.

The existence of alternative donors, with different ideologies, did not suffice - despite the hopes of Rao and Narain (1963, 73) - to keep post-1964 bilateral, above all Indo-US, aid dialogues respectful of national sovereignty, and concerned mainly with national economic policy rather than with international politics. This is the main theme of the 'crisis of macro-leverage' in the mid-1960s. Before we return to it, a few words are needed on a parallel source of tension: the use of aid-linked political relationships to divert economic aid to the commercial advantage of the donor. Bilateral aid, tied by the donor to the supply of otherwise uncompetitive products, seldom revives those product lines in the donor country, (Mosley, 1986; Toye and Clark, 1986)[11] and cuts across the effective use of policy dialogue to increase the economic returns of aid to the recipient. The Bokaro steel plant typified:

> the conflicts between the Indian need to develop and utilise indigenous design and the interests of potential foreign financiers of the plant, often paralleled by the influence of controlling politicians and diplomats. By 1962, India [could] design steel

mills, particularly in Dastur and Company. But no major aid provider, whether the USA or the USSR, would fail to insist that the design be made by its own nationals. This insistence was justified, not by the technical assistance needs of India, but by the political and economic requirements of the donor.

(Mellor, 1976, 229; cf. Desai, 1972).

Not all tied bilateral aid is wrong;[12] the commercial demands of 'tied' exporters may even deter donor governments from otherwise distorting policy dialogue, via 'ideological' or foreign-policy conditions for aid. However – especially in the area of consultancy, technical assistance, and choice of project techniques – bilateral tied aid can induce donor governments to apply criteria inconsistent with genuine policy dialogue.[13]

There are, then, two underlying (if, happily, conflicting) dangers of bilateral leverage: its use for commercial advantage and for international diplomacy. These are dangers, not because it is wrong to use aid to secure gains for the donor, but because these aims (i) do not work, and (ii) subvert the usefulness of aid to the recipient.[14] Even if the donor genuinely believes that its leverage seeks only to increase recipient benefits from aid, it must take extreme care to respect recipient sovereignty. Recipients may define 'effectiveness' differently from the donor, or may have different views of the politically feasible options.[15] Even where the topic for bilateral pressure is well chosen, there are serious risks in concentrating on a narrowly-focused 'ideological' approach (see pp. 99–102). The outcome was well described by Tarlok Singh:

[We needed in 1965–6] a careful analysis of the basic weaknesses of the economy, the assumptions which had gone wrong... reorientation of...policies, and economic discipline. A democratic political system could have posed the issues openly in these terms. Instead, influential criticism from abroad focused on one element, the overvaluation of the rupee, as the prime cause of current difficulties. Encouraged by informal assurances of greater external support, the GoI undertook a hasty and ill-prepared devaluation under exceptionally adverse circumstances.

(T. Singh, 1974, 350–1)

The aid environment, the policy environment, and the nature and concentration of bilateral leverage combined after 1964 to create the conditions for a 'crisis of leverage'. The aid environment involved India's growing reliance on aid, and the growing concentration of that aid on one donor, the USA. The policy environment involved – in the context of the exhaustion of India's supply of readily cultivable and unused land, and of tightening growth of foreign-exchange bottlenecks associated with food supply and capital- (and import-) intensive industrialization – policies discouraging exports, creating economic rents, and persisting in import-intensive growth paths. Bilateral leverage involves dangers of diplomatic (or undiplomatic) pressures based on international politics, of commercial rather than economic interventions, and of over-simple, insensitive ideologizing. Yet these three conditions might not have produced a crisis of bilateral macro-leverage, but for the events of 1965–6: war with Pakistan, a disastrous monsoon, foreign-exchange exhaustion, and hence absolute dependence by India on relief from a single powerful nation.

In Summer of 1965, the USA:

> as a sign of displeasure at the waste of scarce resources in an unproductive war, had indefinitely suspended all aid to both India and Pakistan [and] refused to sign a fresh long-term agreement under PL 480 when the existing agreement expired in August 1965. Instead, the Johnson administration, egged on by Congressional opposition to concessional food aid for India, adopted a 'short tether' policy of doling out stocks sufficient only to meet requirements a few months at a time, and explicitly tying the continuation of food aid to the adoption by India of policies aimed at increasing agricultural production and curbing population growth.
>
> (Frankel, 1978, 287).

The then head of USAID in New Delhi, J.P. Lewis, spoke of 'specific aid offers contingent upon the institution of particular adjustments in indigenous rural policy' (cited in Chopra, 1968).

We thus have two elements of bilateral leverage: tie-up with international politics (the hostilities with Pakistan) and conditionality of aid on specific macro-policy changes. Later in 1965, two further contentious elements were added. With Indian food reserves and foreign exchange almost exhausted, India effectively submitted to foreign macro-economic policy review: in a 'meeting in Rome between [India Agriculture Minister] Subramaniam and US Secretary of Agriculture, Orville Freeman, the specific policy proposals were revised item by item' and pushed through Cabinet 'despite the vehement objections of the Finance Minister'. Second, this review involved the inclusion of items commercially favourable to donors. The Freeman-Subramaniam review 'includ[ed] the plans for incentives to foreign private investment, especially in fertilizers', and shortly afterwards GoI 'announced a new policy of concessions to foreign private companies willing to invest in the fertilizer industry in India' (Chopra, 1968, 287). We are not at all arguing that it is unreasonable for a donor, if even-handed, to refuse aid that finances recipients to wage war on each other; or to insist that, if more food production (as a wage-good) is necessary for progress, the recipient uses resources to that end. All the above pressures (except the commercial one) may well have been perfectly proper, and their outcomes largely desirable for India. But the manner of their effective imposition upon a proud and large country, by a single donor not obviously representing the international community, in the wake of aid suspension in a war and 'short-tether' food relief in a drought, led to 'anger and humiliation' (Patel, 1986, 73) and probably doomed bilateral *macro*-leverage as a route to policy dialogue for India's aid donors.

The cap was put on this by the devaluation saga of 1966 and its aftermath. The above donor interventions – while in our judgement they improved Indian economic policy, not least in its impact on the poor – involved major concessions of Indian economic sovereignty; yet, as regards aid inflows, these concessions had restored no more than the *status quo ante* and that only with respect to food aid. 'A final condition for the resumption of large-scale foreign [i.e. US capital] aid had still to be met, that of devaluation. [T.T. Krishnamachari, the Finance Minister] still refused to consider such a step'. L.B. Shastri's apparently sudden decision[16] to set up a commission of enquiry to investigate the longstanding allegations that Krishnamachari had abused his office to advance his sons, was certain to cause 'TTK' to resign in protest, and was widely seen in India as a bridge to devaluation. Despite TTK's negotiations with the World Bank (pp. 93–4) and the apparent agreement, it soon became clear that the key US 'aid would be forthcoming only after India had acted on her earlier promise to devalue'. This happened on 6 June, 1966, despite major dissension in Cabinet and AICC. US aid resumed ten days later (Frankel, 1978, 228, 297–8).

This was bound to look like extreme bilateral leverage, at the borders of disrespect for sovereignty. Had devaluation been seen to work, such leverage might just have proved acceptable in India. However, price-inelastic supplies of key exports (or of inputs to make them) meant that 'the immediate impact of devaluation proved unfavourable. Although mining and manufacturing exports did increase, stagnant or declining sales of traditional exports produced an overall decline of real foreign exchange earnings of about 8 per cent in 1966–7' (Frankel, 1978, 322). Nor were the pledges of aid, especially those by the USA, made to secure the devaluation/policy reform packages, in fact met (see p.112). Thus GoI had been subjected, in crisis, to extreme bilateral pressures - albeit, in many cases, pressures to do sensible things;[17] had bowed to such pressures; and had found that neither the policies adopted, nor the pledged aid, produced real foreign-exchange inflows to compensate for the wounding realities of bilateral leverage. Although the US use of food aid in 1966 'worked', in the sense that it extracted (probably desirable) Indian policy changes, the process killed bilateral leverage by revealing, not only the uncertain quid (or dollar) pro quo, but also its potential for politicization and abuse. Indeed, in 1971 (during the events leading to the independence of Bangladesh), the USA once more suspended economic aid – this time in a purely political context, for seven years, in the wake of an avowed 'tilt to Pakistan'; but Indian policy was not changed as a result.

Aid 1965–85: towards multilateral sector dialogue

The temporary withdrawal of the US from bilateral aid to India in 1965–6, the lasting wounds left by 'leverage' from that period, and the long US absence in 1971–8, rendered bilateral, aid-based approaches to macro-dialogues with India almost infeasible. No one donor looms sufficiently large. At least one of the largest, the UK, in principle prefers to leave such policy dialogue to the Consortium, and is increasingly prevented, by its emphasis on tying and aid-trade linkage, from entering usefully into such dialogue without meeting commercial objections from exporters. Anyway, a growing proportion of aid to India is multilateral; total gross bilateral aid to India, since 1970 typically below 0.7 per cent of Indian national income, would, even if co-ordinated, be too small to exert major influence on macroeconomic policy.

Also, there are more positive reasons for the move towards sectoral dialogues, with donors' wishes mediated through the World Bank. The Bank has in most years been much the largest donor (via IDA) of concessional funds to India – its pledges in 1981–2, for example, totalled 1307 (Rs crores), or 60 per cent of total OECD aid to India (GoI, 1982–3, 271–2).[18] The Bank's overriding role has increased as other donors, especially the US, became less important. Bank aid has also been more reliable than that of some donors and, through IDA, more concessional than that of most. Through its Delhi office and India-specific staff in Washington, the Bank has many more specialists with long-term expertise and links to Indian experts, in many fields, than any one bilateral donor (probably even than all combined). The presence of many senior, Indian passport-holding Bank staff (in at least one case moving between a senior research position in the Bank and senior policy responsibility in GoI), and of an Indian Executive Director at the Bank (usually a retired senior civil servant), at once strengthens and eases the Indo-Bank relationship, in a way not feasible for a bilateral donor, which can hardly appoint senior Indians to domestic policy-making positions.

Hence many bilateral concerns are expressed through the Bank as Consortium chairman. This had happened already with the Bell Mission in 1964–5. Then, however, several factors – US predominance in bilateral flows to India; Bank liberalizing pressures that seemed to some Indians to take the US side against them; Bank wishes to release public-sector resources for agriculture by re-balancing industrial activity more towards the private sector; a perceived conflict between Bank agricultural strategy of 'progressive farmers' in irrigated areas and stated Indian perceptions of regional and vertical equity – prevented the Bank from adopting the low-key, give-and-take role that it required (and later sought) for effective sectoral dialogue. Most seriously, the Bank and the Consortium were seen by leading Indians as linked with one overpowering donor, the USA (both in seeking to influence Indian macro-policy excessively and perhaps ideologically, and subsequently in not succeeding in mobilizing the aid promised as *quid pro quo*), partly because of high sensitivities on both sides, but mainly because of the 1965–6 crisis. The Bell Mission – while advocating many sensible measures, most of them later adopted independently by GoI – was in some respects a 'false start' for multilateral sectoral dialogue (Frankel, 1978, 271–2; Rosen, 1985, 107).

In the post-1971 situation of many smallish bilateral donors, with the ring held by the World Bank as major donor, even bilateral leverage has tended to be sectoral, tactful, and mediated through the World Bank. For example, the US – which since 1979 has resumed project aid to India at some US$90–100m yearly – has, in preparatory documents discussed at Consortium meetings, pressed for import liberalization, export development, and preference for the private sector. In February 1983 the Bank, USAID and ODA (UK) jointly surveyed training needs for social forestry, and recommended several private initiatives, with the Forestry Department as 'catalyst rather than provider'; these proposals were favourably reviewed in Delhi, itself worried about the expansion of the costs of the Indian Forest Service. The US, mainly via the World Bank, has also encouraged India towards diversified private-sector provision of contraceptives. Such initiatives, because sectoralized and Bank-mediated, have not provoked crises or ideological conflicts.

All is not sweetness and light. Despite evaluations suggesting high economic rates of return to aid for agricultural credit in India (World Bank, 1981a), the USA has stopped aiding NABARD,[19] mainly because of objections that interest-rate subsidies make for a low (or even negative) financial return. The USA has (until 1989 unsuccessfully) pressed the Bank and other donors to do likewise, apparently because conclusions about the scale and inefficiency of subsidized rural credit, partly valid in Latin America, are being applied to India. The US belief in an almost exclusively private-sector role in oil exploration and development led them in 1983 to block the proposed Bank 'energy affiliate' – which could have been of great value to India – and, on some accounts, has led the Bank to overstate, to donors, the private-enterprise preferences conveyed to India and others in policy dialogues about energy. However, it is in general correct to say that bilateral aid relations with India have been improved greatly, in respect of their capacity to 'carry' policy discussions without tension, by their mediation through the Bank.

This is not at all because the Bank has systematically co-ordinated its policy dialogues with other donors. This has taken place only where bilateral expertise and cash, complementary to the Bank's, have flowed – with the Nordic countries on family planning, with Britain on coal. But India has tried to reduce the number of multi-donor projects, where timing and procedural wrangles impel the sort of 'consultation' that can easily turn into 'ganging up' against the recipient. In most sectors the Bank, too, has carefully avoided the appearance of such 'ganging up'.

The difficulties of World Bank-mediated policy dialogue are different and more fundamental. The first difficulty is the growing pressure inside, and upon, the Bank to remove increasing parts of aid to India from IDA terms. The USA, and to some extent the Bank itself, feels that low-income African countries – which, unlike India, have no prospects to borrow commercially – are priority candidates for 'soft' IDA terms. However, the returns to capital aid seem far higher in India than in most of Africa (Papanek, 1972; Mosley, 1987). Most African countries, it could be argued, require research, training, and technical assistance – some of these, perhaps, from India - before large increases in capital aid can work. Aid cuts for India, moreover, seem a sorry reward for steady growth, good aid administration, democracy, and persistent and extreme mass poverty.

If, as is envisaged, Bank funds for India are increasingly to flow on IBRD terms, then an increase in the scale of those funds will not be as much of a compensation to India for the decline in IDA money – nor, therefore, as much of a help in making the transition to more liberal policies[20] – as both India and donors might wish. This is because – while loans from IDA are so concessional as to be worth over 85 per cent of a grant of the same amount – the IBRD rate is now not far below commercial bank rates available to India. If the Bank, its members, or other 'donors' increasingly push India from near-grant to near-commercial terms of capital transfer, then – apart from possibly incurring quasi-Brazilian risks in the long run (see Chapter 1) – they inevitably, and greatly, reduce their power to persuade, or to help, India to improve its economic policies, and hence the effectiveness of capital transfers. This is especially important in view of the growing recognition, in GoI and at the World Bank, that the structure, extent, and quota-orientated nature of Indian import restrictions still severely harm both efficiency and equity – but that, if the changes (on which GoI has long embarked) are to accelerate, supportive aid expansion is needed, both to afford the transitional import increases and to help 'compensate the losers' and thus increase the political feasibility of liberalization (Bhagwati and Srinivasan, 1975, 245; Sukhatme, 1983, 34–6; Krueger and Ruttan, 1983, 4–8 to 4–9). The continuing decline of IDA, and hence of World Bank aid, for India is, in view of this growing consensus, most unfortunate.

The second difficulty arises from the changing images of the World Bank. It has always favoured efficient use of market incentives in development. However, from President McNamara's 'Nairobi speech' in 1973 to his retirement in 1981, the Bank was increasingly seen as liberal, expansionist both in its own lending and in its view of government, and poverty-orientated; under Presidents Clausen (1981–6) and Conable (1986–), the image has become blurred, partly by US pressures on the Bank, partly by its own frequent reorganizations, and partly by public and apparently 'ideological' conservative postures in Bank research and, in Africa, policy dialogue. Such documents as the 1981 'Berg Report' (though not the follow-ups on African policy), and the 1986 and 1987 *World Development Reports* (Lipton, 1987; Singer, 1987), while not reflecting Bank-wide consensus, did sound an unfortunate note of dogmatism as regards the role of government and the sufficiency of price policy. The reality of Bank actions – whether in loan operations (country-desk or project-officer level) or at the top (in formal policy statements (e.g. World Bank, 1986a) or Presidential commitments) – has changed far less than the image. For example, Bank Group lending was only slightly more concentrated on poverty-related sectors or countries in 1973–81 than before or since (Beckmann, 1985), and the poverty focus has been frequently re-emphasized by McNamara's successors, not only (though also) by almost every Annual Speech to the Governors. Most recently the Conable Bank has embraced 'adjustment with a human face'. Yet there is a persistent, nagging feeling among outsiders and aid recipients, including India, that the Bank, in the course of pressing for lower levels of government involvement in several parts of the economy (and of removing barriers to private-sector development), is downplaying poverty issues. Since the 1973–81 Bank positions – expansionism, poverty-focus, etc. – were in close accord with GoI's official stance, the apparent blurring of such positions was bound to impair prospects of smooth policy dialogue, mediated by the Bank, at sector level. The apparently blanket formulae – devalue, deflate, decontrol – applied by donors in Africa, were in reality due more to the Fund than to the Bank, and were in part inevitable, given past African policy errors, worsening terms of trade, and droughts. However, given the increased co-ordination after 1980 between the Fund and the Bank, the smell of dogmatism affected the

Bank as well – and reminded Indians of the macro-leverage of the later 1960s.

There are thus two threats to sectoral, Bank-mediated dialogues with India: a Bank image on occasion dogmatic or blurred; and reduced Bank emphasis on Indian lending via IDA. Such threats are to be regretted for several reasons.

(i) Sector dialogues have produced some desirable outcomes. Urban priorities have moved from so-called 'low-cost housing' (for middle-level officials) towards slum upgrading for the poor. In fertilizer production, electricity distribution, and elsewhere, the dialogue has also been fruitful.[21]

(ii) The Bank's own formulation of its positions in sector dialogues involves a useful learning process.

(iii) Above all – while content in development policy normally matters more than form – the most important lesson from sectoral Indo-Bank dialogues lies in the procedures evolved. These help Indian policy-making and analysis. For instance – even if T and V extension or rotational irrigation have flaws or limitations – Bank finance to test such models, in prolonged consultation between Bank and Indian experts, stimulates counter-models, and debate about just when each approach works or fails (e.g. Moore, 1984; Feder and Slade, 1986). Such procedures need (a) Bank money, and (b) free debate within India. As for (a), a leading Bank irrigation specialist wrote in April 1984:

> I cannot imagine a situation where the Indian irrigation establishment would have been prepared to listen to expatriate advice if this advice, at least in the initial stages of our work, would not have been a condition of our financial contribution to the programme. Today I would guess that some of our technical advice would be accepted even if it would not be concerned with specific lending operations. [Acceptance of our expertise in] data evaluation, training of engineers, training of diploma holders, groundwater hydrology, and even road planning, design and construction have become independent of our lending programme.

This raises a second-generation worry. If bilateral macro-leverage was too invasive and abrasive, has multilateral sector dialogue been too cosy: too much a mutual acceptance, modification, and convergence, through learning, of the assumptions and codes of, for example, the irrigation establishments in the World Bank and the GoI? Do Bank and Indian engineers tacitly agree: to overlook the problem of corruption; to overstress technical fixes, and under-state the need for appropriate, regionally distinct, institutional change; to train at too high a level, neglecting 'the 80 per cent of non-professional staff' who determine day-to-day management of secondaries (Wade, 1982, 181)? Analogous risks apply in other areas of Bank sectoral specialism. Some of the lessons for policy dialogue are discussed below. But the central point is that major experiments, initially financed by aid and then openly evaluated and debated, are the essence of successful dialogue. Free, lively and informed debate in India, notably in the *Economic and Political Weekly*, has been as necessary to good sectoral dialogue as is some experimental use of cash by donors and GoI alike. Uma Lele and George Rosen both contrast 'absence of foreign economists and vigorous discussion of agricultural policy in [Africa] today with the situation in South Asia' around 1960–70 (Rosen, 1985, 231). We doubt the clear linkage between 'foreign economists' and free and informed domestic debates on economic policy, but the latter are probably essential for useful 'policy dialogue' with the former. Freedom of debate on economic policy – except to some extent during the 1975–7 Emergency – *has* prevailed in India; but a cosy, top-down style of sectoral dialogue might muffle such a debate, or listen to it too late.

There is also a worry about how far the Bank – as its lending emphasis on India, and perhaps its total real resources, decline – will choose to maintain in India (not just in Delhi) expert staff in 'critical mass' and with individuals assigned for periods long enough to become really familiar with the sector and with Indian experts (and structures), and senior and assertive enough to carry weight with the Bank HQ in Washington DC Junior line staff are often prone (i) to over-interpret signals, real or assumed, about changing priorities in management or policy[22] and (ii) to give priority – in accordance with banking-style career signals, in this case real and not imagined – to 'getting the money moving' over getting the project and the policy agreed and right. Yet a strong case does exist for more decentralization from 'aid HQ' to senior staff in the Third World. This has been to some extent recognized by USAID in increasing the local cash limits up to which local staff may authorize projects, and by the UK through its Development Divisions located in such capitals as Lilongwe and Bangkok, and each responsible for decisions for several countries. Several donor agencies told us that experienced local staff acted as invaluable 'buffers' against swings of ideological fashion in donor HQs, keeping projects on course and preserving continuity in sectoral dialogue.

While accepting this in theory, donor HQ in practice often enforces its own positions, not those of decentralized country offices, in policy dialogues.

Sometimes this means pushing through central 'standards', even when inappropriate. Sometimes, donor HQ rightly sees the need for ultimate policy overview when the donor's local staff, keen to push projects through, finesse central policy guidelines. In one striking example – a very large irrigation project under construction in India –

local donor staff failed to clarify the compensation of tribals for loss of unregistered land rights in the huge areas to be inundated by the project. Only prolonged campaigning by the agency's sociologists at HQ eventually forced a better outcome. However, in general, donor HQ – like a Foreign Office, fears that senior personnel, based long-term in (for example) India – side with Indian officials against donor agency advice, and are seen by such officials as 'not really meaning it' when they convey agency doubts or criticisms.

So donor HQ does assert itself, sometimes rightly. Also, continuity of senior donor experts is less useful if recipient contacts are often changed, posted, etc. – a more serious problem in Africa, but not unknown in India. And a close, lasting relationship among experts can sometimes degenerate into buddy-buddy establishmentarian setting of a static 'hidden agenda'. Despite such risks and conflicts, the criticisms of Bank positions in policy dialogue, discussed below and in Chapter 7, illustrate the need for more, more expert, more senior, more continuous, more project-localized Bank expertise in India. Pressure in 1988–9 to cut Bank project management costs may waste, not save, money.

The problem of 'ideology' in policy dialogue

'It is important that US goals in India[23] not be framed in a narrowly ideological fashion....The ideological interest of the US is well satisfied by the fact that India is a reasonably effective working democracy... [The] amount of State action or private enterprise is a decision for India to make' (Rosen, 1967, 268). The Bank-led consortium of OECD donors surely shares the interest in democracy in India. Yet India has received much less aid-per-person than most LDC non-democracies. Also, many pressure groups in donor countries felt that democracy was threatened by the State of Emergency in 1975–7; however, although the Consortium countries met shortly after the Emergency was declared, only the UK sought to obtain any response by them to it, and was overruled.

So donor ideology did not link elections or press freedom with aid – as possibly it should have done; the results, most of the time, would have been to raise India's share in world aid. Did, and does, the donor community link 'ideological' views on macroeconomic policy with aid? The Bank was, and is, less vulnerable to this criticism than any one donor. It repeatedly stresses its commitment to efficiency in both public and private sectors, not to any particular borderline between them. However, some of its recent publications – notably on Africa (World Bank, 1981), but see also (World Bank, 1986, 1987; Lipton, 1987; Singer 1987), – alongside its role in structural adjustment loans, have led some critics to believe that, for some senior Bank policy-makers and researchers, 'efficiency' means not only cost-effectiveness plus competition, but also a smaller public sector (Toye, 1987, 47–9). The Bank's close link to the IMF – with its frequent advice, and even conditions for short-run support, favouring reduced public expenditure, devaluation, and decontrol – increases these suspicions. These recent fears reawaken echoes of India's experiences in 1965–70 and 1975. Thus Frankel wrote of the events of April 1975:

> The central government, meanwhile, [in the wake of the oil price explosion and the foreign-exchange shortage], was again confronting pressures from the IMF for 'stabilisation' as a condition of a credit line to cover the massive balance-of-payments deficit. IMF recommended stringent fiscal discipline to control the money supply and complementary economic policies to freeze wages...and provide incentives to private investment. These recommendations were also then taken up by the World Bank as part of the negotiations on development aid then in progress between the Consortium countries and India. The Bank pushed even harder [than the IMF for such changes, and secured] a growth strategy with no more than marginal adjustments in the interests of more equitable distribution.
>
> (Frankel, 1978, 515–6)

Doubt can properly be cast on such accounts of pressures on India by the Bank, other donors, or the Fund. The point, however, is that (as any half-dozen random issues of the *Economic and Political Weekly* will confirm) such interpretations are increasingly prevalent in India. In the early 1970s they led to official unease about aid, clearly expressed in planning documents – and to strident, influential, and politically effective demands on the nationalist Right (Swamy, 1971) as well as on the Left, for 'self reliance' in the sense of near-autarky. The fall in real aid to India, past and proposed, represents in part a response to such unease and demands. Their plausibility has been enhanced since 1980 by the close co-operation between Bank and Fund. This has arisen because the acute, debt-and-drought-linked, balance of payments crises of much of the developing world have induced donors to shift aid from projects to general import support. This has led the Bank to impose conditions less on projects, but more on overall policies, in the context of 'structural adjustment loans' (SALs), and in the process to co-operate more closely with the IMF in medium-term lending operations (e.g. 'extended financing facilities' or EFFs) and conditions in numerous, mainly African and Latin-American, countries. Such operations and conditions are declared to be non-ideological, but in many cases have involved no published analysis (and, in some cases known to us, no unpublished analysis either) of the effects on the poor of implementing the conditions. These conditions almost always convey a standard message, the 'four Ds': devalue, decontrol, deflate, denationalize.

Stabilization support from the IMF – especially short-term loans on the higher tranche, but even EFFs – almost always carry several or all these conditions. They have tended to leak into several sets of conditions for World Bank structural adjustment lending, despite its longer-term explicit goals. 'Cross-conditionality', moreover, impedes Bank lending if Fund conditions are even slightly under-fulfilled. Also, several bilateral donors are little disposed to give new aid, unless Bank or Fund conditions have been met. India has so far not needed to look for foreign help on quite such terms, and both the Bank and the Fund have since 1986 shown increasing interest in 'adjustment with a human face'; however, memories of 1965 and 1975 loom large in India, as do present realities of donors and the 'four Ds' in Africa.

No plausible alternative stabilization programme, radical or nationalist, permitting stabilization in a balance of payments crisis yet not at all involving the 'four Ds', has yet been worked out. The Bank and Fund are bound by their Charters to collaborate. India has not yet needed a SAL–EFF package. Yet such counter-arguments do not quite succeed in defusing the charge of ideology. The charge bites deeper because Indians recall their experiences in 1965–6 and 1974–5 – disturbing precursors of recent African styles of Bank-Fund 'policy dialogue' – and fear that the ideological hardening in the West will bring even tougher conditions in any future crisis (cf. Patel, 1986, 191). Some Bank officials adopt styles closer to those of some prominent western political leaders than to economic analysis. Whether their arguments are right or wrong, they cannot demonstrably be linked to efficiency or equity. Their adoption may reflect pressures upon the Bank by its donor members.[24] It is perhaps more a question of statements and style than of substance.[25] Also, aid donors, even the Bank, have changed the substance less than the IMF which, in the early 1980s, was driven by cash shortages to much more restrictive conditionality than the Bank. For example, in East Africa, the Bank was noticeably more long-term in its conditions, and less sceptical about public-sector activity, than the Fund. Yet the Fund has generally avoided public statements or high-profile documents that smack of paternalism and dogma.[26] Meanwhile, some positions taken by some Bank officials and researchers, especially in 1984–6 – and a quite new sense in some parts of the Bank that alternative evidence, analyses, and persons, however cautious or scientific, were not entirely welcome, even if efficient – have somewhat imperilled the Bank's credibility with many Indians in its attempted dialogues.[27] To avoid such peril is important. In India the dialogue has been impressively successful, and even during this difficult period was carried out by undogmatic Indian and Bank experts well qualified to keep it that way. Also, the Bank's role in policy dialogue with India cannot be filled by any bilateral donor.

There is little prospect that bilateral or commercial transactions might lead to healthier or less arm-twisting dialogue than multilateral aid. Indian officials' fear of excessive reliance on commercial bank flows may have been influenced by alleged US pressure on Brazil to accept, in return for financial support (ultimately from the Federal Reserve), and US military landing rights at Recife airport. One could equally mention successful Soviet pressure on India to repair, and provide spares for, Egyptian aeroplanes during the 1973 war – pressure conditioned upon trade credits as well as bilateral aid. As a general approach, bilateral macro-leverage on India is so discredited, not least by the memories of 1965–6, as to be dead. However, the risk that ideology may be seen by GoI as creeping into Bank relations with it – especially if the poverty-focus seems to recede, while IDA aid to India dwindles – is a serious threat even to Bank-mediated sectoral dialogue. A good sign, in autumn 1987, was the Bank's major new research and policy attention to the impact of structural adjustment on poverty groups; this could be helped and broadened by new Indian research to evaluate the successes, failures, and prospects of transfer to other countries, of their many different programmes, some Bank-aided, for poverty alleviation. A new difficulty since 1987, however, is that the reorganizations of Bank staff may bring to Indian affairs, both in Delhi and in Washington, persons of considerable distinction but limited Indian experience, and some rather prolonged senior vacancies.

Risk of rigidity

The Bank now represents a single conduit for most dialogue with donors above the project level. In India, it is working in a big country with many different physical and political environments. The Bank thus faces a special need to avoid imposing one monolithic view, even if that view appears to Bank staff to be not 'ideological' but purely technical or efficiency-oriented. The responsibility is so great, not because GoI cannot do projects without the Bank or other donors – about three-quarters even of public-sector project funding remains domestic – but because, as the overwhelmingly major cash-linked source of outside advice, the Bank, if rigid or monolithic, risks using its prestige to overpersuade India of spuriously general solutions, sometimes based on small, costly, and regionally specific pilot projects. Yet the Bank's own wish to move money swiftly and at low administrative cost must favour exactly these general, technocratic, all-India approaches. Has this been a serious problem in practice? We concentrate here on the risk of rigid procedures; the consequences at project level are considered in Chapter

5, and the implications for TC and institution-building are taken up in Chapter 6.

In respect of aid to irrigation:

> the World Bank's standard package for improving...canals included (1) lining the main canal, (2) land levelling below the outlet,....(4) rotational irrigation between...sub-outlet blocks, and (5) formation of water users' associations at the outlet level, to implement the rotational irrigation schedule; [and more recently] (6) building the main system so as to allow for 'flexibility' [, i.e. for] varying quantities of water to be delivered to each location over the course of the crop season, in line with changing crop-water requirements. Perhaps the major single weakness [is that] the package is to be applied more or less uniformly everywhere, with little research being done to match the ingredients against the environment. This makes for ease in project formulation and lending.
>
> (Wade, 1982, 171–2)

However, it is too rigid an approach to serve as a good basis for sector dialogue. Such rigidity is especially dangerous where other donors (e.g. the USA) explicitly funnel their views on Indian irrigation policy through a single source of policy advice, the Bank. For example, canal lining (as against telegraphs and other informational improvements) is a cost-effective way to improve water use only in sandy soils with well-managed canals. 'Rotational irrigation below the outlet is a waste of time except in some specific soil conditions and where water is very scarce.' Water users' associations probably make sense only where water is both moderately scarce and rather reliable. 'Flexibility is much too ambitious a criterion [where, as is usual] outside the North-west, canal managers cannot allocate water evenly from head to tail within distributories and minors' (Wade, 1982, 172–9).

Some of these criticisms would be questioned by Bank irrigation engineers; others appear to have been taken account of in recent projects. Even so, it does look as if – in its urge to develop a testable policy model – the Bank for several years over-generalized, from the successful experience in re-organizing the Chambal irrigation system of Rajasthan, to create a blueprint for far less appropriate places and structures, including ones where organizational inputs and Bank help and overview, as well as soil and crop-mix, are far less suitable. This conforms with the description of a leading Bank expert:

> The first objective of our technical assistance was to induce the Indian irrigation [authorities in 1973–7] to use more modern design standards. During this period, we succeeded to upgrade some of the

project designs. We argued with our engineering colleagues in
favour of more and better water control structures, and, water
measuring devices (Personal communication).

Some Bank experts place more stress than do their critics upon the
experimental, learning-by-doing nature of their part in policy dialogue
(while also frankly recognizing the financial sticks and carrots used).
However, the language of the above Bank version – 'modern',
'upgrade', 'better' – does suggest a global technocratic wisdom: a
uniform technical package for, rather than environmentally specific
institutional approaches to, better water management. It is
uncomfortably echoed, in the rhetoric of some Bank officials and
documents, over macroeconomic policy (everywhere): liberalization,
reform, redefined to mean (mostly) not better access for poor people to
assets or services, but smaller states and fewer controls on prices or
private firms (including monopolies?). It is not only Indians who are
concerned by, and may be harmed by, such rigid versions of dialogue.

Over-generalization, from successful pilots to general solutions, is a
widespread problem of rigid policy dialogues, not confined to irrigation:

(i) Community development, in the 1950s, was thus 'generalized' by
US donors and Foundations from Etawah, Uttar Pradesh to places with
far fewer skilled personnel and far less physical potential for rural
development (see p. 218).

(ii) Support for co-operative agricultural product collection and
processing has been similarly generalized by EEC. The original Anand
project succeeded partly because it replaced the local monopolist
(Polsons) in handling milk, for which small producers urgently needed
collection to avoid spoilage, in an area that enjoyed unusually
favourable conditions and personnel inputs. This pilot has been
extended to several other areas and products, based on a national
authority working through somewhat top-down 'co-operatives'.

(iii) Extension reform along T and V lines has, essentially, been
spread out by the Bank from a single tested example of dramatic success
in India – again in the ideal environment of Chambal – to several Indian
(and African) States. The World Bank's references to Chambal, and
advocacy of T and V, apparently make no mention of 'pilot project
effect: that agricultural performance was so good because the World
Bank was intensively involved' and pulled Indian staff out of
less-favoured areas.[28] 'A recent survey in the Chambal Command Area
reveals that the extension system has virtually 'gone to sleep' since the
area ceased to be a focus of interest' (Moore, 1984; see, however, Feder
and Slade, 1986).

In any sub-sector (e.g. extension, agro-processing), there is always a
danger of inferring a single solution for many environments on the basis

of exceptionally carefully managed pilot projects in one or two. The danger is much greater if a single main outside bearer of expertise, cash and 'policy dialogue', able to grant or withhold cash and hence patronage from embattled officials, insists upon such a solution as a condition for sub-sectoral aid. The 'pilot effect', and the unwisdom of generalizing from it, are recognized in general terms. A senior Bank official with wide Indian experience told us:

> Bank projects go better than non-Bank projects. There is an outside source of trouble-shooting in the event of delay, and of appeal if things go wrong within GoI. It is known that, if there is local deficiency, Bank staff will object at State or Central level. There is more kudos for timely fulfilment – and there are more visitors.

However, this general recognition does not always produce due caution in particular areas of sectoral policy dialogue. This is especially important because donors, in seeking to evaluate aid-effectiveness, stress replicability as the key to successful sector dialogue. One good project, in India where aid has ranged from 0.5 to 2.0 per cent of GNP, may simply replace government money that would otherwise have paid for the same project; what is felt to matter most, therefore, is innovative projects that are cost-effectively replicable, and sector dialogue that explores their worth first, and advocates replicability, if appropriate, only subsequently. We concur with this donor assessment. However, despite the Bank's massive expertise, we do see dangers in its sometimes rather rigid transfers, as major protagonist in policy dialogue, from pilot project to national blueprint. Career incentives in any large bank, and in some aid agencies, tend to reward 'moving money' in big amounts; if the project later fails, the rewarded money-mover has usually moved as well, and is seldom penalized.

Changing fashions

It may seem inconsistent to claim both that policy dialogue can impose rigidity – as donors and recipients together come to accept a specific blueprint for general use – and that it is subject to swings of fashion. Unfortunately both claims are valid. Blueprints once set are applied far too generally, but they are re-set every few years, following changes of mood, as much as of scientific evidence, in economics or agronomy or engineering. Development studies are notoriously prone to swings of fashion. Often, these swings are embodied in 'impact statements', on every major project, required by national legislatures from bilateral aid project managers, or sometimes even from multilateral agencies. To insist that all project officers design or evaluate bridges or irrigation schemes with *major* reference to the role of any one sex or age-group, or to non-formal education, or to the preservation (in countries where poor people are endangered medically) of endangered non-human species, is probably not very sensible. Yet such fashions, once formalized into requirements, exert influence long after the next fashion has replaced them. There is thus a real danger that sectoral dialogue – and project preparation – may become cluttered with large amounts of almost empty 'busyness'. More seriously, the fashions can distort projects – as with UN pressures towards the accelerated spread of intra-uterine devices in the 1960s (Cassen, 1978, ch.3) – producing 'successful' dialogue but bad policy outcomes.

The problem is not simple, because at least two 'development fashions' have lasting importance. It matters greatly that the project cycle, at all stages, should investigate and seek to improve the impact of the project – directly and via other activities[29] – on poor children, women, and men. It is also of durable importance that the bias of large capital funding – domestic or foreign – away from rural people, and especially from food-producing smallholders, be exposed and corrected. The language of donors, and of GoI, increasingly reflects these lasting truths. Their new-found place in the fashions of development has therefore done some good to policy dialogue, because rhetoric is heard and quoted back, and carries some commitments. Changing fashions, moreover, can in a healthy dialogue involve mutual learning. Patel (1986, 215) recalls GoI's 'difficulties in the early 1960s in persuading the World Bank that rural electrification was important and deserved World Bank assistance. Later, in the early 1970s, the Bank had begun to criticize us for not devoting enough attention to rural electrification!' By the early 1980s joint analyses had convinced both India and the Bank that remote electrification had grid costs so high as to be a cost-ineffective way to help the rural poor.

Unfortunately, however, if a new policy guideline has been adopted for reasons of fashion, it may be abandoned later even if it was and remains correct.[30] In 1967 – after two droughts had cruelly exposed the effects of India's prolonged under-emphasis on agriculture; and after the new cereal varieties had demonstrated their huge potential – an influential, and otherwise perceptive, expert could complain of:

> pressures [that] have contributed to a set of policies favoring
> expenditure in the low-return sector of agriculture. It is here that
> the weight of American policies associated with the American aid
> program to India can make a difference in the short run. In the
> longer run, the increase in the strength of industrial and urban
> political groups and the pressures and ideas generated within these
> groups would hopefully lead to a different political power structure

and a set of policies that would continuously stimulate industrial growth.

(Rosen 1967, 262–3)

There is hardly a worse use of policy dialogue than to intensify the strong Indian pressures for steel mills before canal maintenance, especially in 1967, but even today. Yet most commercial pressures in donor countries, and many pressures within aid agencies for technically safe spending in big units at low administrative cost, still favour such misplaced heavy-industrial emphases. Similarly, the 'focus on poverty' – apparently a central feature both of World Bank policy guidelines and of the Indian Seventh Plan – remains vulnerable, both to the combine-harvester salesmen and to the genuine, if misguided, believers in trickle-down. Academics may feel they can gain promotion by saying (researching, theorizing) something new: currently that poverty is after all easily cured by growth, or that agriculture responds rapidly to urban development even if governments discourage such responses. While (moderately) new again, such fashions are, however, still untrue. Today's academic fashion is too often tomorrow's blueprint for sectoral policy dialogue.

Choosing sectors and topics for dialogue

The fashions of development analysts play a large part in determining what sectors and topics donors emphasize in policy dialogue. The wish of donors to find blueprints, usable in many different projects at low administrative cost, can lead them to turn these fashionable sectors – and topics for the handling of any given sector – into rigid project guidelines, even in places as big, and as politically and environmentally diverse, as India. The focus of policy dialogue upon one powerful donor, the World Bank, leaves a recipient with few alternatives but to accept yesterday's fashions, turned into today's and tomorrow's blueprints by Bank experts. Fortunately, most of these are highly competent and fully aware of the risks in this process. In assessing the contribution of sectoral dialogue to aid-effectiveness in India, however, we have to enquire whether the key sectors and topics have been correctly specified, and whether there is enough room for flexibility if new facts (not new fashions) challenge the fashions of yesterday.

One major example of how sectoral policy dialogue may be pushed, by development fashions, to seize upon 'wrong issues' is in agricultural credit (see Chapter 2, pp. 58–61) and World Bank, 1981a). Credit is an important sector for agricultural development in some parts of India. Also – because of the research efforts of the All-India Rural Credit Surveys of the Reserve Bank of India (together with many microstudies), together with the long period of experiment with alternative channels of agricultural financing and refinancing – there is major Indian capacity to engage in dialogue in which both Indian and World Bank authorities could learn as well as teach. Further, most World Bank evaluations show very satisfactory rates of return to its lending for agricultural credit, not least in India.

However, the Bank may be focusing its policy dialogue upon the wrong issues. First, in the successive negotiations with the Agricultural Refinance Corporation and its successor, NABARD,[31] the Bank has concentrated almost entirely on the need to reduce and recover overdues. Yet, despite the importance of ensuring adequate financial returns so as to keep lenders viable, it is surely even more important not to choke off credit when – as is amply proven for India, even allowing for past overstatements[32] – the economic rate of return is more than acceptable. Further, research in Tamil Nadu (Ch. 2, p. 59) clearly confirms that many so-called 'overdues' are formal roll-overs and/or are secured against gold or jewels, so that even the financial return is better than it looks. Bank emphasis should surely shift, therefore, to the need to get larger shares of credit to small and/or labour-intensive farmers. That emphasis is implicit in the Bank's 'poverty focus' (and the classification of many of these credit-supportive loans as poverty-orientated 'rural development'), and may even improve repayment rates, which are better among smaller farmers (Lele, 1974; Lipton, 1976).[33]

Second, there is the issue of whether the extra assets, acquired with extra rural credit associated with aid, are employment-generating or otherwise poverty-orientated. A World Bank (1981a) evaluation of ten IDA projects commenced in 1970–3, to support Indian farm credit, takes a very favourable view of loans for tractor hire and purchase, but appears to overlook conclusive counter-evidence (Agarwal, 1980, 1984; Binswanger, 1979; and see Chapter 5 below) that, while privately profitable, the shift from animal to tractor draught displaced labour without raising output in most of South Asia – even in the extremely favourable environment of the Punjab. The Bank and USAID rightly stress collecting overdues, avoiding large subsidies (which tend to benefit almost entirely wealthy farmers), and ensuring that institutional credit can be embodied in extra investments with satisfactory returns. But an opportunity is being lost of re-orienting the discussion towards the means by which – without substantial credit subsidies, which are often diverted to richer farmers (or intermediaries) and which threaten the viability of lending agencies – credit can be focused on smaller farms, and on labour-intensive fixed and working capital. To concentrate the debate on how to collect overdues – instead of on how to select efficient activities, embodying equitable types of credit – is implicitly to weaken Indian resolve to use credit to increase the productivity of poorer farmers.

In defence of the ten IDA projects, they antedated the poverty-focus of Mr McNamara's 1973 Nairobi speech, so that 'the tractor components were not designed to reach small farmers' (World Bank, 1981a). However, there seems in general to be extremely inadequate effort to focus the policy dialogue on the poverty issues, especially where poverty-reduction and high efficiency are compatible. We have mentioned the apparent failure of Bank-Fund negotiators in 1975 to raise the question of how the – doubtless necessary – stabilization measures might be designed to minimize harm to the very poor. Also, although both Indian work and responses by individual Bank staff (see, for instance, Ahluwalia, 1977, 1986) on the 'poverty/basic-needs' debate have been of high quality, such work, even the Bank's own, penetrates too little into the making of aid policy. The Bank's own Report on Consortia and Consultative Groups (1978) makes it possible to see what was placed on the agenda for Consortium meetings. The nutrition, life-expectancy, literacy, or landholding of India's poor – and the likely effects on these variables of alternative aid policies – are not issues with which the Consortium donors appear to have been confronted by the Bank secretariat, despite its excellent, ample staff work on these matters.

Apart from the choice of topics for policy dialogue, the choice of sectors greatly influences aid-effectiveness. We saw how, as late as 1967, a perceptive US specialist actually proposed (even) less agricultural emphasis for India and its major donors. Not until the mid-1970s did that balance begin to be put right; as a former Chief Economist at USAID rightly remarked:

> Foreign aid to India was largely directed to industrial rather than agricultural development...from 1951–2 to 1970–1, only 2 per cent of foreign loans and credits (overwhelmingly aid) were earmarked for agricultural development, compared to 61 per cent for industrial development... GoI, much criticised by foreign observers for underemphasising agriculture, allocated 17 per cent of investment in this period to agriculture and irrigation.
>
> (Mellor, 1976, 244–53)

The proportion of Bank Group lending worldwide that comprised 'agriculture' plus 'rural development'[34] rose sharply in the 1970s, but has fallen quite sharply, in the budgetary projections (made each year for the next quinquennium), since 1982.

While policy dialogue clearly does best by emphasizing the right sectors, it is in India not so obvious what those sectors are. Even though the proportion of public expenditure supporting agriculture, irrigation, etc. remains somewhat too low in India – though the shortfall is nothing like as big or harmful as in most of sub-Saharan Africa – is agriculture, etc., the sector where the industrial donors, and their main conduit for policy dialogue (the Bank), are relatively best placed to engage constructively in policy dialogue? Increasingly, GoI takes the view that Bank expertise, and its capacity to raise appropriate funds and supporting technology elsewhere (especially in the Consortium), are greatest in energy, heavy industry, power and transport. Fortunately the Bank has also established *locus standi* with GoI in several agricultural sectors – irrigation, extension, credit, some aspects of research – but it is more the Bank and other donors than GoI that seek rural emphasis in aid and policy-dialogue. Even the donors' enthusiasm has been damped in the 1980s by the low current and projected world prices (largely created by western farm policies) for major Indian farm products – though in India world prices are probably an imperfect basis for establishing sectoral rates of return.[35]

Despite India's own proven skills in public policy and investment for agriculture and rural development, a major donor input in these sectors, in policy dialogue as well as aid, remains likely to increase aid-effectiveness, for two main reasons. First, while most Indian specialists now recognize that '20 per cent of public investment for 70 per cent of workers and 35 per cent of output' is too low a priority for agriculture, the immediate political pressures for domestic spending – usually less profitably – on industry and infrastructure remain stronger. Foreign cash and policy support for agriculture and rural development, if based on real expertise as is the Bank's, can greatly help GoI to defend, against strong short-term pressures, the larger rural allocations that it knows to be right. Second, India is in many technical, research, delivery, and economic fields a world leader in formulating agricultural policy (if not in mustering resources or power to implement it). 'Policy dialogue' is needed to help the Bank and other donors to learn lessons, about both what to do and what to avoid, for testing and possible application in other developing countries.

The proper selection of topics, and to some extent of sectors, for concentration in sectoral policy dialogue is most effectively advanced by the open discussion, between donor and recipient experts, of carefully conducted project evaluations. However, their contribution to dialogue has been hampered by some donor and recipient procedures: (i) only the Bank, and recently USAID, regularly evaluate returns and other outcomes from major aid projects; (ii) use of the main source of good project evaluation is restricted because objections by recipient governments prevent the Bank from publishing OED's evaluations;[36] (iii) operating divisions within the Bank – and probably other donor agencies – quite often decide to hold up the last few per cent of the cash on large projects; this means that completion reports (and therefore evaluations) cannot be prepared; (iv) in general, evaluations take place much too soon after project completion: comparison of the very thorough analysis (much fuller than an ordinary evaluation) of the Muda project in Malaysia carried out shortly after completion (Bell, Hazell, and Slade, 1982), and the OED's (also excellent) impact study based on research done a few years later (World Bank, 1981b), shows that a few years of full operational experience reversed many of the apparently favourable equity effects of the project; (v) many evaluations are hit-and-run jobs in which an expert, genuine but often in a quite inappropriate discipline, is given a quick tour of many sites by persons with clear initial positions or special interests. A major bilateral donor's 1976 evaluation of tractor aid to India appears to have been carried out in a couple of weeks, by an agricultural engineer untrained in economics, guided by local tractor distributors; (vi) most seriously, there is no systematic attempt, by such agencies (or LDCs) jointly, to compare evaluation documents and draw lessons for future project cycles. Nor do most big projects in LDCs – aided or not – begin, as they should, by reviewing relevant evaluations.

Bank, US and (recently) UK project evaluations have reached high standards of professional competence, but too much aid to India is still evaluated in unsatisfactory or unpublished forms. In 1982 a major EEC evaluation of aid to dairy development (see p. 193) allowed itself to be almost entirely guided by Indian project administrators who, while known to be dynamic and competent, are widely regarded in India as being somewhat reluctant to release information, and rather mistrustful of objective research. A British official evaluation of aid for a private-sector fertilizer factory erected for an Indian subsidiary, IEL, with a majority shareholding held by a British company (ICI), fails to disclose the extent of the interest-rate subsidy to the donor country firm involved, presumably on the grounds that it was commercially sensitive information (Haley and Hesling, 1986). Aid effectiveness would be improved by frank, published evaluations of past projects. However, the Bank evaluations are generally full, fair, and accessible (though unpublished). Aid effectiveness would also gain if, whenever major new projects or sectoral policy-dialogues were being considered, systematic review of good evaluations of past projects in that sector were first jointly undertaken by donors and recipient together.

Can the dialoguer deliver?

Most assessments of policy dialogue (including the World Bank's OED evaluation of structural adjustment loans, e.g. those to Turkey and Kenya) use, as the major criterion, whether the professionals – donor and recipient – are satisfied that each party has 'delivered' according to the conditions agreed. In the India-Bank dialogue: (i) Bank doubts about financing NABARD centre upon repeated Indian failure to deliver the promised reductions of overdues; (ii) Bank satisfaction about lending to irrigation centres on successful Indian 'delivery' of proposed design changes, and appreciation by senior Indian engineers of the virtues of these changes; (iii) the case for assigning 'substantial (Bank) lending resources to the industrial sector' is made in a 1984–5 Country Programme Paper in terms of a long series of liberalizations during 1981–3 – of imported inputs; of investment licensing; of coal, steel, and cement pricing – together with the need to compensate GoI for the political and perhaps distributional costs of these consequences of past sectoral dialogue.

There is something worryingly self-confirming about such assessments, whether they end up praising India for delivering, or blaming India for not delivering. One should also evaluate whether what is delivered secured the desired results cost-effectively: i.e., whether the conditions were well chosen. (i) In rural credits, should NABARD be helped (or pressed) to collect overdues, or, rather, to redirect resources to intermediaries in ways that favour small farmers – anyway better repayers – as final borrowers? (ii) In irrigation, were the 'delivered' design changes really more important than institutional changes? Did they really provide good results cost-effectively outside north-west India? (iii) In industrial policy, while the Bank praises the liberalizations, should it be justifying and structuring further aid to the sector in terms of the need to relax the political constraints upon 'how much further and faster the GoI can move', and the need for aid 'to support and sustain the adjustment process which has now been initiated'? Should not the Bank rather address – by the structure of its industrial lending – the recognized 'concern from both the Left and the Right that in a world of rising protectionism, it will be increasingly difficult to [offset] import liberalizations with export expansion [and] that the burden of adjustment inevitably falls most heavily on those least able to bear it' (World Bank, pers. comm.)?

On the Indian side, confidence in policy dialogue is imperilled when donors do not deliver aid that has been pledged, after GoI has accepted the short-run political cost of (possibly economically desirable) changes. In 1964–5, the Bank's 'Bell Mission' secured commitment to a package of liberalizing reforms, and provided 'informal assurances of a significant increase' in aid to US$1.5bn a year by the end of the Fourth Plan. After the 1965 war and drought, the June 1966 devaluation took place 'encouraged by informal assurances of greater external support' (T. Singh, 1974, 351), and following up the April meeting at which 'Asoka Mehta placed virtually all of India's major Fourth Plan schemes before George Woods for his consideration and approval, (obtaining) assurances of a five-year aid commitment (at) US$1.2bn a year' (Frankel, 297–8). However;

> By November 1967...[the USA] had to inform the Consortium it could not keep its April pledge to provide US$380 million of the US$900 million already promised for 1966/67. Thereafter, actual new commitments by the US for non-project aid to India showed a steady decline from US$300 million in 1966/67...to US$200 million in 1968/69. Reflecting America's reduced role, total new commitment for project aid [exclusive of food] fell from US$888 million in 1966/67 to US$534 million in 1967/68 and US$594 million in 1968/69 [including debt relief].
>
> (Frankel, 1978, 322)

Indeed, partly reflecting 'sharp increases in debt repayment' (Mellor, 1976, 223), net aid to India fell much more sharply, from US$1.3bn in 1964–5 and 1965–6 to US$0.5bn. in 1970–1 and 1971–2 (Chaudhuri, 1978, 99).

It is absurd to expect aid donors to put up and shut up. They owe their taxpayers evidence that the aid voted has been well used. But most aid to India has comprised loans, with a grant-element of total aid that has been really high (over 80 per cent) only for a few years. Especially in that context – at least as much as donors have the right and duty to see that India 'delivers the goods' – so the recipient has the right to expect that aid pledges, made in return for policy changes, will be fulfilled. The substantial cuts in the 1980s in the real value of IDA aid – plus major redirection (actual and planned) of IDA aid away from India, largely in response to US judgements and pressures – render it rather unlikely that, at least, implicit pledges made in past sectoral dialogues will be fully honoured on time. Even a big rise in IBRD (non-concessional) flows to India can hardly make up for significant falls in IDA flows. If Consortium members wish to provide signals favouring liberalizations, they will have to deliver the promised *quid pro quo*, whether through IDA or otherwise. A repeat of the 1964–9 experience could damage the (generally 'aid-effective') sectoral multilateral dialogue, perhaps as terminally as non-deliveries of pledged aid then wounded the (much less satisfactory) bilateral macro-leverage. It is worrying that, since 1985, successive Bank 'progress reports' on sub-Saharan Africa – while praising many of its governments for policy reforms – have repeatedly, but fruitlessly, upbraided donors for not delivering the promised capital flows in return. Both Africa and India since 1985 suggest that donors might usefully re-examine the lessons of India in 1965–71. Conditionality cuts both ways.

113

References

Agarwal, B. (1980) 'Tractorization, productivity and employment: a reassessment', *Journal of Development Studies*, 16:3.

Agarwal, B. (1984) 'Tractors, tubewells and cropping intensity in the Punjab', *Journal of Development Studies*, 20:4.

Ahluwalia, M.S. (1977) 'Rural poverty and agricultural performance in India', *World Bank Reprint Series* No.60.

Ahluwalia, M.S. (1978) 'Rural poverty and agricultural performance in India', *Journal of Development Studies*, 14:3.

Ahluwalia, M.S. (1986) 'Rural poverty, agricultural production, and prices: a re-examination' in J. Mellor and G. Desai (eds), *Agricultural Change and Rural Poverty*, Delhi, Oxford University Press.

Bell, C., Hazell, P. and Slade, R. (1982) *Project Evaluation in Regional Perspective*, Baltimore, John Hopkins University Press

Bhagwati, J.N. and Srinivasan, T.N. (1975) *Foreign Trade Regime and Economic Development: India*, New York, Columbia University Press (for NBER).

Binswanger, H. (1979) *The Economics of Tractorization in South Asia*, New York, Agricultural Development Council.

Burch, B. (1979) *Overseas Aid and the Transfer of Technology: a Case Study of Agricultural Mechanization in Sri Lanka*, Ph.D. thesis, Brighton, University of Sussex.

Cassen, R. (1978) *India: Population, Economy, Society*, London, Macmillan.

Chaudhuri, P. (1978) *The Indian Economy: Poverty and Development*, London, Crosby Lockwood and Staples.

Chopra, P. (1968) *Uncertain India*, Bombay, Asia Press.

Desai, P. (1972) *The Bokaro Steel Plant: A Study of Soviet Economic Assistance*, New York, American Elsevier.

Farrington, J. and Abeyratne, F. (1980) *Farm Power and Water Use in the Dry Zone of Sri Lanka*, Part I, Research Study No. 43, Colombo, ARTI

Farrington, J. and Abeyratne, F. (1982) *Farm Power and Water Use in the Dry Zone of Sri Lanka*, Part II, Research Study No. 52, Colombo, ARTI.

Feder, G. and Slade, R. (1986) 'A comparative analysis of some aspects of the training and visit system of agricultural extension in India', *Journal of Development Studies*, 22:2.

Frankel, F. (1978) *India's Political Economy 1947-1977: the gradual revolution*, Princeton, Princeton University Press.

Government of India (1982-83) *Economic Survey*, Delhi, India Press.

Haley, G. and Hesling, S. (1986) *An Evaluation of Indian Explosives Ltd.'s Expansion of Fertilizer Production at Kanpur*, EV 308, London, ODA.

Herring, R.J. (1983) *Land to the Tiller*, New Haven, Yale University Press.

International Labour Office (1971) *Matching Employment Opportunities and Expectations* ('Ceylon Report'), Geneva.

Jha, P.S. (1980) *India: a Political Economy of Stagnation*, Bombay, Oxford University Press.

Krishna, R. (1983) 'Growth, investment and poverty in mid-term appraisal of Sixth Plan', *Economic and Political Weekly*, 18:47.

Krueger, A.D. (1974) 'The political economy of the rent-seeking society', *American Economic Review*, 64:3, June.

Krueger, A.D. and Ruttan, V. (1983), 'Trade sector policies and the impact of assistance', in Vol. I of A. Krueger and V. Ruttan (eds) *The Development Impact of Economic Assistance to LDCs*, Economic Development Center, University of Minnesota/ USAID/Dept. of State.

Lele, U. (1974) 'The role of credit and marketing in economic development', in N. Islam (ed.) *Agricultural Policy in Developing Countries*, London, MacMillan/IEA.

Lele, U. (1979) *The Design of Rural Development: Lessons from Africa*, (revised edition with postscript), Baltimore, Johns Hopkins University Press.

Lele, U, (1987) 'Growth of foreign assistance and its impact on agriculture', in J. Mellor *et al*. (eds) *Accelerating Food Production in sub-Saharan Africa*, Baltimore, Johns Hopkins University Press.

Lipton, M. (1976) 'Agricultural finance and rural credit in poor countries', *World Development*, 4:7.

Lipton, M. (1985) 'Indian agricultural development and African food strategies: a role for EC?', in W.M. Callewaert and R. Kumar *EEC – India: Towards a Common Perspective*, Netherlands, Peeters-Leuven.

Lipton, M. (1986) 'Aid-effectiveness, prisoners' dilemmas and country aid allocations', *IDS Bulletin*, 17:2, April.

Lipton, M. (1987) 'Agricultural price policy: which way at the World Bank?', *Development Policy Review*, June.

Mellor, J. (1976) *The New Economics of Growth: a Strategy for India and the Developing World*, Ithaca, Cornell (for Twentieth Century Fund).

Moore, M.P. (1984) 'International development, the World Bank, and India's new agricultural extension program', *JDS*, 20:4.

Mosley, P. (1987) *Overseas Aid: Its Defence and Reform*, Brighton, Wheatsheaf.

Papanek, G. (1972) 'The effect of aid and other resource transfers on savings and growth in less developed countries', *Economic Journal*, vol. 82.

Patel, I.G. (1986) *Essays in Economic Policy and Economic Growth*, London, MacMillan.

Rao, V. and Narain, D. (1963) *Foreign Aid and India's Economic Development*, Delhi, Asia Press.

Rose, T. (1985) *Crisis and Recovery in Sub-Saharan Africa*, Paris, OECD.

Rosen, G. (1967) *Democracy and Economic Change in India*, San Francisco, University of California Press.

Rosen, G. (1985) *Western Economists and Eastern Societies*, Delhi, Oxford University Press.

Singer, H.W. (1987) 'The World Development Report 1987 on the blessings of 'outward orientation': a necessary correction', *Journal of Development Studies*, vol. 24.

Singh, A. (1973) *Impact of American Aid on the Indian Economy*, New Delhi, Vora.

Singh, T. (1974) *India's Development Experience*, London, Macmillan.

Sukhatme, V. (1983) 'Assistance to India', in vol. II of A. Krueger and V.

Ruttan (eds) *The Development Impact of Economic Assistance to LDCs*, Economic Development Center, University of Minnesota/USAID/Dept. of State.

Swamy, S. (1971) *Indian Economic Planning*, New York, Barnes and Noble.

Toye, J. (1987) *Dilemmas of Development*, Oxford, Basil Blackwell.

Toye, J. and Clark, G. (1986) 'The aid and trade provision: origins, dimensions, and possible reform', *Development Policy Review*, 4:4.

Wade, R. (1982) 'The World Bank and India's irrigation reform', *Journal of Development Studies*, 18:2.

World Bank (1981) *Accelerated Development in sub-Saharan Africa: an Agenda for Change*, Washington DC, The World Bank.

World Bank (1981a) *Agricultural Credit Projects: A Review of Recent Experience in India*, Report No. 3415, Washington DC, The World Bank (Operations Evaluation Division).

World Bank (1981b) *Impact Evaluation Report – Malaysia: Muda and Kemubu Irrigation Projects*, No. 3587, Washington DC, The World Bank (Operations Evaluation Division).

World Bank (1982) *Focus on Poverty: A report of a task force of the World Bank*, Washington DC, The World Bank.

World Bank (1986) *Poverty and Hunger, Policy Paper*, Washington DC, The World Bank.

World Bank (1986a) *World Development Report*, Washington DC, Oxford University Press for the World Bank.

World Bank (1987) *World Development Report*, Washington DC, Oxford University Press for the World Bank.

Chapter 4

The Systemic Effects of Aid and Donor Procedures

Introduction

So far aid to India has been examined in a number of partial aspects – its implications for macroeconomic management, for the alleviation of poverty and for the development of Indian policy-making. In this chapter, a more holistic approach to aid is adopted, focusing on the question of whether aid has important 'systemic effects' on India's political economy, and whether particular procedures of aid-giving could or should be modified in order to reduce adverse systemic effects, or increase beneficial systemic effects. The reason for asking questions like this is the fear that foreign aid may, in certain circumstances, have strong distorting effects on the recipient's economy, and therefore that an evaluation method which concentrated only on the results of individual aided projects would fail to detect something important about the overall aid-giving process. Before proceeding to an analysis of aid project evaluations in the next chapter, it is necessary to tackle these larger and more comprehensive questions.

One would expect, as a first guess, that the distorting effects of foreign aid on India's political economy would not be large, especially in comparison with small, poor sub-Saharan African countries which receive aid. The first reason for this is the smallness of the aid flows to India relative to the size of her economy, as illustrated in Chapter 1. They are simply not large enough to be the cause of 'Dutch disease', the loss of competitiveness in tradeable goods brought on by a major discovery of oil or natural gas, or a major rise in a commodity price or (by analogy) a major inflow of foreign aid. The second reason why one would not expect aid-induced distortions to be large in India is India's thirty-year experience of managing aid inflows precisely to avoid the worst forms of microeconomic distortions. India's strong administrative capacity relative to other developing countries (particularly, again, countries of sub-Saharan Africa) has permitted an effective learning process to take place in the field of aid management.

117

The broad conclusion of this chapter is that India has succeeded in minimizing the adverse systemic effects of foreign aid. A relatively sophisticated set of defences has been established over the years to buffer the wide variety of political and economic pressures that can emanate from aid donors. Although a number of problems remain unresolved between the Indian Government and the aid donors, they are not likely to be a major disruptive force in the overall aid relationship. Two key components of the defensive strategy should be noted - the multiplication of the number of donors combined with the centralisation of control over the channelling of aid to the domestic economy. By encouraging the giving of aid by a large number of countries, and using aid from the USSR and its allies to create extra room for manoeuvre in its relations with the Aid-India Consortium (which represents the bulk of donors), India has side-stepped many of the more extreme problems of aid-dependency. By centralizing its own relations with donors through one government department, it maintains a tight control over the aid process and creates an important buffer between donors and the internal agencies that are associated with aid-funding.

In order to simplify the discussion of systemic effects, a basic distinction is made between multilateral and bilateral aid. This is a reflection of the fact that aid-giving procedures vary significantly as between the multilateral and bilateral agencies, and therefore the types of problems and conflicts which can be created are also different in each case. A secondary distinction is made between project aid, where some discrete developmental activity is being wholly or partly financed, and non-project aid (which includes debt relief, food aid, and general balance of payments support). Within these broad categories, it should be noted that, quantitatively speaking, multilateral project aid is the largest category of aid to India. Generally speaking, India's relations with the multilateral agencies have (after the conflicts over the 1966 devaluation) been fairly smooth ones. Some friction has been experienced over the requirement for international competitive bidding. But this subsided as the agencies conceded a margin of price preference to bidders in the recipient country and certain other developing countries. The multilateral agencies have also increasingly moved towards a more relaxed attitude to the financing of local costs and this has reduced another potential area of conflict. With the abandonment of attempts to use aid leverage to influence macroeconomic policy, such leverage as now exists operates at the more acceptable level of sectoral policy. The long gestation period of multilateral projects remains their most substantial systemic drawback.

The most serious systemic drawback to bilateral project aid has been source-tying, i.e. the requirement that the imports which the aid finances should come only from supplies within the donor's own country. This is objectionable to the recipients because it can confine their choice to a range of goods that is unsuitable in design or quality for their project's purposes, or because by limiting competition it allows the donor-country suppliers to charge higher prices that would be possible against the full force of international competition. Bilateral project aid is the second largest component of India's aid, and in the period up to the 1970s, source-tying was widespread and represented a serious problem for India. During that time, however, India managed to accumulate a considerable expertise in comparing aid offers for projects with ruling international prices, and did not hesitate to reject offers which involved heavy price-loading by donor national suppliers. Since the mid-1970s, the extent of *formal* source-tying has changed. The United States, a major bilateral donor, now permits procurement in India and other developing countries, although not from its major industrial competitors. The Netherlands and Scandinavian donors, along with the Germans and Japanese, impose relatively few procurement restrictions.

But just as the removal of tariff barriers can be followed smartly by the erection of non-tariff barriers, so the reduction of formal source-tying can be, and in some cases has been, accompanied by new donor practices which have the same effect as source-tying. Certain bilateral donors have in the 1980s set aside part of their aid budget for high-visibility export promotion purposes. These involve an increase in the intensity of aid-tying, because procurement is not tied merely to the donor country's suppliers, but is given to clinch a contract for a particular national firm, as in the recent UK aid for sales of power stations and helicopters to India. Often here not only is international competition eliminated, but also intra-national competition among firms in donor countries. In addition, it can be argued that there is less control over whether the aided project is sound from a developmental point of view. Another donor practice which can be an effective informal method of tying aid that is formally untied is the rapid switching of country aid between different sectors. Failure to publicize calls for tenders and the specification of donor country consultancy firms are other methods which also have the same restrictive impact as source-tying. All of these methods of informal source-tying remain a serious impediment to the recipient of aid achieving value for money in its spending of aid.

The absence of much finance for the local costs of projects has been a cause of project delay and inappropriate project choice until recently. Now, alongside the multilateral agencies, both the UK and the USA have found ways of significantly increasing the local cost element of their bilateral aid. But, to the extent that local costs are usually also recurrent costs, this favourable development has raised a new problem. Are recipients of local recurrent cost aid being committed by donors to large expenditures in future years which their fiscal systems may not be ready to cope with? The previous exclusion of local costs was designed to finesse this problem, but now aid can require future commitment of recipients' revenues. But whether the recipient will wish to withdraw from that commitment ought to depend on the social profitability of the project. If the project has been well chosen in the first place, finding the necessary revenues from internal sources ought to be an attractive proposition.

In marked contrast with the experience of many aid-receiving developing countries, especially in Africa, India does not appear to have had serious problems with donor procedures of project appraisal, monitoring and reporting. Although these procedures do differ quite markedly among donors, and although they are compatible neither with each other nor with India's own internal project procedures, the Indian authorities appear to have coped well. However, if some standardization of procedures between donors could be agreed, this would probably cut down administrative delays and be welcomed by the Indian side.

An important choice which faces donors is whether to support its aid programme by a substantial local mission. Practice on this varies between donors, with the World Bank and USAID being well represented in India, but the UK High Commission being very short-staffed for handling aid issues and relying heavily on intermittent special missions sent out from London. Local missions are a costly use of aid money and their effects are far from predictable. However, if donors are committed to making a reality of 'policy dialogue', an effective local mission is probably indispensable. If this is so, it might be worthwhile to consider the idea of a joint mission of aid donors, as the way of minimizing the cost of keeping the policy dialogue working well. A joint mission of aid donors could help by raising the average quality of aid field staff and of standardizing the functions which they would perform in relation to the recipient government (which presently show the same inter-country variety as do other donor procedures). This suggestion, however, does have political implications for the recipient, which may be reluctant to countenance a 'united front' by donors on aid policy issues. This reluctance could be reduced if dialogue was confined to project or sector issues, but may still be a stumbling block in India, which has always shown itself anxious to maintain a distance between its policy-making and the views of particular donors, either as individuals or as groups.

Many donors: help or hindrance?

Does the number of donors from which a developing country accepts aid matter? Does it make any difference whether a certain amount of aid is given by three donors or by thirty? The effect of larger numbers of donors works in two opposing directions. On the one hand, the proliferation of donors can strain a recipient's administrative capacity to co-ordinate all the different forms of aid activity to the benefit of the economy, rather than to its distraction and disruption. Ultimately, a recipient can suffer from 'aid overload' when donors are allowed to start up too many different activities and to compete for scarce domestic resources in a vain attempt to complete them all. On the other hand:

> There may be some benefit in multiplicity (of donors) when it widens the recipient's choices and permits a range of innovation which might not arise if only a few agencies were in the field.
>
> (Cassen, 1986, 223)

Thus it is not the absolute number of donors that matters, but the number relative to the level of administrative capacity. Further, the greater a recipient's competence in aid management, the more it can gain the advantages of many donors – in terms of choice and innovation – without having to pay the serious costs that can arise. Essentially, India is an example of a country with the administrative capacity to take full advantage of a multiplicity of donors.

Before considering that judgement in greater detail, it may be useful to sketch in some information about the main sources of aid and their trends over the last decade. Table 4.1 shows the distribution of utilizations of aid among the four groups of donors which are conventionally identified separately. These are the Aid-India Consortium, consisting of thirteen nations plus certain international organizations, whose activities are co-ordinated by the World Bank; the USSR and East European countries (of which the USSR is by far the biggest contributor); the OPEC countries and related organizations; and the 'others', notably the European Community (EC) and Switzerland. Table 4.1 also shows the shares of each group in India's aid flow in percentage terms.

It is clear from these figures that by far the greater part of India's aid derives from the Aid-India Consortium which, even after the dwindling US contributions in the mid-1970s are taken into account, never provided less than 70 per cent of the total. The share of the USSR and its allies is normally very small. Their unusually high 10 per cent share in 1973–6 reflects emergency wheat assistance during the bad harvests of that time and this peak has not been regained since. After the oil price rise of 1973, OPEC and individual oil-rich Middle Eastern states made a significant contribution to aid flows, but with the falling oil prices of the early 1980s this is unlikely to be a permanent feature of the composition of India's aid. The 'others', including the European Community, are at best a make-weight in the total.

121

Table 4.1 India: aid utilization by source

Rupees (crores)	1970–3 (average)	1973–6 (average)	1976–9 (average)	1979–82 (average)	1983–4
Aid-India Consortium	728.3	1,006.7	1,121.7	1,674.3	2,309.9
USSR and East Europe	301.1	138.0	52.1	35.2	150.5
OPEC and related	0.0	199.7	184.9	40.9	80.0
Others	5.5	52.4	26.2	69.4	35.8
Total	763.9	1,396.8	1,384.9	1,833.2 [a]	2,576.2
Percentages					
Aid-India Consortium	95	72	81	91	90
USSR and East Europe	4	10	4	2	6
OPEC and related	–	14	13	2	3
Others	1	4	2	4	1
Total	100	100	100	100	100

Source G.O.I., *Economic Survey, 1982-83 and Economic Survey, 1983-84*, Table 7.3.
Note a Total greater than components due to error in source

But the significance of the role played by the USSR and allies in giving aid to India is somewhat larger than its small share in total aid flows seems to indicate. This is for three reasons.

(i)Soviet government aid has been concentrated on sectors (steel, power) which the Indian planners have regarded as particularly vital in their strategy for economic development; (ii)The bulk of India's aid derives from a group of western donors whose aid policies are harmonized – not fully harmonized, needless to say – through their participation in the Consortium. Soviet aid contributes more to widening the Indians' choice of projects than would one additional western donor; and (iii)because of geopolitical competition between the USA and USSR, the latter is particularly keen to substitute for the former when sometimes American promises of aid fail to materialize.

The classic illustration of factors (i) and (iii) is provided by the history of the Bokaro steel mill in the 1960s. In a fit of liberalism, and despite its considerable scepticism about the Indian heavy-industry, public-sector strategy of the Second and Third Plans, the US Administration of the day agreed to finance the construction of Bokaro. But it failed to secure the necessary legislative approval for this aid. At this point, the Indian Government was able to turn successfully to the USSR for the necessary funding. The manoeuvre was costly, both in terms of the delays in the implementation of the project and the subsequent indifferent performance of the plant, but the presence of the USSR as an aid-giver did help to maintain the Indian plan strategy basically intact (Kothari, 1970, 413).

As has been argued previously, the ability to benefit from the multiplicity of aid donors depends partly on there being many donors willing to give or make concessional loans, but – granted such an international environment – it then depends on establishing the administrative machinery to control the aid giving process in the recipient's national interest. The main features of the Indian Government's aid management policies have been:

(i)Responsibility for all negotiations with donors, for administering the documentation of aid inflows and for monitoring the implementation of aided projects is centralized in the Department of Economic Affairs within the Ministry of Finance. The DEA operates procedures which aim, as far as possible, to stabilize project spending even when the level of aid fluctuates – i.e. to separate as far as possible decisions on the size and composition of the investment programme from the arrival or non-arrival of aid for specific projects.

(ii)The concessional element in aid finance is largely withheld from the agency in India whose project is being funded with aid money. The aim here is to dampen the incentive of state and local government, parastatals and other agencies to alter their development programmes just in order to take advantage of a new facility being provided free by a donor. That is regarded as being disruptive of overall planning priorities and an incentive to use sources of supply (i.e. donor country suppliers) which might otherwise not be chosen (Cable, 1980, 75). Of course, it is not possible to maintain this position entirely. Since aided projects do involve an abnormal level of work and documentation, agencies must be given some incentive to participate in them. As a result the central government normally retains 75 per cent of the concessionality of aid finance, while passing on 25 per cent to the agency concerned.

(iii)Where aid is capital aid, the Indian Government operates a series of controls over the policy of public sector financial institutions which ensure that the end use of the aid is in line with pre-determined plan priorities.

(iv)Where aid is in the form either of sectoral aid or aid for maintenance imports, the Indian Government has almost complete discretion over its use, with the result that donors will normally not be told exactly what it has been used for.

As a result of aid management practices such as these, the Indian Government has exercised great care and vigilance over the absorption of aid. Her success in this regard has been widely recognized. In a book that summed up India's aid experience in the 1960s, it was said that 'the multiplicity of donor agencies, each with their several points of view, gives India ample room for manoeuvre in obtaining a balanced pattern of aid. Cold War differences and the policy of non-alignment enhance her bargaining power still further' (Eldridge, 1969, 70). At the end of the 1970s, the UK Select Committee on Overseas Development 'were impressed by the determination of the Indian authorities not to allow aid to distort their priorities. The Indian authorities have maximized their own room for manoeuvre within existing resource constraints at the same time as they have minimized their dependence upon aid donors' (House of Commons, 1979: xvii). Kalecki had also included India among the 'intermediate regimes' of which he wrote:

> (They) are the proverbial clever calves that suck two cows: each block gives them financial aid competing with the other. Thus has been made possible the 'miracle' of getting out of the United States some credits with no strings attached as to the internal economic policy.
>
> (Kalecki, 1972, 167)

The second half of that assessment, written in 1967, was just ceasing to be true. In the mid-1960s, the question of economic policy strings was placed firmly on the western donors agenda. Faced with the tight Indian system of aid management, what options were and are available to donors? They can usefully be classified according to the terminology developed by Hirschman (1970), that is, options of 'exit', 'voice', and 'loyalty'. Loyalty was the initial option, a willingness to support India's development effort even (in the case of the United States) contrary to better judgement. When loyalty had eroded, as it had by the middle of the 1960s, the options were 'exit' or 'voice', or some combination of the two. Some donors have indeed exercised the option to exit in their dealings with India. The exits have been of two distinct kinds. Some major bilateral donors have exited in order to try and exercise leverage over political developments in the South Asian region. Both the US and the UK cut off aid in response to the outbreak of the Indo-Pakistan conflict of autumn 1965, the UK giving in to pressure from the USA., which had treaty obligations to Pakistan under CENTO. When the Indo-Pakistan conflict surfaced again over East Pakistan/Bangladesh in December 1971, the British this time did not follow the USA's 'tilt towards Pakistan', and the USA was alone in cutting off new aid authorizations until 1978. Clearly, at times of international conflict, India, like other aid recipients, has felt the effect of the 'leverage' which dominant aid donors, like the USA at that time, can exert, both directly on their own account and (sometimes, but not always) through their closer allies who also give aid. Such leverage caused great nationalistic resentment in India, which was convinced of the correctness of its international actions *vis-à-vis* Pakistan. Donors who exit inevitably point to the fungibility of aid and the feasibility of using aid finance indirectly to fund increased military expenditure (by directing aid to projects that would have been undertaken in any case and thereby releasing resources for military uses). It is difficult to assess the impact of the US exits from aid to India. In geopolitical terms, the USA probably did more to ensure the limitation of the conflicts by denying Pakistan rapid rearmament after the first bursts of armed conflict. But perhaps, in order to be able to do that, some 'even-handed' action against India was also necessary for reasons of successful political presentation.

The other type of 'exit' – or rather leverage achieved by threatening 'exit' – was a joint multilateral and bilateral manoeuvre aimed at major changes in economic policy in the period 1964–6. For various reasons discussed at length in Chapters 3 and 7, this attempted manipulation came to grief, causing further resentment in India – even in moderates like I.G. Patel (1986, 73) – and has not been repeated. Threats of exit have now been replaced with the use of 'voice', Hirschman's third option. Voice operates more gently, but also more continuously, through the institutions of 'policy dialogue', the nature and effects of which are discussed separately in Chapter 3. Policy dialogue takes place much more at sector and project level, than at national level. But to be effective, donors still need to co-ordinate their views at whatever is the relevant level. A multiplicity of donor voices favours a recipient government that wants to go its own way, without regard for donor opinion. Pure multilateral exit is also a logical possibility, although one most unlikely to affect India. In Latin America, some multilateral lending appears to have been responsive to the policy stances of would-be borrowing governments (e.g. Peru in 1969–73, Chile in 1970–3, and Nicaragua in 1979–82), particularly on questions concerning the nationalization of foreign private assets (Van de Laar, 1980, 33; Hayter and Watson, 1985, 214–23). India has dealt very circumspectly with such matters and accordingly has not run into these types of difficulties, and is not likely to encounter them in the immediate future.

Systemic aspects of multilateral aid

The Aid-India Consortium provides the great bulk of India's aid and co-ordinates the overall level of future aid commitments by major Western countries. Through the Consortium both multilateral and bilateral aid is given, and each broad category is subject to markedly different conditions, procedures, and arrangements. Table 4.2 provides details on the composition of Consortium aid, in this respect, as well as a country breakdown of bilateral aid and the mixture of loans and grants. This table gives a good picture of the diversity of forms of the Consortium's aid, although unfortunately it does not give detail on the breakdown between project and non-project forms of aid. Loan figures are shown gross rather than net, because at this point we are more interested in the spread of donors and types of aid than in the level of overall transfers between the Consortium and India. The gross figures indicate more accurately the complexity of the aid-giving process.

Table 4.2: Gross loan and grant disbursements by Aid-India Consortium (5-year averages) US$m

	1976–7 to 1980–1 (average)		1981–2 to 1985–6 (average)	
Bilateral	Gross loans	Grants	Gross loans	Grants
Austria	1.6	–	2.8	–
Belgium	10.2	0.1	4.8	–
Canada	24.8	22.4	37.0	12.1
Denmark	3.8	12.8	12.6	14.2
France	36.2	–	46.4	–
W. Germany	156.6	3.9	144.8	0.9
Italy	4.4	–	3.4	2.1
Japan	95.4	12.6	102.2	11.0
Netherlands	75.2	17.2	43.0	36.3
Norway	–	18.1	–	20.8
Sweden	1.6	56.7	–	47.4
Switzerland	3.2	9.1	0.6	16.0
UK	12.0	229.0	–	155.3
USA	56.2	132.5	52.2	106.8
Total	*481.2*	*514.4*	*449.8*	*422.9*
Multilateral				
IBRD	146.8		359.8	
IDA	478.2		927.8	
EEC		37.9		76.6
UN		94.4		109.7
IFAD	–		–	
Other	12.2		17.8 ·	
Total	*637.2*	*132.3*	*1,305.4*	*186.3*
Aid-India Consortium	1,118.4	646.7	1,755.2	609.2

Source World Bank (1987) *India: an Industrializing Economy in Transition*, Report 6633–N, vol. 3, Tables 4.3(b) and 4.3(g) adapted.

From Table 4.2, one can conclude that, over the decade 1976–86, Consortium aid was more multilateral than bilateral. Multilateral aid to India at this time was almost exclusively project aid. When the World Bank began after 1980 to offer balance of payment support through its Structural Adjustment Lending (SAL) facility, it was recognized both by the Bank and by the Indian Government that such a facility for non-project aid would not be appropriate for India. This form of lending carried with it conditions, that is, specific economic policies which the borrower promised to adopt in return for the right to borrow. It is difficult to think that the Indian Government would have relished borrowing on such terms, and difficult also to imagine that the Bank would have wanted to resort to sanctions, if India had borrowed but failed to meet the conditions of the loan. In the absence of SAL (or similar policy-based) lending, most multilateral aid has been of the traditional project type. The procedures for multilateral project aid are therefore the most important determinant of the systemic effects of Consortium aid.

Major types of problem arising from multilateral project finance have been classified by Harvey (1983, 23–6) as follows:

Currency problems

The World Bank does not lend dollars just because its loans are denominated in dollars. It lends those currencies which it has borrowed on world markets, and thereby insulates itself from problems of currency fluctuation. The currency of its Bank borrowings does matter to the borrower, because that is the currency which has to be repaid. Thus if it is a hard currency, which subsequently strengthens against other currencies, repayment will become more onerous.

Procurement problems

Multilateral loans normally include a condition that procurement financed by these loans is subject to a procedure of international tendering. This is designed to give all the contributors to the multilateral finance (and indeed all other countries' suppliers) an equal opportunity to win the contract, subject only to normal commercial criteria. The recipient country may believe that, for various reasons – including the need to encourage domestic industries – a full international tender procedure is not appropriate.

Delays

Delays arise from the lengthy project cycle of identification, preparation, appraisal, and negotiation of project lending. This cycle requires agreement between the multilateral institution and the borrowing government and its agencies on a very wide range of matters thought likely to affect the ultimate success of the project (Baum, 1982). Borrowers thus face a choice between accepting substantial 'interference' in project design in order to reduce delays, or accepting substantial delays in order to gain more agreement to their own conceptions of correct project design.

Project bias

When the multilateral lender lends only to cover foreign exchange costs and not the local costs in domestic currency, there may be pressures towards choices of excessively capital intensive and/or excessively import intensive techniques, despite a general awareness that an 'appropriate' technology is what is required.

The currency aspects of multilateral project finance have not been a major source of difficulty for India. There are various reasons for this. First, the currency exposure problem was essentially confined to the 1970s. Under the regime of fixed exchange rates which lasted until its collapse in 1971–3, the exposure problem was confined to the risk of an occasional revaluation: it was rare and dramatic rather than chronic and continuous. After 1980–1, the Bank changed its currency policy, pooling its available currencies and lending to each borrower roughly the same mix of currencies. This spread each borrower's exposure into a basket of currencies, and virtually extinguished the exposure problem. Even during the 1970s, however, India was in a relatively fortunate position to deal with currency risks from aid loans. As a regular borrower, any inability on its part to forecast the currency of the loans would have been offset by the acquisition of a basket of different currencies through repeated borrowing. As a borrower with good access to IDA funds in the 1970s, India enjoyed long grace periods before repayment started, which allowed the debt burden to be eroded by inflation. These two favourable factors moderated considerably the currency exposures generated by multilateral finance in India during the 1970s.

The procurement conditions of multilateral loans, like currency exposure, posed problems most severely in the 1970s. This was because the requirement for international tendering is most obviously in the interest of the aid recipient when the project is of a conventional turnkey kind, for which there is no domestic manufacturing capability. Examples are power stations or textile mills. Such projects dominated multilateral lending in the late 1950s and 1960s and international tendering therefore provided a substantial safeguard in securing value for money for India, particularly compared with bilaterally funded projects. However, as the purposes of multilateral finance began to change in the early 1970s, and as India's own productive capacity diversified under the impact of import substitution, so the advantages of the international tendering rule became less clear-cut. Some friction between the Government of India and the multilateral agencies ensued. As agriculture (and specifically irrigation) grew in importance as a sector for multilateral aid, so some disagreements occurred between the Government of India and the World Bank about whether the rule requiring international competitive bidding should apply to canal construction. The Bank wished the rule to apply in this case, while the Government of India considered that value for money would be sufficiently ensured by competition for these contracts among domestic civil engineering firms. For a period in the 1970s, this failure to agree may have influenced the Bank's lending policies, leading it to favour a strategy of land levelling and channel construction rather than heavy investment in main canal systems (Wade, 1982, 172).

More generally, the Bank's international tendering rule has been a controversial one in India. Critics, both inside and outside India have made a variety of claims about its effects on project choice. These claims are often contradictory, but that does not allow us simply to ignore them. It is sometimes argued that, where India has the capability to produce a required project component, the domestic version should be purchased, in order to 'reduce imports of technology' (Economic and Political Weekly (EPW), 1982, 1590). The question of relative cost and value for money is simply ignored in this line of criticism. This surely is not in India's interest. A different argument is that the Bank unduly favours foreign main contractors, even when Indian bidders are equal in competence and competitive in price and that the choice of a foreign main contractor introduces a bias in favour of imported equipment. Thus, of three equivalent fertilizer plant projects (Nangal, Sindoi, and Haldia), the first two, financed by multilateral aid had a 25 per cent higher foreign exchange content than the latter, which was bilaterally funded and undertaken by a domestic main contractor, the Fertilizer Corporation of India (Payer, 1982, 143; EPW, 1982b). This alleged bias is interpreted as an attempt to hobble India's development of an independent technical capability. The Bank's position is that the imported equipment is more advanced, more reliable, or less expensive, and that fair foreign competition is a stimulus, not a brake to the transfer of technology. This dispute thus boils down to the question of whether the existing procedures ensure a 'fair' competition. It does not seem useful to try to come to a general conclusion on this. All one can say is that conclusive evidence of systematic unfairness is lacking.

On the whole, the GoI does not incline to endorse these more sweeping criticisms of international competitive bidding. Certainly the

Ministry of Finance sees this practice as helpful in limiting the pressures which arise from domestic suppliers which have spare capacity and which believe that they are *ipso facto* entitled to government orders, regardless of their high production costs and prices. It is a way to avoid the perpetuation of the effects of past unwise investment decisions. The Ministry of Industry naturally has a different perspective, being responsible for the entities created by past investment. In an important round of discussions about a new set of super thermal power stations, it found itself taking up cudgels for Bharat Heavy Electricals against the Ministry of Energy but it proved to be fighting a losing battle (EPW, 1982a). The GoI's anxieties about international competitive bidding have thus been effectively limited to peripheral areas, such as civil engineering or irrigation. By the early 1980s, these anxieties had been resolved successfully by a change in World Bank policy on procurement conditions. A 15 per cent margin of preference was granted to domestic contractors in both areas; in order, as the Bank's semi-official pamphlet describes it, 'to foster the development of local capabilities' (Baum, 1982, 21). However, international competitive bidding remains the means by which the Bank believes that efficient and economical procurement can be achieved 'in most cases' (Baum, 1982).

Systemic aspects of bilateral aid

Multilateral aid is free from the problem of source-tying precisely because of its requirement in most cases for international competitive bidding. In contrast, bilateral aid's major disadvantage for the recipient is that it is 'tied' in various different ways. Source-tying is the requirement that the foreign exchange value of the aid should be spent only with the donor country's national suppliers (or, in some cases, a restricted set of other specified geographical sources of supply). Project-tying is the limitation that aid must be spent only on an agreed, identifiable 'project'. (Reverse-tying is advantageous for the recipient, because it allows loan repayments to be made in commodity exports rather than free foreign exchange.) Bilateral aid is less project-tied than multilateral aid in India, as Table 4.3 shows. But it is seriously source-tied, in a way that multilateral aid is not – see Table 4.4. The bilateral donors' reason for the double-tying of aid is primarily the need to demonstrate in the domestic political arena the concrete results of aid, which is much easier with the 'project' format, and the visible list commercial contracts from aid projects. However, donors are also concerned that their aid should secure their national suppliers additional exports, that is, exports over and above the level which would have been purchased in the absence of aid. At first glance it might appear that extra exports must necessarily be generated by double-tied aid. This is not the case, because aid is to some extent fungible in the hands of the recipient, i.e. the recipient may be able to use aid money for a project which would have been undertaken anyway in the absence of aid, and thereby free resources for another purpose (unspecified). When aid is fungible in this sense, the giving of aid may not produce additional exports for the donor country – it would depend on what the other unspecified purpose or project actually was. Naturally, given that national commercial advantage is a major political motivation for aid-giving, donors are unhappy about fungibility, which even double-tying does not always eliminate.

Table 4.3 Gross disbursements of Consortium aid in 1979–80 (US$m)

Consortium member		Project	Debt relief	Food	Other	Total
Austria			1.4		0.4	0.4
Belgium					7.8	9.2
Canada		22.9		17.1		40.0
Denmark		12.1			3.8	15.9
France		29.2			11.8	41.0
W. Germany		91.5			56.1	147.6
Italy						
Japan		53.5	4.0		23.5	81.0
Netherlands			0.4		99.5	99.9
Norway		10.4			10.4	20.8
Sweden		7.7			33.5	41.2
UK		102.4			149.2	251.6
USA		56.0		165.3		221.3
	Sub-total	*385.7*	*5.8*	*182.4*	*396.1*	*970.0*
IBRD		148.7				148.7
IDA		546.7				546.7
	Sub-total	*695.4*				*695.4*
Total		*1,081.1*	*5.8*	*182.4*	*396.1*	*1,665.4*

Source World Bank (1981), Economic Situation and Prospects of India, Report 3401–IN, p.241, Table 4.2(a).

Purchases made with tied aid funds tend to be more expensive than if the same items were acquired by worldwide unrestricted sourcing. Even those commentators who claim that multilateral aid has no advantages over bilateral aid have to acknowledge that tying 'reduces the real value of aid below the nominal value' (e.g. Bauer, 1984, 66). Those who have tried to estimate the extent of price inflation as a result of aid-tying in the Indian case come up with estimates of price differences of between 20 and 30 per cent (Riddell, 1987, 209). If these figures are anywhere near correct, and they have not been seriously challenged, then it is clear that source-tying of aid provides a means of support for donor country export industries which are relatively uncompetitive in the world market. This inference is consistent also with the data in Table 4.4 on inter-country differences in the extent to which bilateral aid is source-tied. It is clear that, with the sole exception of Italy, countries which are relatively liberal in their tying arrangements are either those which are very firmly committed to progressive aid policies (the Scandinavian countries, the Netherlands), or those who have reason to regard their export industries as very competitive across the whole range of exports (West Germany, Japan).

Table 4.4 Tying status of DAC bilateral aid, 1982–3 (Percentage of bilateral ODA gross disbursements)

	United	Of which: Technical co-op	Of which: 'Cash'	Partially untied	Tied	Of which Technical co-op
Consortium member	(1)	(2)	(3)	(4)	(5)	(6)
Austria	3.3	1.0	0.4	–	96.7	14.6
Belgium	24.7	–	4.6	–	75.3	53.4
Canada	17.0	3.2	–	–	83.0	13.0
Denmark	63.9	40.2	19.0	–	36.1	7.5
France	36.6	11.3	19.3	9.1	54.2	45.3
W. Germany	70.4	19.9	13.1	–	29.6	14.7
Italy	54.8	31.7	11.7	1.1	44.1	3.3
Japan	55.3	–	3.5	21.4	23.2	13.4
Netherlands	57.1	33.5	17.2	25.9	17.0	–
Norway	65.1	–	56.0	–	34.9	16.5
Sweden	81.2	24.1	45.7	–	18.8	–
Switzerland	66.0	5.6	60.4	–	34.0	12.9
UK	23.7	0.5	23.1	1.1	75.2	35.9
USA	36.8	–	36.8	16.5	46.7	11.4

Source OECD (1985) Twenty-five Years of Development Cooperation: a Review, Paris; adapted from Table 11, 244
Note DAC members who are not Consortium members (Australia, New Zealand, and Finland) are not included. Tying status relates to all bilateral aid, not just aid to India

What effects does this variety of tying behaviour have on the Indian system of planning and budgeting? As previously indicated, once the GoI has approved a project for inclusion in its development spending budget for a given year, it attempts to implement it to plan, without close regard to the timing of the arrival of the foreign funds intended to finance it. In the period up to the mid-1960s, the long delay between the authorization and the utilization of aid tended to be blamed on the fact that much bilateral aid was project-tied and source-tied. Certainly, at that time the Indian administration was in the process of learning how to manage aid inflows sensibly, and from 1966 onward, the utilization rate of authorized aid markedly improved (Sukhatme, 1986, 20–1). Despite this improvement, it still remains normally the case that aid receipts arrive after the project outlays have been made. It is possible in principle that delays in the arrival of aid receipts could cause delays in the implementation of the project. But that would normally happen only if, in a particular year, the country was experiencing an overall foreign exchange constraint. In many recent years, that has not been the case. In the absence of an overall constraint, the existing stock of foreign exchange can be managed to cover the interval between the project's requirement for foreign exchange and the arrival of the earmarked foreign funds.

A number of more difficult management problems do, however, arise in connection with offers of bilateral project aid. An important one is how to choose which of the available project aid offers to accept. When donors express interest in financing a particular project, the Ministry of Finance has to decide whether to accept in the light of estimates of the effects which the donor countries' tying procedures will have on the prices charged by their countries' supplies. Clearly, a multiplicity of donors, with a wide variety of different tying procedures, makes this a complicated choice. Choosing correctly requires a detailed and up-to-date knowledge of competitive world prices of the relevant products.

India is much better placed than many small African countries to marshall this information and to act upon it. She has indeed on occasions refused offers of aid on the grounds that the donor's suppliers' price quotes were highly inflated and at least one case was reported to us where such a refusal was quickly followed by a renewed offer at half the original quotation! But there are also cases reported in the late 1970s when India accepted bilateral aid almost reluctantly and without enthusiasm because of the combination of the low priority of the project and the inflated price of the goods: purchase of the UK merchant ships with bilateral aid might be cited in this connection. The Indian Government successfully created the impression that they were doing the UK a favour by accepting the ships, rather than that the UK was doing India a favour by giving the ships. Indian aid officials are said by some to believe that they can out manoeuvre bilateral donors (Hayter and Watson, 1985, 245). On this occasion at least, such a belief was vindicated.

Behind the public manoeuvrings, however, lie serious issues about the distortions which tied bilateral aid can cause. One often encountered is a bias towards excessively capital-intensive and foreign exchange-intensive projects. Such a bias was evident in Indian plans of the 1950s and 1960s. But it was almost certainly not caused by bilateral aid, although the latter may have given it some minor sustenance. The chosen development strategy of rapid industrialization without careful regard for employment considerations was the major reason for excessive intensity of capital and imports in early Indian development projects. Bilateral aid merely underwrote this strategy at the margin. Another frequent distortion arising from tied aid is the absence of normal standardization in imported equipment, with consequent problems of raising the local cost requirements for maintenance and staff training. This distortion is most serious in small countries with no indigenous capacity to manufacture capital goods. The Indian strategy of rapid industrialization was helpful in ameliorating this problem. The proliferation of imported equipment types was often followed by the licensing of foreign manufacture of a reduced number of types, and finally by the emergence of a small number of successful suppliers, either foreign or Indian-owned. The sequence did not always work smoothly or in the manner expected – but visible progress was made in standardization, as for example in the production of an indigenous tractor (Bhatt, 1979). Thus on the whole, aid has not been responsible in India for these two well-known non-price distortions, which often accompany aid in African economies.

Nevertheless, the onset of recession in the late 1970s undoubtedly intensified the complexities of choosing between alternative tied offers. As spare industrial capacity increased rapidly in donor countries, some tying practices have become stricter, countries like West Germany which were liberal have become resentful of the tying practices of others and entirely new forms of commercially-oriented aid have been brought into existence. Examples are the mixing of aid with export credits and the creation of new ultra-soft loan facilities. These practices are embodied in France's *credit mixte* scheme, Japan's soft loan finance, Canada Aid Trade Fund and the UK's Aid and Trade Provision (ATP) (Toye and Clark, 1986) India, like other recipients, has been affected by these general trends. Though the share of tied aid has not risen, the cost of not being able to spend a unit of aid freely has gone up, because in a more competitive world market better bargains are available for those who can shop where they wish.

Three additional dangers arising out of the recessionary pressures should be noted. Commercially-oriented aid begins with one donor country firm identifying a business opportunity for a capital goods sale in the recipient country. It is 'firm-led' for that reason, with the donor government acting merely as a facilitator of export sales. In this situation, there is real difficulty in ensuring genuine competition between all competent firms within the donor country. Firms may even enter into informal understandings about which aid-financed export sales are to be regarded as 'theirs'. When this happens, the aid is effectively 'triple-tied' – by project, by national source and by firm. Donor country governments have no particular incentive to prevent this happening. An export sale is an export sale, regardless of which firm makes it and, if the price is inflated, this is positive from the donor government viewpoint because it actually improves the export statistics. This situation can be a tempting opportunity for corruption, and the manipulation by unscrupulous firms of both donor and recipient aid processes.

Commercially-oriented aid can also lead to highly inappropriate purchases. Its standard justification is that 'even the poorest countries need railways, power stations, transmission equipment, construction materials, or water supply and irrigation systems' (Hurtado, 1984). No doubt they do. But inappropriateness does not normally manifest itself at that level (although commercially-oriented aid has in fact been used to sell sophisticated aircraft to very small, very poor, African countries). Inappropriateness arises because, in the drive for sales, the recipient country is sold the wrong type of bus, power station etc. for its environment; or it is sold the right type for an environment which itself needs changing. India has certainly become increasingly involved with this type of commercial aid from the UK. The £230m Rihand coal-fired power station (1982) and the recent £150m captive power station for the Bharat Aluminium Company (1984) are examples. Here the UK Government was more anxious about gaining orders for GEC and NEI than about the development consequences for India.

The third danger is that aid agencies alter their policies in the non-commercial component of their aid, with the aim of gaining commercial advantages. The aid financing of India's purchase of twenty-one Westland helicopters in 1985–6, at a time when the UK company was on the verge of collapse has been cited as an example of the osmosis effect of ATP aid on non-ATP aid (Toye and Clark, 1986, 312, note 1). A single-firm deal, which puts the presumed interests of the firm ahead of the likely developmental benefits for the recipient could become more acceptable in the normal bilateral aid programmes of donors in the wake of the expansion of explicitly commercial aid schemes. In India, this may already be happening. Apart from this spillover effect, there are other ways by which donors can design aid programmes to capture extra commercial benefits. It is possible for donors to make rapid switches between project areas, moving funds from one to another every two years or so. This leaves the recipient locked into the purchase of further capital equipment and maintenance imports which can only be bought from the donor country and which have to be funded with free foreign exchange. India appears to have experienced this problem also with one or two donors.

If source-tying remains the major negative systemic feature of bilateral aid in India, what are the prospects for its significant relaxation? One frequently suggested method is the so-called 'additionality alternative'. This is a proposal that aid-recipient countries should endeavour to ensure that they purchase additional exports from the donor country of a value related to the amount of aid given. 'Full additionality' would imply extra exports equal to the value of aid, but lesser ratios might also be mutually agreeable. As is clear from the discussion at the start of this section, the additionality alternative is – at least in the form of full additionality – an attempt to get to grips with the fact that aid is to some extent fungible, even when double-tied. It is far from clear that this is possible, even in principle, for it seems to require counter-factual knowledge, i.e. knowledge of the level and composition of imports under 'normal' trade relationships, defined by the absence of aid. Apart from this, serious problems would arise in the mechanics of carrying out the additionality undertaking. In India, the private sector has the dominant role in making import decisions, and there are powerful arguments for further relaxing import controls rather than reinforcing them to achieve additionality objectives. Within the public sector's direct area of control over imports, additionality would have to operate mainly with respect to bulk items rather than capital goods and components; it might interfere with procurement associated with multilateral aid finance, where as already discussed, competitive international tendering is required and it would be a positive disadvantage where the donor country had an over-valued currency – because then all exports bought additionally from that country would be over-priced. All in all, the bureaucratic requirements of ensuring that additionality is effective appear to be insurmountable even in a relatively well-organized country like India. This judgement is confirmed by India's brief experience. Between 1967 and 1969, the USA attempted to impose the concept of additionality on to its bilateral aid relations with India. It did not succeed: this 'episode was short-lived but costly in economic terms and in political good will' (Sukhatme, 1986, 19). There does not seem to be any realistic way of getting around the aid fungibility problem.

If additionality is not a genuine alternative, some donors may cling to source-tying as a surrogate safeguard for their commercial interests. Other donors, more subtly, may proceed with formal un-tying, in the expectation that it will have little impact on the export benefits they achieve through aid. Just as, when tariffs are dismantled non-tariff barriers can have a similar protectionist effect, so the formal untying of aid can be neutralized by other non-tying means. Two examples of such 'other means' are worth remarking. First, even when bilateral aid donors do not source-tie their aid, they usually do not adopt the same requirements for international competitive bidding as the multilateral donors. It is often the case that invitations to bid for bilaterally aided projects are publicized only in the donor and the recipient country. Thus if the project calls for equipment in which both donor and recipient countries' industries are internationally uncompetitive, the economic benefits of untying the aid will be effectively frustrated. There is a case for changing donor procedures with regard to publicity and tendering to bring them fully into line with those of the multilateral agencies to ensure that untied bilateral aid produces the best value for money for the recipient. Second, the role of project consultants is also likely to be important. Consultancy assistance, under bilateral aid, is almost always provided by donor country nationals, selected by the donor agency. The use of donor national consultancy firms can often result in procurement being tied *de facto*, although it is not tied *de jure*. For the import-content of project aid, therefore, some of the untying which the statistics show may be illusory.

Local cost finance

As we have seen in Table 4.3, about two-thirds of aid to India is normally project aid. Apart from international tendering and problems arising from tying, the chief remaining cause of friction in the project aid relationship concerns local cost finance. Tied aid automatically precludes local cost finance, but even when aid is not linked to a given geographical source of supply, it may still be given for spending on imports rather than domestic expenditures. These expenditures may be either complementary capital expenditure or maintenance and running costs. Historically, aid agencies have fought shy of meeting such costs, for two very powerful reasons. They have argued that long-term political support for aid in donor countries depends on not eroding the commercial benefits which flow back to their national suppliers. Secondly, they see local costs as a continuing commitment which they are unwilling to accept in the light of the legislative requirements for public expenditure control in donor countries. A number of Consortium countries, including Belgium, West Germany, Japan and the USA are known for their reluctance to finance local recurrent costs (Jennings, 1983, 514–5).

There are various ill-consequences of this reluctance. Firstly, the search for local counterpart funds can seriously add to the delays in the implementation of a project. Thus:

It would be reasonable to assume that a shift in a donor's policy with respect to the provision of funds for local expenditures would enhance an aid agency's capacity to minimise the time required for project completion.

(OECD, 1981, 12)

Second, the absence of donor finance for local expenditures can distort investment programming, with too many resources directed towards new capital investment and too few towards the maintenance in good operating order of previous slices of investment. Third, lack of local cost finance biases investment against projects which directly and explicitly benefit the poor. This last effect has been extensively commented on. For example, it has been stated that:

It is possible to cite a number of cases, (including) all UK aid to India until the introduction of Retrospective Terms Adjustment, in which a country-specific upper limit on the extent to which aid could be given in local cost form caused potentially poverty-focussed projects ... to be delayed, truncated or else simply passed over in favour of other projects with a lower local-cost content.

(Mosley, 1981, 221)

When discussing the extent of restrictions on local or recurrent cost finance in aid to India, it is again necessary to distinguish between multilateral and bilateral aid sources. For multilateral sources, particularly the World Bank and IDA, the pressures for greater local cost financing of projects were held at bay in the 1960s by the IDA decision to grant India 'programme aid'. These were credits to be used for miscellaneous industrial imports. Programme aid released domestic resources, which would otherwise have been required for these imports, to be used to meet the local costs of aided projects. The Bank itself, however, did not view this IDA experiment very favourably, because it did not see its function as one of giving balance of payment support only distantly related to specific projects, particularly as it harboured some doubts about the overall success of Indian planning. It therefore gradually relaxed its criteria for providing local cost finance for projects.

Gradual widening of the criteria has had the effect that local currency financing became the Bank's preferred method, compared to programme loans, of contributing to the foreign exchange component of development programmes sums over and beyond those required to buy the imports on Bank-financed projects.

(Van de Laar, 1980, 48–9)

How much local cost finance is permitted in any Bank loan is a matter of judgement by the Bank in relation to individual loans and the overall portfolio of loans to a country at the relevant time. The need for the borrowing country to have an important stake of its own in any project is one key influence in the judgement, as is the Bank's wish to be able to shape the organization and execution of the project and the policies in the sector to which the project belongs.

In certain areas of recent lending to India, the Bank has been criticized for not getting this balance right. In its US$200m package of loans for agricultural extension between 1977 and 1982, the Bank's loans amounted to half of the total costs of the projects. It is suggested that this aid 'has committed the Indian taxpayer to considerably enhanced recurrent expenditure on agricultural extension once the World Bank disappears from the scene' (Moore, 1984, 2, 12–13). This is not disputed by Bank officials (e.g. Feder and Slade, 1984, 35). They argue, however, that the new style of extension is more effective than the old, although the increment in effectiveness and the cost/benefit ratios have not yet been comprehensively assessed. But it is on such assessments that the affordability of these aided projects will depend.

For Bank Group aid, the issues of local cost finance and international competitive bidding were linked to each other. Even when a specified portion of local currency financing had been agreed for a project loan, it could be reduced as a result of the ICB requirement, if foreign contractors could compete effectively in activities which had been set aside for local expenditures – e.g. construction. This was one of the factors that fuelled the dispute between the GoI and the Bank over the ICB rule in the early 1970s. This dispute was effectively settled in 1973 with the grant of a 7.5 per cent margin of price preference to Indian domestic civil works contractors. This has since been raised to 15 per cent.

Aid from bilateral sources, because of its initial high degree of tying, was much slower in making provision for a local cost element than was multilateral aid. For example, as late as 1977, only 2 per cent of UK aid to India was local cost aid (House of Commons, 1979, xxvii). A major change of UK policy occurred in 1979, when significant debt relief was granted to India (the so-called 'Retrospective Terms Adjustment' or RTA). Debt service payments were made available to India in rupees to meet local costs associated with UK aid projects. As a result, local cost aid rose to over 30 per cent of UK aid to India in 1982–3 and is likely to remain at approximately that share for the next twenty years. This is much more closely in line with the local cost proportion characteristic of Bank lending.

When US aid to India was resumed in 1978, it was even more dramatically 'untied'. India was allowed to spend aid funds either in

India, or in the US or in a developing country. The only sourcing that was definitely ruled out was from suppliers in developed countries other than the US itself. Even this might have proved restrictive if the projects supported necessarily had a high foreign cost element. But that has typically not been the case. Project choice has centred on irrigation, social forestry, and primary health care, including family planning and child nutrition. As a result, by far the largest part of current US aid now consists of local cost finance. These local cost expenditures include some recurrent costs in certain health and irrigation projects. It has been thought necessary to offer this in order to get the projects concerned accepted by the GoI. Fears about excessive commitment have been met by stipulating a maximum percentage for recurrent costs and entering into an understanding with the GoI that the recurrent element will gradually taper off over time. Clearly, here is a bilateral aid example of committing the GoI to enhanced recurrent expenditure in certain fields once the pump-priming of aid has been completed. Again, whether this is or is not a problem depends on the social profitability of the aided projects in the longer term.

As the percentage of local and recurrent costs has grown in aid finance in the 1980s, increasing attention has been paid by donors to the cost recovery aspects of projects. Taxation reform is again on the Bank's priority agenda (see, for example, Newbery and Stern, 1987). But improved tax raising is seen as only part of the solution to the sustainable financing of recurrent expenditures. In several important aided sectors in India, cost recovery has not been good. Repayment of rural credit and of housing loans in site and services urban projects have been notorious for low recovery rates. But by moving away from foreign costs-only rules, the donors have almost necessarily involved themselves in seeking to raise cost recovery rates across a wide spectrum of public activity, including irrigation and transport, health and education. This involvement brings with it some difficult decisions which centre on the need to reconcile cost recovery with the poverty-orientation of projects. This is an area which will demand much detailed empirical analysis of beneficiaries' genuine ability to pay, or re-pay, as well as sensitive judgement on where to strike the balance between financial sustainability and poverty alleviation.

Donor procedures

Since the mid-1970s, donors have become increasingly aware that their own procedures of aid-giving may impose significant avoidable cost on the recipient of aid. By 'procedures' is meant the whole cycle of political and bureuacratic activity that accompanies the actual transfer of resources. It is a wide-ranging term covering the donor country's method of authorizing its aid budget, making aid policy, programming aid by country and sector, project preparation and approval, the actual disbursement of funds, and the ex-post monitoring and evaluation of aid-funded activities. Complying with these procedures requires effort and resources from recipients, in terms of negotiation and documentation. Failing to comply also imposes costs, either in terms of delays to existing projects and programmes, or in terms of lost opportunities of gaining additional foreign resources.

Some of these costs would appear to be imposed unnecessarily. Although these procedures all have the basic aim of the efficient mangement of aid funds, they assume a great variety of different forms as between different donor countries. The supposition must be that some standardization between donors is possible and would be beneficial in reducing recipients negotiation and compliance costs. The standard argument against this has been that standardization of procedures cannot be carried out without very difficult changes in the constitutional frameworks of the donor countries. However, a recent study of the problem concluded that this explanation was not entirely valid, on the grounds that:

> During the course of this study, a small number of donors have made changes in their procedures which appeared previously to be impossible from a legalistic point of view (e.g. multi-year commitments, field missions) without major revisions in the bureaucratic or legislative framework of their aid programmes.
>
> (OECD, 1981, 73)

Thus there does appear to be some scope for beneficial co-operation between donors, to agree standard formats for project appraisals, disbursement certifications, evaluation reports, etc.

Project appraisal methodology has often been identified as a source of difficulty for aid receiving developing countries. This is partly because these methods are often too sophisticated for domestic planning capacity and partly because donors (e.g. the Bank, the EC, Sweden, and Japan) insist on the use of distinctly different appraisal methods (Murelius, 1981, 91–3). It is clear that these difficulties are much less severe for India than for a range of other countries, including Brazil, Peru, Nigeria, Tanzania, and Thailand. Nevertheless, the Indian Governments capability for project appraisal does not appear to be particularly strong. In the mid-1980s, the Project Appraisal Division of the Planning Commission consisted of only fifteen mainly junior professionals, handling a total of only 150 project appraisals per year (Little, 1987, 44). Despite the limitations in the scope and quality of the work of the division, its existence is sufficient to ensure that the Indian Government no longer sees the variety of donors' project appraisal requirements as a major issue of aid policy, compared with the tying of aid. Needless, if donors can standardize their requirements for appraisal in a way that reduces India's compliance costs, this will be welcomed.

Especially difficult procedural problems can arise from having several donors involved in a single project – the 'multiple-donor project'. The co-ordination requirements here are much more stringent than for the single-donor project and failure to meet them can lead to additional sources of delay in project implementation. The GoI has, as a matter of policy, tried to minimize its involvement with multiple-donor projects.

On the few occasions when avoidance has not been possible, steps have been taken to reduce the dimensions of the co-ordination problem. When IDA has collaborated with bilateral donors, an attempt has been made to break down the whole project into components that are separable for managerial purposes, i.e. the completion of one part is not critical in the sequence of other parts and joint activity on a single site is not necessary. Nevertheless, some delays have occurred, because separability is rarely absolute, but these have been only minor irritants within the whole scheme of aid-financed projects in India.

One important area of procedure where donor practice varies noticeably in India is with respect to the use of locally-based aid agency staff. The World Bank mantains a local mission in New Delhi as does USAID. The UK in marked contrast, has very few permanent staff handling aid in its High Commission, and relies on *ad hoc* visits of aid staff based in London or its Asian Development Division in Bangkok to handle the peaks of aid work.

These differences derive from donors' differing evaluation of the costs of local missions in relation to their benefits. The costs are considerable and have to be deducted from funds that could otherwise be used for resource transfers. The benefits are unpredictable but can be considerable. Clearly, if policy dialogue is to become a major feature of the aid relationship, there are great potential benefits in conducting it locally, continuously and through personnel who have been doing the job long enough to possess deep local knowledge and to be trusted by the recipient side. Having a local mission does not, unfortunately, always ensure that this happens.

Three major difficulties are: (i) merely having a local mission does not ensure that it has the authority necessary to be effective. If headquarters has strong priorities and is not prepared to permit a realistic decentralization, the local mission will be frustrated in its attempts to mould country policy. It has been alleged, for example, that the Bank's large resident mission in India is allowed only to supervise the implementation of Bank aid projects, and that the big decisions on initiation and appraisal are deliberately reserved for headquarters in Washington (Hayter and Watson, 1985, 72).

(ii)For a task where much depends on personal relationship, the right quality of top staff is essential to success. Lack of leadership will leave the mission ineffective. Here again, it has been alleged that all is not well within the Bank's India mission, because of conflicts and jealousies between expatriate and local Indian staff (Hayter and Watson, 1985, 74).

(iii)Familiarity may breed contempt of a local mission. Suggestions or criticisms may be discounted by the recipient government as being ritualistic only in nature. The Indian Government's position (reflected by Patel, 1986, 215) is that the dialogue is mutually educative, and that India has learned, for example about integrated strategies for agricultural development, from the aid agencies. Off the record, Indian officials can give the impression that they believe that they are cleverer than aid officials, and can always out-manoeuvre them (Hayter and Watson, 1985, 245).

None of these difficulties needs to be viewed as insurmountable. If the best way of making aid bear good developmental fruit is the policy dialogue, it does seem desirable that donors with an aid programme beyond some minimum size should take the trouble and expense to have an effective local mission. From a simple cost-reducing perspective, it would be economical and effective for aid donors to fund and staff a joint mission, sharing the costs and co-operating in an international search for high quality staff.

Such a proposal, however, despite its technocratic attractiveness, would face an obvious political disadvantage. It could easily be seen by the Indian Government as the formation of a 'common front' of donors to put pressure on it for policy changes on the issues the size of the public sector, trade liberalization and the treatment of foreign private investment which have cause disquiet with western aid donors intermittently over the years. By relatively prudent macroeconomic management, India has avoided the situation of many developing countries, which are borrowing from the international financial institutions on terms which contain detailed and explicit conditions for policy changes. Even when it borrowed 5 billion SDR from the IMF Extended Fund Facility in 1981, the Bank played a very minor role and only normal forms of IMF conditionality applied: there was no question of Bank/Fund cross-conditionality to bring about changes in India's economic policies. Having successfully avoided such cross-conditionality in the aid process, the Indian Government would need to assure itself, before accepting a joint local mission of aid donors, that it was not also accepting aid cross-conditionality by the back door.

References

Bauer, P.T. (1984) *Reality and Rhetoric: Studies in the Economics of Development*, London, Weidenfeld and Nicolson.
Baum, W.C. (1982) *The Project Cycle*, Washington DC, IBRD.
Bhatt, V.V. (1979) 'Indigenous technology and investment licensing: the case of the Swaraj Tractor', *Journal of Development Studies*, 15:4, July.
Cable, V. (1980) *British Interests and Third World Development*, London, Overseas Development Institute.
Cassen, R. and Associates (1986) *Does Aid Work? Report to an Intergovernmental Task Force*, Oxford, Clarendon Press.
Economic and Political Weekly (1982) 17: 40, 2 October.
—— (1982a) 17: 44, 30 October.
—— (1982b) 17: 25 December.
Eldridge, P.J. (1969) *The Politics of Foreign Aid in India*, London, Weidenfeld and Nicolson.
Feder, G. and Slade, R. (1984) 'A comparative analysis of some aspects of the training and visit system of agricultural extension in India', Washington DC, mimeo.
Harvey, C. (1983) *Analysis of Project Finance in Developing Countries*, London, Heinemann.
Hayter, T. and Watson, C. (1985) *Aid: Rhetoric and Reality,* London and Sydney, Pluto Press.
Hirschman, A.O. (1970) *Exit, Voice and Loyalty*, Cambridge, Mass, Harvard University Press.
House of Commons (1979) *The Pattern of United Kingdom Aid to India*, First Report from the Select Committee on Overseas Development, Session 1978-79, London, HMSO.
Hurtado, M.E. (1984) 'The hard-nosed touch', *The Guardian*, 11 May.
Jennings, A. (1983) 'The recurrent cost problem in the least developed countries', *Journal of Development Studies*, 19: 4, July.
Kalecki, M. (1972) *Selected Essays on the Economic Growth of the Socialist and the Mixed Economy*, Cambridge, Cambridge University Press.
Kothari, R. (1970) *Politics in India*, New Delhi, Orient, Longmans.
Little, I.M.D. (1987) 'A comment on Professor Toye's paper', in Emmerij, L. (ed.), *Development Policies and the Crisis of the 1980s*, Paris, OECD.
Moore, M. (1984) 'Institutional development: the World Bank and India's new agricultural extension programme', *Journal of Development Studies*, 20: 4, July.
Mosley, P. (1981) 'Aid for the poorest: some early lessons of UK experience', *Journal of Development Studies*, 17:2, January.
Murelius, O. (1981) *An Institutional Approach to Project Analysis in Developing Countries*, Paris, OECD Development Centre.
Newbery, D. and Stern, N. (1987) *The Theory of Taxation for Developing Countries*, New York and Oxford, Oxford University Press for the World Bank.
OECD (1981) *Compendium of Aid Procedures,* Paris.
OECD (1983) *Development Co-operation: Efforts and Policies of the*

Members of the DAC, Paris.

Patel, I.G. (1986) *Essays in Economic Policy and Economic Growth*, Basingstoke, Macmillan.

Payer, C. (1982) *The World Bank: a Critical Analysis*, New York, Monthly Review Press.

Riddell, R.C. (1987) *Foreign Aid Reconsidered*, Baltimore and London, John Hopkins University Press and James Currey, in association with ODI.

Sukhatme, V. (1986) 'Assistance to India', mimeo, September.

Toye J. and Clark, G. (1986) 'The aid and trade provision: origins, dimensions and possible reforms', *Development Policy Review*, 4:4, December.

Van de Laar, A. (1980) *The World Bank and the Poor*, Boston, The Hague and London, Martinus Nijhoff.

Wade, R. (1982) 'The World Bank and India's irrigation reform', *Journal of Development Studies*, 18: 2, January.

World Bank (1981) *Economic Situation and Prospects of India*, Report 3401-IN for official use only.

Chapter 5

Project Aid to India

Role and evaluation of project aid

Net aid to India, by 1985–6, was only 0.8 per cent of GDP. However, project aid matters much more than this suggests. As the Appendix to this chapter shows (pp. 204–6), in India (unlike most other LICs): (i) the role of foreign capital is best assessed by the ratio of gross aid to public development investment (21 per cent in 1985–6) or to imports (11 per cent); (ii) a large, growing part of aid is project-linked; (iii) its relatively hard terms (tied loans rather than grants) mean that project returns must at least raise GNP enough to cover loan repayments; and (iv) heavy concentration of aid on key sectors, past (steel) and present (irrigation), further increases the importance of good project performance.

It might be objected that projects, nevertheless, do not matter – that only policy dialogue matters – because aid is money, and as such (even if nominally linked to a given activity) is fungible. If so, the recipient might merely use the donor's money to divert its own elsewhere – i.e. the recipient might 'put up for aid' projects that it would undertake anyway, even with no aid. Thus aid allegedly finances, not 'really' these projects, but marginal and only-just-worthwhile public expenditure, for which it releases funds.

This objection is plausible for some small projects. However, for aided projects as a whole – or for any big project – the fungibility argument makes sense only to the extent that the recipient has ready access to other, non-aid resources: i.e. to the extent that aid forms a small part of a recipient's total relevant resources. It would be absurd to suggest that all aided projects would be done even without aid in a country where aid provides most[1] project finance; but aid at 5 per cent of gross investment, the current Indian norm, might seem too small to avoid fungibility. But 12 per cent of public investment is less clear; not all this 12 per cent would be done without aid. Moreover, most aid finances public development investment, of which it comprises about 20 per cent; this is, as a whole, surely not fungible. Such significant project-linked resources, accompanied by technical assistance with

146

useful messages that earn respect, have plainly altered the project-mix. Far from being a poor second-best for effective policy dialogue, they have comprised a necessary condition for it. In principle, agreed and cash-linked conditionality could emerge from sectoral, not project, aid; in practice, both India and donors want to see that a proposed approach works on the ground, in the project. If projects fail, how can people be sceptical about them yet hopeful about 'policy dialogue'?

A project cycle comprises identification, preparation and design, appraisal, approval, implementation, and evaluation-cum-monitoring (Baum, 1978). If we are to go beyond exciting but atypical tales of triumph or disaster, we require a systematic 'evaluation of evaluations' of projects' performance.

The large number of Indian aid projects and donors compelled us to concentrate on to a few major donors. The World Bank, the USA, the UK Overseas Development Administration, West Germany's Bundesministerium für Wirtschaftliche Zusammenarbeit, and the Directorate-General 8 of the European Commission kindly made relevant documents available to us, and we also reviewed two overall Swedish analyses of their aid projects (Swedish National Audit Bureau, 1976; Macedo and Eduards, 1987). However, the World Bank evaluations available to us were much the most numerous (38 evaluations of 43 projects), covered a longer period (completions in 1969–85) and cost more money (US$2.0 bn. of Bank Group aid, plus over US$5 bn. of GoI capital outlay). Also, these evaluations are closely comparable in method, and in our view are genuinely independent judgements. They include highly critical comments, and replies from GoI officials. Partly for this reason, they are not in the public domain. Therefore, although we concentrate on the World Bank evaluations, we have tried to avoid identifying specific projects or persons, and have not referred by title to project documents.

Weaknesses of all the agencies' evaluation documents should make us cautious about drawing conclusions from them. They were usually prepared after visits of a few weeks, made within months of completion. Later and fuller 'impact studies' often show different results.

Evaluations rarely include points of comparison – whether 'baseline studies' of pre-project conditions, or ongoing 'control studies' of otherwise similar, but non-project, areas. Thus changes in levels or distribution of output or income among persons reached by the project – even if correctly estimated at evaluation – may not reflect the results of the project.[2]

Surprisingly few of the evaluations, except those of the Bank group (The World Bank), assess the expected economic rate of return.[3]

Therefore, many evaluations read like laundry lists – seven objectives achieved, six not achieved, all to varying degrees, with no

147

way of judging the net effectiveness of the resources used up by a project.

Few evaluation documents look seriously at the project's impact on poverty, income distribution, or even employment – despite explicit policy commitments, in most aid agencies, to emphasize these issues.[4] The Bank group in 1986 decided to monitor the poverty impact of major projects even outside those conventionally seen as falling into poverty-orientated sub-sectors. Poverty monitoring is not easy; nobody wants bogus number-spinning. However, if the problems of isolating a project's growth effects can be overcome (and economic-rate-of-return estimates made) in a rough-and-ready way, so can the problems of assessing its poverty impact.

Some evaluations tend to assess projects through the eyes, and with the statistics, of persons whose incomes directly depend on the projects' public support or repute. Sometimes, aid agencies tend to evaluate only their smaller projects.[5]

The remedies are obvious; some are under way.[6]

Nevertheless aid project evaluation is clearly unsatisfactory – albeit less so in India than elsewhere. Some donors, notably the EEC, do not seem prepared to devote significant expert in-house resources to the task, nor to allow genuine independence to the assessors.[7]

Although cross-section studies of countries (Papanek, 1972; Mosley, 1987, 133) allow us to be fairly confident that aid as a whole, at least to Asian countries, has provided growth, evaluation of aid projects has generally been insufficient to draw firm conclusions about what sectors, donors, regions, scales, techniques, or institutions are best, or worst, either at achieving growth or at reaching the poor. However, some significant lessons about what makes for good or bad aid project management – by donors and recipients – do begin to emerge from the Indian experience.

A major priority, for donors concerned with aid-effectiveness, should be to make better use of evaluations. This need goes beyond ensuring that at least a sample of projects from all donors is evaluated comparably and competently, with proper baselines and controls, for their effects on growth and poverty (and for their institutional sustainability). Each aided project also needs to be compared in such respects with non-aided public-sector projects and with private-sector projects that include foreign lending, in roughly similar sectors and areas. Good evaluation is costly (one to three per cent of project costs; the UK spends below 0.1 per cent) and has a long lead time, especially as baseline data are essential to good evaluations. However, the above process could be made into the beginning of a proper feedback system. In this, a donor (or a LDC government), seeking to appraise, design, or implement a specific project, could readily collate information on project successes and failures in similar environments. At present, even the World Bank, with its rich store of evaluations, does not do this systematically; no other donor, as far as we know, does it at all; and there is no body of accessible project knowledge upon which an Indian State, or a smaller LDC (or donor), could usefully draw. India – with excellent research institutions, many varied projects, different donors, comparable aided and non-aided public and private activities, and some receptive governmental agencies – is the obvious place to start. Co-ordination by computer renders ready access to a body of knowledge feasible; widespread problems in SSA make it necessary.[8]

The World Bank Group's project sample

Projects and evaluations

The Operations Evaluation Division (OED) of the World Bank kindly made available to us 38 evaluation documents, covering 42 Bank/IDA-aided projects completed in India. One evaluation (23 of Table 5.1) was published in November 1973; the other 37 between 1977 and 1985. Apart from one long-drawn-out project, the remaining 37 evaluations refer to 41 projects on which disbursements were commenced between 1969 and 1978, and completed between 1974 and 1985. Details of the projects appear in Table 5.1.

There are substantial formal safeguards of OED independence in its evaluations and OED is often very critical of recent project practice. All the evaluations used here include project completion reports (PCRs), either by non-OED Bank staff (sometimes also involved at earlier stages of the project cycle), or by Indian executive agencies. Almost all the PCRs used here are supplemented by project performance audits (PPAs) by OED itself, often supported by outside consultants. Some PPAs involve only assessment of in-house documents, interviews, and write-ups. Most projects, however, and all problem projects, were also reviewed in the field by OED missions before these PPAs were finalized.

Various involved GoI and state agencies are shown the draft PCR and PPA. Their comments are added to the reports. The openness of the whole process is impressive; however, this might have to be reduced if there were much exposure of exactly who said what about which specific project; hence some necessary vagueness in what follows. In particular, it should not be assumed that any comments in this text have any official support, either from GoI or from the Bank.

Table 5.1 World Bank projects in India

Project number	Date loan effec.	Years to phys. compl.	Time over-run %	Compl-etion %	World Bank group credits US$m	Project cost		Credit as % of total		Econ. rate of return		Remarks on project performance	Overrun indexes:[a]	
						Appraisal	Actual over-run %	Appraisal	Actual	App-raisal	Act-ual		Cost	Time
Fertilizer factories														
1	8.74	3.5	41	100	50	60	76	84	66	16	17	Dearer fertilizer +, dearer transpt ± Impl. efficient	127	141
2	2.75	4.7	36	100	91	174	187	52	48	16	5	Parameters too optimistically estimated. Less than satisfactory.	107	136
3	7.71	5.0	87	100	20	47.2	72	42	28	14	14	1,000–2,000 constr. jobs, 800 perm jobs. Dearer fert +, low capacity use −.	153	187
4	5.73	4.6	72	100	58	100	140	58	41	15	12	Increased costs due to delays but satisfactory.	140	172
5	4.72	3.7	yes	100	10	16	23	63	43	19	19	Increased operating costs but satisfactory.	144	>100
6	5.75	5.0	50	100	109	220	247	49	44	16	11	Shift to dearer feedstock (naphtha) but satisfactory.	112	150

Table 5.1 World Bank projects in India (continued)

Project number	Date loan effec.	Years to phys. compl.	Time over-run %	Completion %	World Bank group credits US$m	Project cost Appraisal	Actual	Cost over-run %	Credit as % of total Appraisal	Actual	Econ. rate of return Appraisal	Actual	Remarks on project performance	Overrun indexes:[a] Cost	Time
Agricultural credit projects															
7	4.79	5.7	77	207	32	60	58	-4	53	55	21–32	17–40	103,000 gainers,	46	85
8	8.75	2.0	0	100	75	168	179	6	44	42	14–49	18–50	80,000 jobs. 210,000 gainers (56% small farmers). Employment up.		
9	6.77	2.5	0	100	200[b]	467	488	34	43	41	27–50	23–50	530,000(59% small farmers).	134	100
10	10.73	3.2	0	100	33	60	70	16	55	47	17–100	41–50	150m workdays 44,000 farm gainers, 8m workdays.	155	100
11	10.73	4.6	38	219	38	72	80	10	52	48	16–35	25–39	300,000 farm gainers (66% 1–3ha.), 25m workdays	50	63
12	9.73	4.5	55	160	40	70	74	6	57	54	12–41	21–50	1,900 perm. workers, 400,000 workdays.	66	97
13(i)	9.70	7.3	200	100	27	40	43	7	69	64	14	50+	18,000 gainers.	107	300
13(ii)	11.71	4.7	66	100	25	44	53	19	56	47	15	50+	36,000 gainers.	119	166
14(i)	10.71	4.6	100	100	24	45	47	4	54	52	30	37	95,000 gainers.	104	200
14(ii)	11.71	6.0	100	100	35	62	62	0	56	56	28	35	56,000 gainers.	100	200
14(iii)	1.73	3.0	30	100	30	43	57	7	56	53	33–50	17–50	100,000 gainers.	107	130

Table 5.1 World Bank projects in India (continued)

Project number	Date loan effec.	Years to phys. compl.	Time over-run %	Compl-etion %	World Bank group credits US$m	Project cost Appraisal	Actual	Cost over-run %	Credit as % of total Appraisal	Actual	Econ. rate of return App-raisal	Act-ual	Remarks on project performance	Overrun indexes:[a] Cost	Time
Irrigation															
18	11.71	8.0	30	80	39	127	211	67	31	18	14	14	Better cropping intensity + prices offset cost rise. 10,000 person-years' employment.	209	162
19	7.70	8.0	60	50	35	67	183	100	52	19	14	12	Cost overrun vs. crop price rise.	400	320
35	8.78	5.2	0	<100	111	222	222	0	50	50	32	25	20m person-days, 550,000 farm family gainers	>100	>100
36	1.78	?	?	?	58	116	116	0	50	50	20	19	175,000 farm family gainers. Crop price rise offset implementation delay.	?	?
39	3.78	7.0	79	?	70	140	183	31	50	38.2	17	17	15,000 farm family gainers	?	?
33	7.75	6.4	34	65	34	67	59	-12	51	58	55	42	Huge fluctuations in performance of (minor) works. 120,000 families gained.	135	206

Table 5.1 World Bank projects in India (continued)

Project number	Date loan effec.	Years to phys. compl.	Time over-run %	Compl-etion %	World Bank group credits US$m	Project cost Appraisal	Actual	Cost over-run %	Credit as % of total Appraisal	Actual	Econ. rate of return App-raisal	Act-ual	Remarks on project performance	Overrun indexes:[a] Cost	Time
Agricultural marketing															
16	7.72	7.0	17	100	14	23	29	24	60	49	29	11	Land acquisition delays; only 19 of 47 markets operational.	124	117
30	9.73	9.3	48	100	8	12	16	42	67	50	15	0–7	Construction delays. 'Success-ful' despite low EROR.	142	148
32	9.74	8.0	100	35	13	22	19	–11	60	68	23	1	Delayed implem-entation, weak institutional per-formance, yet major impact claimed.	254	571

Table 5.1 World Bank projects in India (continued)

Project number	Date loan effec.	Years to phys. compl.	Time over-run %	Compl-etion %	World Bank group credits US$m	Project cost Appraisal	Actual	Cost over-run %	Credit as % of total Appraisal	Actual	Econ. rate of return App-raisal	Act-ual	Remarks on project performance	Overrun indexes:[a] Cost	Time
Other agricultural and rural development[c]															
15	11.72	7.3	158	100	5	16[d]	20	27	31	25	25	15	Land acquisition delays, higher costs, but significant contribution	127	258
17	9.69	9.0	50	100	13	22	22	-3	58	60	17	18	Product quality better than expected. User income rose (c.400,000).	97	150
20	6.75	6.0	20	95	35	103	84	-18	34	41	12	Neg-30	281,000 farm gainers 36,000 person-days' employment. Uncertain impact	86	126
31	5.76	6.6	31	?	3	8	6	-27	49	50	?	?	Bad project type? Weak institutional performance.	?	?
34	2.78	5.1	11	?	13	239	217	-9	5	6	?	?	2,000 perm. staff 2.8m farm families to benefit.	?	?

Table 5.1 World Bank projects in India (continued)

Project number	Date loan effec.[e]	Years to phys. compl.	Time over-run %	Compl-etion %	World Bank group credits US$m	Project cost Appraisal	Actual	Cost over-run %	Credit as % of total Appraisal	Actual	Econ. rate of return App-raisal	Act-ual	Remarks on project performance	Overrun indexes:[a] Cost	Time
Infrastructure[e]															
26	7.71	6.0	51	?	75	126	126	0	59	59	?	?	Unsatisfactory finances, States', institutions.	?	?
22a	4.72	3.0	0	100	75	1,084	1,200	11	7	6	10–20	10–20	Incomplete info Early results only.	111	?
22b	1.74	1.3	?	?	80	?	654	?	?	?	10.20	13		?	100
23	1.61	11.0	?	?	50	?	?	?	?	?	?	?	Prevented closure of key infrastructure facility.	?	?
24	7.69	6.0	High	?	105	652[f]	463	−29	16	23	16	19[g]		?	?
25	8.73	5.1	84	60	80	534[h]	545	2	15	15	13	17[g]		170	307

Table 5.1 World Bank projects in India (concluded)

Project number	Date loan effec.	Years to phys. compl.	Time over-run %	Compl-etion %	World Bank group credits US$m	Project cost Appraisal	Actual	Cost over-run %	Credit as % of total Appraisal	Actual	Econ. rate of return App-raisal	Act-ual	Remarks on project performance	Overrun indexes:[a] Cost	Time
Social and other[j]															
21	9.63	?	?	?	19	40	59	47	48	33	?	?	Unsatisfactory.	?	?
27	1.74	6.0	High	56	35	59	112	90	59	31	10	?	Widespread but not calculable gains to poor groups.	339	>200
29	5.73	?	?	?	32[j]	?	?	?	?	?	?	?	Good implementation.	?	?
37	6.73	10.5	82	98	12	19	?	?	62	?	?	1[k]	Satisfactory.	?	186
38	3.74	7.2	-60	59	58	280	251	-10	21	23	1[k]	5–6[k]	Satisfactory.	130	68

Notes

a Cost overrun index: 100 + [(% cost overrun)/(% completion)].
  Time overrun index: 100 + [(% time overrun)/(% completion)].
b Co-financed with 3 other donor agencies, adding £111m to the Bank Group's US$200m.
c One each extension, forestry, rural works, seed production, storage
d Plus a further US$5m from another donor agency.
e Ports, power, railway, telecom.
f Another donor agency provided a further US$35M.
g *Financial* rate
h Two other donor agencies added US$24m
i Population, sewage, universities, urban development, plus one iron and steel
j Another donor agency provided US$11m also
k Incremental *financial* rate of return

Table 5.2 summarizes the financial role of the World Bank in the large sample of its projects where we were able to see evaluations. The US$2bn or so of Bank Group credits, reviewed here, appear to have covered less than one-third of project costs (Cols 8 and 10). Only a small part of this 'shortfall' was due to cost overruns (Col. 9) and a tiny proportion to co-financing by other donors (fns. b, d, h, j). Most of it is due to the large role played by GoI in project finance. However, the figures are greatly influenced by four big infrastructure projects (Table 5.1, 22a, 22b, 24, and 25) in which the World Bank played a small role. If these projects are excluded, the total Bank input into Indian projects with full cost information, recorded in Table 5.2, was US$1.5bn, comprising 45 per cent of appraised total cost (US$3.3bn) and 40 per cent of actual total costs (US$3.8bn).

Although not necessarily a random sample of the PCR-PPAs – either in timing or project-mix – the projects that we have reviewed roughly represent the Bank's project performances and priorities. Moreover, these are not very different from those of non-Bank aid flows (insofar as the latter can be assessed from the very limited information available).

Good returns, long delays

The first lesson from these projects is that overall performance has been satisfactory. Real returns expected at post-evaluation – normally economic rates (ERORs) – were assessed in 34 cases, and were in double figures in all but four; three of these four had major redeeming features. Where no rates of return were evaluated, 5 out of 8 reports portray a generally adequate performance. The four clear failures or near-failures (Table 5.1, 2, 32, 26, 21) absorbed 10 per cent of the US$1.97m of World Bank group credits evaluated in these documents, and 6 per cent of the approximate US$6.9bn total actual costs (see Table 5.2, notes g and k) of the sampled projects. A lower proportion of failures would have implied an unduly conservative attitude to project finance.

Of course, the estimated real ERORs, etc., have major weaknesses. The rates evaluated for farm credit projects are overstatements, since – as one of the PPAs makes clear – some private investments, financed by these projects, would have been financed otherwise without them (but ERORs on most such projects would remain high even if this could be allowed for). Tractor components in projects show seriously overstated ERORs because comparison of net farm income between tractorized and non-tractorized farms neglects the higher degree of irrigation on the former (Agarwal, 1980, 1984). One evaluation complains that the EROR estimates often show a distressingly large 'judgemental' range.

Table 5.2 Bank role in funding some projects

1 Sector	2 Evaluation documents	3 Projects reviewed	4 Bank Group credits (US$m)	5 Bank Group credits (US$m)	6 Total project costs (US$m)	7 Total project costs (US$m)	8	9	10
	Nos.	Nos.	Total	Fully costed projects	Appraised	Actual	Col. 5 + Col. 6	Col. 5 + Col. 7	Col. 5 + Col. 7
							%	%	%
Fertilizer	6	6	338	338	617	754	55	83	45
Ag. credit[b]	8	11	559	559	1131[c]	1211[c]	49	93	46
Irrigation	6	6	347	347	739	974	47	76	36
Ag. marketing[d]	3	3	35	35	57	64	61	89	55
Other ag./forestry[d]	5	5	74	74	338[e]	349[e]	22	97	21
Infrastructure[i]	5	6	465	335[g]	2396[h]	2334[h]	14	103	14
Social sectors[i]	4	4	137[j]	93[k]	339	363	27	93	26
Total[l]	38	42	1,974	1,800	5,657	6,099	32	93	30

Notes

a For projects in which both appraised and actual costs are given in the evaluation documents.
b Two national (ARDC/NABARD) and nine state-level projects.
c Includes US$111m from other donors.
d Storage is included in 'other agriculture'.
e Includes US$5m from another donor.
f Rail, ports, telecom, power.
g This (and all subsequent figures in this row) are for four projects only.
h Includes US$59m from 2 other donors.
i Education, populations, sewerage, urban development
j another donor agency provided a further US$11m, for a project not included in cols 5–10 (no appraisal or actual costs available).
k This (and all subsequent figures in this row) are for two projects only.
l The early, atypical Project 21 (Table 5.1) is here included only in this last row of numbers.

Four of these evaluations warn that their EROR estimates are especially risky because they had to be made very soon after project completion. Another four warn about their ERORs because these reflect sub-systems – parts of substantial infrastructural or social-service programmes – whose performance cannot really be separated from that of other sub-systems. All the same, the numbers and comments suggest strongly that the true rates of return on projects embodying World Bank aid to India have, on the whole, been satisfactory.

Time overruns, however, pervade these projects (Table 5.3), averaging 51 per cent of scheduled time for the 34 projects with available data. These time overruns delayed the operation of, and hence returns from, the projects. Normally this tends to cut back ERORs, particularly if inflation affect costs more than returns. However, time overruns sometimes reflect correct changes in project design – or even GoI's decision to increase its input into an apparently successful project, so that completion exceeds 100 per cent, as with three agricultural credit projects in Table 5.1. Conversely, if a project is under-fulfilled by x per cent (completion is 100 minus x per cent), then a time or cost overrun is worse than it looks; thus the last irrigation project listed in Table 5.1 overran by one-third of its planned completion time and cost 12 per cent less than expected, but was 35 per cent under-fulfilled. Table 5.3 attempts to standardize for these facts, giving time/completion and cost/completion ratios – and also, in the data for 'all projects' in each sector for which calculations are possible, to allow for the fact that delays or cost escalations do more harm for big than small projects.

Nevertheless, the picture of delay and under-completion is worrying. A unit of 'real' project implementation appears to be taking 1.5 to 2.5 times as long as planned, except in rural credit (1.25 times as long). Comparison of the sixth and the last columns of figures in Table 5.3 shows that the corresponding rise in cost, per 'real' unit completed, is considerably less serious, except for irrigation projects; in other sectors, delayed completion probably affects mainly 'finishing touches' which do not add so much to costs. The relatively good timekeeping and cost-containment of credit aid are, of course, the counterparts of weaknesses: bad recovery of overdues, and little certainty that the extra credit (let alone the aid for it) is indeed necessary and sufficient to add the farm-level components assumed at appraisal and evaluation.

Even if persistent delays and cost escalations do not greatly harm a project's EROR or poverty-focus – and on the latter effect we have little evidence – it is desirable, if feasible at reasonable cost, to reduce them. They must damage financial and personnel planning, not only in donor agencies, but also in GoI, which pays much of the cost of these projects. If trains are persistently late, perhaps the timetable should be changed. The trouble is that one can seldom predict how late a train or a project will be, but Table 1 does suggest that timetables have been more realistic (i.e. delays are less) on recent projects. In any case, we need to know when, and why, delays did not harm ERORs.

Often, it was because the projects' output prices so outpaced input prices that the gap between the two increases (raising EROR) outweighed the effect of delayed sales of output (reducing EROR). This effect is reported for three fertilizer projects and four others. However, first, rises in a sector's output prices – creating a good EROR estimate at evaluation, e.g. after an oil shock has increased output values from a fertilizer project – can be reversed later; impact studies of the price history of aided projects, comparing input and output prices with those prevailing at appraisal and evaluation, could improve future project selection. Second, price forecasting at appraisal requires more attention; it has not always been consistent with price projections from the Bank's own commodity specialists. Third, the sensitivity of expected returns on an aided project to errors in price projections should be explored at appraisal and evaluation. This is especially important if a country looms large in a particular market, and/or if there is much investment, by the country or overall, in producing for that market.

General features of Bank Group projects

Regionally, although of the 38 evaluations only four or five reported results clearly less than satisfactory, three of these were in one especially 'difficult' state. There, only two of the five projects with Bank Group aid were satisfactory. This reflects the difficulties experienced by GoI and other donors with that state, despite considerable natural resources. Perhaps this difficulty is related to donors' special problems in tackling some thorny issues, notably that of corruption.

The financial structure reflects very little donor co-financing: a repeat of a tested success (Project 9); a new donor invited to break a GoI–Bank bottleneck (15). In the only other case (24) the evaluation stated that major problems of donor disagreement and co-ordination, of the type familiar in Tanzania and Bangladesh (van Arkadie, 1986), caused serious delays. The rarity of multi-donor aid projects, then, reflects the expressed, and justified, reluctance of GoI to incur the problems of timing, conflicts of laws, and consistency that habitually bedevil such projects. Multi-donor, non-Bank projects are even rarer.

Due to the delays and consequent cost overruns, GoI had to bear a larger proportion of capital costs than was estimated at appraisal. Total Bank group aid on all the projects in Table 5.1 was US$2.0bn; total scheduled project cost was US$5.0bn; total actual project cost was

US$7.1bn. (US$0.2bn. from non-Bank donors). Hence heavy extra costs, far in excess of inflation and often in foreign exchange, were imposed on GoI by the delays.

Information on employment and income-distribution effects is very scanty. Also, as we shall see, the analysis on these matters is sometimes questionable. One evaluation stresses that these projects were generally designed before 'GoI and IDA policies changed in favour of generating more employment and reaching smaller farmers'. However, these evaluations show rather little trend, over time, for project documents to become increasingly concerned with labour use or with poverty-focus.

There was a trend in the 1970s in the Bank, as in other donor agencies, to shift the structure of lending towards countries, sectors, and even beneficiaries with acute poverty problems (World Bank, 1983, 1–3, 24–5). But this trend was seldom expressed in clear-cut choices, either within projects or in the policy dialogue. For example, the use of income-distribution weights in cost-benefit analyses was outlined in a clear way by Central Projects Staff, following Squire and van der Tak (1975) – but only as an advisory guideline. It has never (so far as we know) been used in practice in any major project cycle. The recent Bank decision to monitor poverty impact more widely (see p.148) is of limited effect because (after rising steadily from 1968 to 1981) the share of Bank Group activity in 'poverty sectors' (Beckmann, 1986) has since been in decline. To judge by these evaluations, so has the degree of poverty-focus in monitoring Bank Group projects even within these sectors. From 1988, however, the poverty emphasis has revived.

Many lessons of the projects, outlined in the PPA/PCRs, cannot be simply read off from Table 1. We consider three sets of issues. The first set concerns project cycle procedures, donor and Indian, especially in appraisal, supervision, evaluation, and mission composition. The second set deals with analytical choices, in matters such as technology; the use of non-Indian standards, equipment, and consultants; the trade-off between moving money swiftly and achieving long-term goals flexibly; and the level and nature of intermediation between a big aid donor and many financially miniscule 'target' beneficiaries. The third set of issues concerns policy goals: ultimately, benefits to the poor, fuller use of labour, efficiency, and growth; more immediately, learning effects for donors via pilot projects, and for recipients via institution-building.

Project cycle procedures

Post-evaluations detected (inevitably) some slips in pre-appraisals. (A bilateral donor has conceded similar arithmetical errors that would, if detected sooner, have avoided a clearly unsuccessful manufacturing project). Encouragingly, such simple appraisal errors are not recorded, in evaluation documents seen by us, for projects appraised after 1970. The lack of systematic post-evaluation of project-cycle procedures by several donor agencies, however, still leaves cause for concern.

Lessons can also be learned from more subtle mistakes. First, integration among aided projects needs more systematic attention, especially at pre-appraisal. The post-evaluation of one surface-irrigation project points out that the ineligibility for credit of many farmers greatly delayed the whole process of on-farm land development; yet a simultaneous farm credit project covering the same area, also Bank-financed, was confined to loans for tractors and groundwater development, and was thus apparently precluded from meeting such farmers' credit needs. More generally, the calculation of ERORs on all Bank projects is entirely from the standpoint of the particular developing country receiving advice, yet many Bank projects to raise output of the same product in different developing countries can reduce each other's EROR by glutting each other's markets. Apart from international integration of project effects, it is not clear that in practice the Bank's estimates of project-specific ERORs deduct for the effects of draining key personnel away from other parts of the national system – e.g. towards the new Training and Visit system and away from conventional extension – nor 'add on' for the effects of training personnel who can then usefully serve that system outside the project area. These objections apply at least as forcibly to donors other than the Bank – and above all to the donors and projects where evaluations are not done, not available, or not numerate.

Second, many appraisals, through their procedures, projections or assumptions, made future project work less fruitful. (i) In several cases, inadequacy of baseline data prevented proper subsequent calculation of ERORs; (ii) sometimes farm budgets at appraisal assumed that all farmers used the same mixes and amounts of all inputs, so that such problems as the unequal, and hence patchy and inefficient, distribution of irrigation-water offtake were not foreseen; (iii) sometimes, assurances by persons eager to proceed – perhaps by staff eager to move the money – were allowed to override careful assessment of likely implementation difficulties; this was reported in four evaluations, two each in respect of conflicts over land acquisition and of inadequate incentives to use project capital. All these three problems are reported in the more recent batch of evaluations seen by us (post-1984, of completed projects that had been pre-appraised in 1973–9), as well as in the earlier batch (1969–74).

Third – although the Bank group has shown exemplary flexibility in permitting major redesigns during project implementation (these affect over 75 per cent of its agricultural projects and outlay) – the delays, conflicts, patching-up, and hence reduced ERORs, involved in such flexibility, could have been mitigated by remedying the lack of adequate consideration, at the design and appraisal stages, of alternatives.

In general, project designs have usually narrowed down the appraisal process to a yes/no – cynics would say a yes/yes – decision, with scant scope for shifting the hardware within a project, let alone for moving to a less hardware-oriented approach altogether. There are welcome signs in some recent Bank projects in India, notably in agricultural marketing, that alternative design ERORs (and sub-project ERORs) are being estimated at appraisal, but this still seems to be the exception; such breakdowns are seldom presented when the project appraisal report reaches the Board. Still less are poverty impacts set against ERORs for alternative design/component sets, leaving the Board to decide. The Bank is probably the best of all donors here, because the least subject to the wrong sorts of commercial pressures, and the most systematic and independent in its post-evaluations.

A final problem about pre-appraisals, revealed by these post-evaluation documents, applies also to other stages of the project cycle. It is that the composition of the team, its duration, and its field procedures often militate against obtaining a 'feel' for crucial, sometimes non-quantifiable issues. These could sometimes be handled by better team composition.

A lawyer might best sniff out problems of land acquisition. An anthropologist could have helped many appraisal missions: to reject such absurd assumptions as that, in two large states reviewed for long-term rural credit projects, there was no problem of short-term credit (and therefore no likelihood that long loans would be diverted to finance current inputs, or even consumption); to assess the impact of forestry development on tribals; and to explore the unregistered land rights, and alternative opportunities, of persons displaced by big irrigation projects. An appropriately trained economist could ensure that proper baselines and control groups are prepared, especially in pilot projects. One evaluation reveals cost increases due to rock faults – a risk that a hydro-geologist would have foreseen at appraisal. A recent evaluation comments on the lack, at pre-appraisal, of a specialist on the cropping patterns feasible under the project's irrigation system.

A recurring problem with infrastructure projects is the failure to include, in project missions, staff with appropriate macro-planning expertise to ensure that project and system are correctly matched.

The cost of such errors and omissions is huge. It would justify expanding the disciplinary base of a hundred six-week appraisal missions with (on average) one extra expert each, even if only one major project improvement, worth as little as US$3m, resulted; we would anticipate a total improvement worth at least five times this sum. Once again, the readiness of most donor agencies to expand appraisal missions, imaginatively but selectively, beyond the most conventional disciplines and ranges of experience is certainly no greater than the Bank Group's – and their readiness to reveal their appraisal procedures and expertise is usually much less.

A wider range of mission staff can complement improved mission attitudes and organizational forms in improving the project cycle, but it cannot substitute for such changes.

First, more time by individual agency staff in the project area, less turnover, more 'field feel', are essential, if aid agencies wish to learn how efficient but poor beneficiaries are to be identified and reached. One large agricultural project, lasting over five years and costing over US$100m, exemplifies the problem. Evaluators pointed out that, although missions every five to six months would have been desirable, considerably longer intervals elapsed between some visits. Compounding this problem was the high turnover among Bank staff, most of whom visited the project only once before responsibility was delegated to someone else. Similar criticisms are quite common. Such brief periods in the field lead to systematic under-estimation of project-threatening patterns of tenure and credit, since these patterns are concealed.

Second, even local, competent, motivated, full-time implementing agencies can fail to meet targets, if obsessed by hardware-oriented approaches and/or by top-down management structures that seldom make contact with the needy.

Third, project teams cannot achieve the best results, if they persistently evade sensitive, but central, issues affecting the behaviour of both beneficiaries and bureaucrats: civil-service power struggles between new and old agencies; lack of clearly enforced guidelines about what each level of decision-making has to provide for, as well as to exact from lower levels (as when the unreliability of the main system of gravity-flow irrigation discourages water users from taking time on co-operation below the outlet); and sometimes the existence of serious corruption.

These three sets of issues are responsible for apparently technical problems in many aided projects.[9] Faced with such problems, donors, eager to avoid accusations of meddling in domestic politics, either seek solely techno-economic solutions at project level (changes in physical design of systems, or in pricing of their outputs to users), or try to impose policy conditions at sectoral, state, or national level. However, if the power structure stays much the same, such tactics are likely to be partly frustrated, as abuses or distortions helpful to groups with power will often emerge in other forms, expressing more or less the same power balance. Donors of project aid tread a fine line: how are they to strengthen the forces of efficiency, rationality, and responsiveness in

165

project cycle procedures, without improperly intervening in local or state politics? At least India, unlike many African countries, has enough local expertise and open debate to ensure that extreme political or administrative distortions of techno-economic guidelines are publicly questioned. However, the (self-?) delusion that the issues really are just techno-economic is unlikely to help donors. Although the choice of technique on a project can indeed change the amount of damage done by unclear lines of authority, or by over-centralization, or by corruption, this is possible only if project designers explicitly allow for such non-technical issues.[10]

In India, the above problems are eased by a competent, long-serving group of Bank experts in Delhi, who move around major projects often, and who usually have relations of mutual respect with similarly competent and long-serving Indian experts. However, much more responsiveness to, and day-to-day local contact with, the intended beneficiaries of big aid projects – often, even if very poor, interacting in complex ways with such power groups – is required than this technocratic model suggests. In this context, two recent evaluation documents may be in error in stressing the advantages of a resident Bank staff in working with Centre officials to promote Bank Group projects in India across departmental boundaries and with less effect from personal and political pressures. Such advantages are likely to be achieved at the cost of slower progress on non-aid GoI investment activities (and on development activities on current account) which lack these special favours. And Bank Group projects, if thus insulated and protected from 'normal' administration and politics, are themselves vulnerable after the evaluation is over and the donor has left. The way to better project-cycle procedures lies through much greater presence in the field.

The problems in project-cycle procedure should not obscure the general success of Bank Group aid in India. There has been much learning by doing. However, many criticisms recur in recent evaluations; Bank project procedures in other developing countries, notably those with less Bank presence and shorter learning, are usually less satisfactory than in India; and other donors' project procedures are usually inferior to the Bank's – not least at evaluation. However, the problems raised on pp. 147–8 appear in Bank evaluations too – especially the problems that project performance audits (PPAs) represent swift overviews, often too soon after the event; that project completion reports (PCRs) partly reflect the views of staff involved in the project cycle; and that baselines and control groups are absent or inadequate. All this is especially damaging to pilot projects.

Analytical choices in projects

Technology

The first such choice concerns technology. We have stressed that technical choices appear to be foreclosed too early in project design, generally leaving the appraisal to assess just one way of doing the project. That 'one way' - given the backgrounds of donor project pre-appraisers, the pressures to obtain project approvals that seem to move money quickly, and the wish to reduce apparent risk – is too often the way of high technology. In a fertilizer project, an incompletely developed process, based on an untried combination of sub-processes, caused losses from severe delays and foregone production. Another project suffered similar effects from complex slip-form silo construction. Such approaches greatly increase the need for special technical and managerial skills. In some earlier aid projects, this directly delayed critical works. India's large and growing pool of skills has reduced such problems, but several evaluations of recent projects still show high-tech choices causing indirect delays. The cause of indirect delay is often a prolonged dispute between the GoI and the potential donor about whether the high technology of the project necessarily requires foreign consultants and foreign procurement of supplies.

Donors' and consultants' penchant for high technology not only causes delays and losses. It also, at first, diverts attention from beneficiaries' preferences and, later, helps to channel such preferences more towards superficially 'modern' approaches, rather than towards cost-effective ones. This can imperil the very objectives of aid. The distortions of high-tech affect not only hardware, but even rural credit projects.

In one case, farmers' own tested and cost-effective preferences (for bamboo over conventional steel tubewells) were not analyzed at appraisal, and were only to a small extent financed by the project. In another project for credit to minor irrigation, farmers' wish to avert risk by using low-input, low-output dug-wells (rather than more elaborate tubewells) was not foreseen at appraisal.

Sometimes, credit projects have so defined beneficiaries as to exclude the really poor from credit or benefit, at the same time as claiming that all remaining beneficiaries, even 'poorer' ones, are sufficiently advanced and capital-intensive to prefer the most advanced technique. Thus the post-evaluation of a project offering credit for wells reported that so-called small farmers, as readily as large farmers, adopted mechanical pumping rather than the improvement of traditional methods; yet farmers operating less than three acres – 70 per cent of all farmers in the project area, and those likeliest to prefer the more labour-intensive, lower-risk method – had not been permitted to borrow under the project.

Generally the emphasis in credit support upon capital-intensive modern technologies not only 'unemploys' workers, but also discourages adoption among the smallest, labour-intensive, unskilled, and risk-averse entrepreneurs – especially if, apart from scale and indivisibility, the equipment is experimental, or new to its environment or culture. Both employment and income distribution tend to suffer from high-tech, unless very carefully selected to suit the requirements of local poverty-groups or symbiotic with non-aid, labour-intensive investments..

Sometimes it is – even though many in the government believe that western donors' comparative advantage in India lies precisely in high-tech. First, the benefit/cost (EROR) pre-appraisal of all Bank Group projects allows for the fact that under-employed labour, which is likelier to be used up by a less high-tech approach, is less costly to India than its market wage suggests. However, even this does not allow for the benefits of labour-intensive methods in respect of poverty alleviation. (It would do so, if the Bank would only make mandatory its guidelines on incorporating income-distribution weights into ERORs.) Nor, perhaps, has the Bank Group done enough to mitigate undue predetermination (largely by engineers) of project technology in the design stage – which almost certainly discourages low-tech.

Second, large programmes – such as five years' worth of total Indian investment, or even of IBRD/IDA loans to India – should take some risks, aiming at a high average EROR on projects rather than a safe but lowish EROR on each one. Hence, such programmes should aim to install some technologies that look towards India's more skill-intensive and capital-intensive future.

Finally, some Bank projects have shown institutional flexibility and ingenuity in 'learning-by-doing' how to provide access for very small and poor operators to efficient large-scale and/or 'high' technologies. For example, the importance (not least for employment) of timely supply of improved seeds – delivered via a complex and sophisticated 'high-tech' system – initially dictated a large-farm approach to producing the seeds for use by smallholders. Later, after piloting, it was spread successfully to seed-growers with small farms, through a 'compact area' approach.

Nevertheless, in most cases high-tech, large scale, capital intensity, and few jobs (per US$1m of project investment) do go hand in hand. They do, also, match the preferences, manuals, and working experience of most engineers trained in western-style institutions – not least those in developing countries. The Bank Group's ingenuity in sometimes seeking to offset the worst effects of these biases has not wholly removed the damage via delay, lost output, high costs, and foregone jobs.[11]

Incorporation of project economists throughout the design stage, presentation of alternative designs at appraisal, and use of income-distribution weights in both design and appraisal, appear to provide possible remedies.

Foreign expertise

A pervasive cause of delay, and hence of lowered ERORs, has been Bank Group insistence that, for some purposes, recipients use foreign expertise or equipment. Such insistence usually raises project costs and delays completion, but can in principle raise ERORs if it improves project performance by enough in compensation. Often, however, this seems not to have been the case, though the Bank's evaluations point to a learning process.

This problem – while much less frequently reported in evaluations of Bank projects completed since 1983 or so – is probably persistent among other, less frank donors. It ties in with the wish of bilateral donors to respond to their own exporting firms. For most donors, even for the Bank Group, the problem is typically compounded by donor pressure for 'modern' technologies.

For example, in a big fertilizer project, the Bank Group appears to have objected to an economically adequate, if perhaps not optimal, process proposed by the Indian executing agency, and to have withdrawn its objection only after long and costly delays. In another example, the Bank's initial insistence on an (eventually uneconomic) high-tech approach (slip-form silos) was also the ultimate cause of 'an inordinate amount' of delay to a storage project, due proximately to GoI-Bank disagreements about whether local consultants could be used.

We reject a simplistic framework of 'good' local expertise versus 'bad' high-tech consultants and hard donor agencies. Sometimes, a donor can take too soft a view on local expertise; a Bank-aided fertilizer project was seriously penalized by the GoI's decision to force the Indian executing agency to purchase some equipment from a manufacturer in India without adequate experience, against the recommendations of IDA. Sometimes, it is the recipient government that impedes local input; in an irrigation project, both the Bank and the Indian executing agency were frustrated in their wish to rely upon local inputs by GoI delays in counterpart funding, though GoI comments on the evaluation suggest that this cannot happen nowadays. India now has a wider range of competing inputs – and of consultancy skills, often under-employed – and the Bank Group has by now learned to use them better. In a project completed in the early 1980s, for example, foreign and local consultants worked well together, with an exchange of roles: in the later years of implementation, the local firm took over prime consultant responsibility, and the foreign firm supplied the project with specialized assistance on contract. Yet, on balance, donors have not gone far enough in using Indian expertise and equipment.[12]

Move money or improve project?

A third analytical choice in aid project management is between getting the money moving quickly, and achieving long-term goals flexibly even at the cost of some delays. Donors, especially the Bank, are normally accused of overstressing the former. Usually the career incentives in any donor agency are to move money swiftly and at low administrative cost: banks want to lend, and aid agencies want to use the money voted to them by governments – otherwise these funds may be lost to the agency at the end of a fiscal period, and the vote next time may be reduced. If the project turns out badly, the quick-spending officers partly responsible are unlikely to be 'punished' in career terms. Often, indeed, they will not be in the same part of the same agency when their chickens come home to roost – though in India, aid agency staff are more likely to stay in the same group of offices. Bank Group project delays do not suggest a mad rush to move money fast.

However, using speed as a criterion for efficiency can be misleading. Undue speed at design or appraisal might, in principle, slow down implementation later on. In several projects, a wish to move money early has indeed meant long delays later. However, it remains sensible to have some high-risk projects in a big portfolio, to keep average ERORs high. Delay in beginning implementation of a good project is a real cost; reduction of such delays justifies *some* hurry at the appraisal stage. The questions are: how much? And should more attention be given to identification and design?

The balance between two targets that both raise ERORs, but are in direct conflict – moving money fast and getting projects improved – is a fine one. Despite some exceptions, we do not believe that the Bank has pushed too fast in its Indian loans. One clear example of care is shown in a farm credit project in the 1970s. The evaluators point out that the local executive agency by which the project was 'carried out [was] known to have major weaknesses. [The] comprehensive package of manpower and financial reforms insisted on by the appraisal team, even at the cost of a significant delay in project processing, [is] to their credit'.

Intermediation: overdues, externalities, federalism

It is the GoI, not the project authority, that guarantees repayment of aid loans – essential if donors are to be able to pick projects with high

ERORs even if the recoverable commercial returns are low or negative; and desirable to avoid excessive caution in project selection, which would produce a safe but low EROR on the donor's portfolio. Formally, therefore, aid loan agreements are between GoI, or its financially guaranteed agents, and a donor, such as IDA. There are three crucial issues, however.

First – despite the formal aid agreement – in substance the money passes through a series of intermediaries, often ending in the private sector (Chapter 7). For lending in support of rural credit or minor irrigation, the series might be: IDA; GoI; Reserve Bank of India (RBI); NABARD (formerly ARDC); a state-level land development bank (LDB), or else a commercial bank; a primary land development bank (PLDB), village co-op, or a rural branch bank; and finally private borrowers, mostly farmers. (Analogous series apply where money passes via an industrial development finance corporation such as ICICI).

Second, each 'link' in the chain has access to other sources of cash. For example, given the level of aid, the GoI can enable the Reserve Bank of India to increase its on-lending to NABARD, so the latter can re-lend to commercial banks in support of their rural lending; farmers can borrow from commercial banks or from village moneylenders, both financed privately. Neither the Bank Group nor other donors can influence this directly.

Third, though the loans are normally destined for medium-term to long-term producer credit, extra cash is in reality to a large extent fungible between this use (for which aid is nominally intended), short-term credit, and consumption; and it is fungible at each stage of intermediation.

Many of the problems besetting aid loans – notably the problem of overdues – are related to these three interwoven issues: serial intermediation, parallel sources of cash, and fungibility.

First, if intermediation is serial, it is hard to apply incentives and disincentives at the right level. Typically a commercial bank, faced with excessive overdues from a rural branch bank serving several hundred borrowers, can threaten to close the branch, or at least to reduce or delay new lending to it (and therefore by it). However, this penalizes not just wilful defaulters, but also (i) the unlucky; and, above all (ii) borrowers who have succeeded in keeping up repayments. Such good payers, indeed, are encouraged to default after all, by the threat that even if they repay they will be unable to borrow from their bank branch next year, because it has effectively been bankrupted, by the defaults of other borrowers. Moving one stage up, the ability of a particular rural bank to on-lend is reduced, if NABARD decides to cut its support because it has done badly in retrieving overdues from village branches (at least three substantial cases are reported in the World Bank's evaluations of rural credit projects). But this incentive to good credit management for the board of directors (of a commercial bank or of a land development bank) is a direct disincentive to a local branch (a village bank or a primary land development bank). If the managers of a branch bank feel that head office – because it has been penalized by NABARD for the past poor performance of its branches as a whole – will be unable to lend it much money for the next crop anyway, why should the branch struggle to repay this season? At the level of the aid donors, by threatening NABARD with the disincentive of reduced funding, they indeed encourage it to penalize each commercial bank head office more heavily for its overdues; but such penalties not only create incentives to default among 'innocent' local branches of each bank, and among non-defaulting farmers, but also allow bad financial returns on a project, due partly to intermediation problems, to choke off funds when economic returns may be excellent. This problem is not confined to farm credit (as one evaluation of a large infrastructure project makes clear). Nor has it a neat answer: simply to continue unlimited funding not only leaves the aid donor in the position of appearing to encourage financial indiscipline, but also puts the GoI in the same position, and drains its resources, because the aid commitment to the project is fixed in cash terms, as is GoI's commitment to finance the gap between donors' contributions and total project costs, unless all parties agree to reduce the size of the project.

Apart from this serial intermediation problem, appropriate incentives are hard for a donor to apply when recipients at each level can respond by turning to parallel, competing sources of funds. The Bank has taken the view that institution-building, in farm credit, involves it in gradually raising the 'level' of its lending, from state-level institutions to NABARD (ex-ARDC). However, each time the level of donor support is raised, its influence on base-level actions by borrowers is further diluted, because there is one more intermediary lender who can turn to parallel sources of funds.

Is all this 'healthy competition' in credit markets? Only if price incentives, information, externalities, and distribution of income and power are such as to translate maximization by each agent (farmer, village formal financial institutions, commercial banks) into socially desirable equity and efficiency outcomes. Several evaluations suggest otherwise. In one state credit project, for example, the structure of borrowing for minor irrigation led to a much less labour-intensive pattern of works than IDA had envisaged. Since each borrower had many alternatives, IDA could exert very little influence (even if it has wanted to do so). In many cases, borrowers' access to these lending alternatives prevented IDA, NABARD/ARDC and commercial-bank/ LDB from controlling negative externalities.

Most notably, Bank-ARDC-LDB rules on spacing of wells designed to conserve groundwater (and thus to ensure both the farmer's return to his well and the lender's repayment), are not enforcible if alternative credit sources are readily available. Evaluations of IDA aid to rural credit in two states, and a general OED review of such aid, specify this problem.

Apart from credit projects, much Bank support for specific rural investments contains credit components, and faces the same difficulties. Thus a 1986 review by the Bank Group of groundwater development in an Indian State pointed out that 'unregulated private development may have a serious limiting effect on usable groundwater'; that 'poor recovery [of credit for] private investments' in such [over]use is typical; and that 'a substantial part of investments through World Bank supported institutional credit are used for private groundwater investments'.

Non-enforcibility of economic incentives, due to parallel and serial intermediation, and to fungibility, is a challenge to aid-effectiveness extending far beyond the Bank Group, credit, the rural sector, or India. It is the basic challenge posed by economic externalities – benefits reaped by one party, while costs are borne by another – to market-based approaches to development (of which use of aid is a small part).

The choice of level of intermediation, and of appropriate incentives, is complicated in India (and some other countries) by federalism. The World Bank's early agricultural credit projects sought to help GoI to strengthen state-level local development banks (LDBs) and commercial banking institutions, alongside ARDC's capacity to supervise and evaluate them. Only later did the Bank move towards direct support of ARDC/NABARD, citing the advantages of greater flexibility, and of capacity for reachout to remoter states and smaller projects. The long, careful build up meant that gains probably exceeded losses from this upward shift in the level of intermediation. Where a donor straight away operates at the centre, at the highest level of intermediation – and especially where its share in the project is small – relations of donor and recipient tend to be less successful. In the case of an infrastructural project in several states, for example, the evaluators found that, 'IDA's lack of a (direct) contractual relationship with the state (authorities helped to ensure) that IDA's influence at state level was minimal or non-existent'.

Goals of Bank Group project aid

Institutional learning: recipients

Most PPAs – and indeed the earlier appraisal documents – express great concern with helping Indian institutions to improve their performance. The increasing use, in the Bank's own analytical work, of Indian consultants (e.g. of ARDC/NABARD itself, to prepare several PCRs following credit projects) exemplifies this concern. In most fields where there have been several Bank Group projects – credit, fertilizer production, extension – major, and in many respects successful, institution-building efforts have been made. There was plenty to build on; in many areas, e.g. fertilizer technology, the Bank Group may well have learned more from the institutions than it has taught them.

A major success of the Bank has been as 'marriage broker' – or catalyst – showing how different institutions can work together on projects. Bank Group credit support in the mid-1970s was critical, for example, in the development of operational links between ARDC and commercial banks, and hence helped to make feasible the GoI's planned shift from a rural credit system based on co-ops and LDBs, to one based largely on commercial banks. The Bank's population project has also twinned each of two Population Centres with a different, prominent Indian management institute. A third example has been the use of an IDA loan to 'catalyze' the combination of research expertise in an agricultural university with the commercial tasks of seed-farming and processing.

In any country, foreign visitors are usually better than insiders at uncovering – and financing – unsuspected prospects for co-ordination. Hence, institutional marriage is a donor strength. Lack of attention to locally reared institutional 'children', however, is a donor weakness. Water users' co-operation is discussed in several evaluations, but with reference to exogenous groups or formal co-operatives. The evaluators seldom say much about informal, local, traditional institutions for such co-operation, let alone of the circumstances that sustain such institutions: e.g. some scarcity, but not too much, of the co-operatively allocated resource (Wade, 1979). Nor, at project level, is much attention paid to informal credit sources. Not only moneylenders (where competitive), but also rotating credit and savings associations could well sometimes function as intermediaries with local knowledge (and low costs of securing loan recovery), and could thus perhaps alleviate some of the credit constraints on rural projects, reach more of the rural poor, and avoid some of the problems experienced with conventional, formal intermediaries.

Another area of institution-building, normally initiated by Indian official agencies but at least supported by donor projects, needs to be questioned. 'Island projects' with exceptionally high levels of services, run by special project-based authorities and with independent resources (often dependent on donors), are against GoI policy as aid media. But this policy appears not to rule out island programmes.

One such programme, for a group of areas with similar ecology, is stated by OED to have had 'good institutional support' from conventional GoI line agencies. Yet it suffered 'frequent changes of administrative staff' at higher levels. Also, 'lack of technical expertise' in the central unit was a problem, because such professionals were 'almost entirely centred in the [line] Ministry' – with which 'co-operation did not materialize to the extent desirable', impeding the programme's 'development of technical packages'. Moreover, 'line department officers who were seconded to district' authorities of the programme had to implement project 'activities [not] supported currently by their departments'. Conflicts of authority and interest led to serious consequences, with little effective remedy. These are standard problems faced by island programmes and projects isolated from national systems of line administration, secondment, and finance. Such programmes, though not projects, have a long history in India – especially in rural India (Lipton, 1987). They represent recurring, often courageous, usually well-intentioned efforts to break bottlenecks in, or among, traditionally proud, separate sub-bureaucracies – different states and the centre; different line departments; IAS and IFS – but face major problems. Perhaps donors should be more careful when supporting such programmes, especially since their post-donor life is usually poor and short. When aiding such organizations as Command Area Development Programmes, donors may show insufficient awareness of the possible conflicts between donor-dependent programmes and stronger traditional line ministries. At least one evaluation reveals the seriousness of such problems.

This is not to say that island programmes and projects never work, or that new, top-down organizations, supported by 'Christmas tree' donor projects, are always wrong. A major evaluation of a Bank Group input into an urban development programme – an exciting, analytical, well-written document that deserves a wide audience (not the 'restricted distribution' to which all OED project-specific work is sentenced) – documents a big and dramatic exception to many current platitudes about development projects. This programme mixed most of the metaphors for the undesirable: island, Christmas tree, top-down – yet it has clearly worked in itself, though probably less so as a pilot (see pp. 176–7).

Institutional learning: donors

Much of the history of aid projects in India comprises pilot projects:

examples from the Bank Group include the projects above and at least one project each centred upon urban sanitation and upon irrigation. Other donors have also supported pilots, e.g. the UK-aided project on dryland farming systems. In pilot projects, the donor may often be tempted to try out numerous project components, even if they have 'no essential linkages or interrelations'. With such projects the only connecting item, on which sub-projects are hung, is the stem of the Christmas tree: donor cash and influence. These often sustain a local organization that has little support in – indeed is seen to rival – line ministries, and is therefore unable to survive, in any strong or integrative form, the transition from donor to domestic funding.

The transition from support of statewise agricultural credit to direct support of ARDC/NABARD was a relatively successful instance of piloting. Farm credit can in principle support many things; the Bank Group's nine state credits, of which a Bank Group impact study was made in 1981, were limited mainly to two sorts of purchase by final borrowers; minor on-farm groundwater equipment, and tractors. The evidence shows that the former was narrow but productively cost-effective (although a Bank evaluation in late 1986 shows that such privately- owned tubewells can be inequitable and may overuse both groundwater and electric power), but tractor credit was often inappropriate. In any event, the relatively narrow range of approved objects for lending (even allowing for fungibility), and the concentration on permanent (indeed almost, though not in the standard ministerial sense, 'line') agencies, did permit successful donor evaluation and learning. The nine-project impact study shows that Bank credit projects tackled several, in some ways increasingly difficult, states – and, under GoI guidance, assessed and improved the capacity of the apex organization (ARDC/NABARD) – before the long and costly pilot stage was transformed into direct support for ARDC.

A massive piloting exercise in India – a project seeking to upgrade a whole range of services and housing in a big city – was a success as a project but probably a failure as a pilot. Two reasons for these linked facts – the uniqueness of the city served, and the ingeniously opportunist 'situationism' of both Indian project management staff and Bank authorities – are well discussed in the PPA. The executing agency was initially an engineering-based, strong, non-participatory body – in essence a reaction or successor to the functional near-breakdown in that city of the traditional modes of local government. It was seized on for flexible Bank Group support, according to the evaluation, in 'patch-up and fix-up style', as 'a bold experiment formulated quickly in response to manifest and immediate need'. Thus the executing agency was allowed to get on with the jobs in hand without the usual Bank insistence on appraising each sub-project. This led to charges of 'Christmas Tree' status, charges justified in form but not in substance. There was no sign of the increasingly fashionable participatory, bottom-up consultations. Institution-building took priority over project specification. The outcome was almost certainly excellent by measurable criteria, and the pilot led to two further large projects in the same city.

This apart, however, the initial project piloted very little. The authors of the PPA recognize that the centralized, engineering, non-participatory management style usually 'works' only during reaction to extreme conditions associated with perceived failure of older institutions. The PPA stresses that institutions of city government in India must normally be much more democratic – as in an ongoing Bank-aided urban development project in another Indian city, with 'a flat-structured [Indian implementing] organization that relies on negotiation rather than a vertical-structured [one, that relies on] authority'. Such democratization is seen as the pilot city's future also; an authoritarian island in a democratic sea is hardly a useful pilot. Even within India, the recognized uniqueness (and extremity) of the 'pilot city' rendered it a somewhat doubtful pilot.

But the major problem with this pilot is the absence of timely provision for control groups, baselines, and evaluations. Crude ERORs were attempted at appraisal, but were estimated only for some sub-projects. They are going to be very hard ever to verify, because only well after the pilot (i.e. during the successor project) did the executing agency 'initiate an evaluation of the impact of past investments' – inevitably, 'based on available, and in some cases limited, data'. There are enough indicators (e.g. death-rates), measurable over time in comparison with other areas, to be fairly confident that overall success was achieved. But it is almost impossible to determine what parts of this large project worked best, and why.

This is not said to attack a project that, rightly, gave first priority to a cost-effective attack on extreme need in one Indian city. However, with a pilot project, proper baselines and controls, to permit full evaluation of performance, should have been estimated. Probably, an independent local research institution should have been selected and helped to work with the executing agency in monitoring; that might have added 0.5 to 1 per cent to the cost of this vast project, but would have added much more to its usefulness as a pilot. Lacking such evaluation, one must conclude that this pilot is exceptional; and that, as a rule, many purposes, islands of organization, non-participation, and Christmas-tree styles do *not* conduce to project success, nor lack of baselines and controls to piloting and donor learning.

Ultimate goals: fuller labour use

It is chiefly by increasing the prospects for and returns to work – and thus the amount of work that people are willing to do and to hire, and also the amount they can produce and consume per hour worked – that developing countries and aid donors can best advance, simultaneously, the causes of efficiency and equity. It is, however, not surprising that aid projects have often been bad at increasing the incentives and prospects for work. Donors' own internal incentives and technologies (and consultants) often militate against labour-intensive design choices.

Another serious impediment to clear thinking about the employment impact of projects has been the rapidly changing theory and evidence about the work-productivity-poverty nexus in the developing world. In the 1960s many believed that vast idle labour reserves existed, waiting to be tapped for development. In the 1970s the pendulum swung, and for many economists involuntary unemployment was almost defined out of existence. Only fairly recently has clear evidence come in that involuntary unemployment – as opposed to withdrawal from labour compelled by illness, hunger, domestic 'duties', or the costs of job search – is significant, fluctuating, increasing, but heavily concentrated on the poor, especially casual employees and women (Lipton, 1983).

It is not surprising that aid project work often: (a) has incorrectly analyzed the impact on work duration and hourly work income – the example of tractorization is discussed on pp. 179–81; (b) has incorrectly compared pre-project and post-project circumstances of labouring groups, using 'partial equilibrium' methods where these are likely to involve major errors (see pp. 181–2). More surprising, however, is the insensitivity often shown to issues of employment.

In particular, most donors, including until very recently the Bank Group, have tended to 'hive off' analytically the big, capital-intensive projects – major transport links, factories, etc. – and to confine analysis of employment (and income distribution) to more diffuse projects such as rural credit or slum upgrading. On the former group of projects, several evaluations strikingly omit any discussion of ways to expand, consistent with economy, the use of unskilled labour. In other cases, the Bank Group evaluation even takes credit for reducing the numbers of unskilled workers.

There is a real tension here, between project efficiency (and financial viability) and social efficiency, although the latter is never advanced by adopting a technique that uses more unskilled labour, at a given level of use of all other inputs, than is needed to produce a given output. However, social efficiency *can* be advanced by adopting labour/capital ratios considerably higher than would be implied by maximizing financial or even economic returns without income-distribution weights. On top of income-distribution weights – i.e. even for projects or techniques justified with such weights – appraisals should allow for the indirect costs when people become unemployed in societies with little 'social security' other than crime or beggary.

Far from this, it does not look as if, once a project is in operation, labour is even priced at social cost by Bank (or other donor) advisers on staffing levels. Nor, when advising against 'overstaffing' in some operations, are consultants automatically asked by donors to look for socially cost-effective, and financially tolerable, ways to expand unskilled employment elsewhere in the project. Under-used capacity and excessively high-tech are common and costly faults in large Indian projects, aided or not. This suggests that incentives to labour-intensity in construction and use – perhaps associated with attempts to negotiate 'high-employment, wage-restraint' deals with major labour unions – could well be explored early in many project cycles. Should donors, linked with that part of GoI which sees their comparative advantage in high-tech, press India to be even more dualistic, half high-tech (with aided projects that aim to slash 'overstaffing') and half poverty-focused (with aid projects aiming at labour-intensity)? This would seem unwise; Japanese development since 1945 (perhaps since 1880) suggests that such patterns are feasible, but require a degree of corporate political control over business far beyond what is acceptable in India. The World Bank's move in 1986, to extend the monitoring of poverty impact to major project cycles outside the traditionally poverty-focused sectors will if implemented be an important move away from such dualism. So could the incorporation of income-distribution weights into project design choices.

Even in rural and small-scale projects, donors' analytical styles may miss out major employment-linked problems. The impact study of Bank Group credit projects – much of which financed tractor purchase by non-poor farmers – points out: 'In southern states, tractor owners interviewed saw as main benefit the ability to manage large (16–20 hectare) holdings without depending on burdensome permanent labour. [There], tractorization has at best no or even a negative effect on employment'. While the problem is recognized, the tone is rather too hopeful, and the following statement that elsewhere in India tractorization 'created more employment than [it] displaced' is almost certainly incorrect (see Binswanger, 1978; Farrington and Abeyratne. 1982). Tractor aid is important because it is popular with donor exporters and because it typifies the problems of evaluating aid that finances potentially labour-displacing equipment.

One major IDA agricultural credit project implemented in the 1970s was intended to finance mechanization only – 8,000 tractors (plus implements), 40 self-propelled harvesters, and 200 tractor-drawn harvesters and spares. The analysis of mechanization is confined to the tractors, however; the much more questionable and employment-reducing (and itself much reduced) harvester component is not evaluated.

The evaluators reported that as a result of investment in tractors, cropping intensity rose from 140 per cent to 160 per cent and the cropping pattern changed to high value crops. Also cropped area rose by 20,200 ha. and the gross value of production increased by US$30 million per year in the two states combined. However, there are four basic errors in the evaluation. First, the only study specific to this agricultural credit project covered just twenty-five tractor-owners and twenty-five non-owners, spread across six villages in one district of one of the two affected states. Second, it is not correct to assess the output gains from tractors by comparing output levels as between owners and non-owners of tractors instead of between users and non-users. This is to assume that all and only owners are users. In reality, plying for hire is a major use of tractors.

Third, the method of analysis assumes that differences in farm output and returns, between tractor-owners and others, are entirely attributable to tractors. In reality, tractor-owners are much likelier than non-owners to have access to irrigation and other inputs, as affluence is a cause of both tractor ownership and other advantages.

Finally, the survey contained no pre-project baseline data, but only data after project completion. So the evaluators cannot safely conclude that the cropping intensity increased from 140 per cent to 160 per cent. All we can say is that tractor owners had a higher intensity, after the project, than non-owners; they may well have had an equally elevated intensity before the tractors arrived. Identical remarks apply to claimed 'rises' in yields and area. These are not rises but differences between rich and poor farmers at a moment of time. Such differences prove nothing about changes in the relative status of users and non-users of tractors over a period.

Yet it is on this series of mistakes – echoed in most donors' and recipients' evaluations of such equipment – that the high claims for IDA tractor credits rest.[13]

The failure of tractors to raise output, and the generally negative impact on employment, are fully borne out by other studies of the area, not associated with the PPA itself but (very properly) reviewed there – and even more strongly by more recent work (Agarwal, 1984).

The general lack of independent contribution by tractors to output – except where they enable new land to be cultivated – is, indeed, crucial to employment effects. For a major component claimed for the 'economic benefits', in this PPA, is 'labour savings through lowering labour costs per unit of (crop) output'. If the claims for higher total crop output due to tractors as such are unfounded, as seems to be the case, then this 'benefit' operates wholly through raising unemployment. In such a case, true project benefit depends wholly on the ability of the economy to absorb the released labour productively. Even in those rare circumstances where tractors, although reducing labour use per unit of crop output by a proportion, raise crop output by a higher proportion – almost invariably an area effect, not a yield or an intensity effect – we would ask whether similar expenditures on other methods of relieving draught-power constraints, or indeed on other inputs (such as water, seeds, or fertilizer) raising yields despite such constraints, might have raised output by as much, or more, with a greater share in total benefits (and in input use) for the poor (and under-employed) labourers.

In this joint evaluation of two nearby tractor-credit projects, the PPA is generally much more cautious than the PCR about employment effects. Nevertheless, it also accepts the conventional wisdom that 'labour has become increasingly scarce'. (Sceptics like ourselves read this as a claim that employers do not wish to pay market wages, nor governments to use resources to support seasonal migration from depressed areas.) 'Labour effects were not incorporated in [the] survey but it was *assumed* that there was incremental labour demand. During the mission's field visits displaced tenants or farmers were *said* to have found alternative employment. All persons the mission asked were of the *opinion* that on balance tractors had created employment' (our italics). It is unlikely that the Mission met migrant workers who had returned to very poor nearby areas. Such workers are the likeliest to be displaced by tractors (and by the, unevaluated, threshing machines also provided).

A related problem to donors' over-estimation of employment effects is that evaluations – and other project documents – often just compare 'beneficiary' and 'control' farmers after the project. But one also has to know the two groups' pre-project (baseline) levels of family and hired employment. Otherwise, one cannot exclude the possibility that the groups' different post-project levels of labour use are due to differences in endowments between the groups not controlled for.

Suppose the latter is not the case. It is still not possible to infer that – because 10.6m. extra family workdays and 14.5m. extra hired workdays are created in one Bank project on the farms receiving credit for extra irrigation – this is the employment effect; it may be more, or less. The family farm-workers who benefit from the project may respond to extra on-farm work chances by supplying less labour for hire off the farm. This will reduce their hired workdays; part of that gap will be filled by extra labour from hired workers without farms, or with farms not benefiting from the project. Numerous other effects, some very large, are feasible, depending on income and price elasticities of labour supply by family and hired workers; and on cross-elasticities of labour supply for one use to changes in attainable wage-rates in other uses, both among and within households; and also on demand elasticities.

The only way to compare employment effects is to compare pre-project and post-project income, and levels of hired and family labour, as between two roughly comparable communities (e.g. groups of villages), with separate but initially similar labour markets. Baseline and control sample areas, not just households, are therefore needed. Only thus can the total effect of a project on its area – not just the effect on project households – in respect of, say, family work and hired work, be compared. This is not a nit-picking point. Unfortunately it means that evaluation estimates of the employment effect of projects – whether or not aid-financed – may overstate or understate by a factor of two to one. The absence of information in most evaluations about whether extra work required is in the slack season or in the busy season – i.e. about whether such work is likely to add to existing employment, or to substitute for it – makes the problem even more serious. Not only in Asia, but increasingly in Africa too, the poverty impact of rural projects depends less on the effect on 'small farmers' than on the contribution to work chances for landless and near-landless labourers. Proper assessment of that contribution is thus a top priority for 'evaluation reform'.

Ultimate goals: less poverty

Most of the projects, recently evaluated, were designed and appraised a decade or more ago. Then, many experts believed that growth would usually 'trickle down' to the poor, so that projects that efficiently produced growth were the best way to alleviate poverty. Since the mid-1970s, much counter-evidence has appeared. Chapter 2 rehearses the evidence that, at least until the late 1970s, steady growth in India brought no significant decline in poverty incidence or severity – especially when skill-intensive and capital-intensive (as often with foreign-funded projects), growth can fail to benefit poor people for long periods, and can even harm them. An environment of rapid increase in the workforce, and of price policies that discourage the use of labour-intensive commodities or inputs – while not the fault of aid donors – can interact harmfully with aid projects that 'go for growth' on the assumption that this alone will ease the task of poverty alleviation. Rather, these two goals are *usually* complementary; for example less-poor workers are healthier and better-educated, and thus more growth-inducing. But are 'projects' appropriate to employ them?

Issues of aid and poverty are treated in Chapter 2. Here, we look only at three project-specific issues, exemplified in Bank Group project evaluations. How do projects define potential participants, and with what effect on poverty groups? Do regional patterns of aid affect its poverty-focus? Does the choice between projects with mainly technology-based, institution-based, or market-based approaches affect the impact on poverty?

First, 'small farmer', 'poor beneficiary', etc. are often defined in ways that exclude many of the poor, and all of the poorest. In one state credit project in the mid-1970 – for example, the evaluation points out that 'marginal farmers' – apparently defined as those operating below 3 acres, not 2.5 acres as in standard GoI practice – 'were not permitted to borrow under the project'. Yet, even in 1970–1, of all operational holdings in the state that were wholly or partly in agricultural use, over two-thirds were smaller than 2.5 acres (Naidu, 1975). Thus, by project completion in the late 1970s, the smallest 75 per cent at least of operational holdings must have been excluded.

In another state, a 1970s Bank Group project for credit to on-farm minor irrigation specified a 'minimum benefiting area of 1.5 ha' for dugwells; but the 1971 land distribution in that state would have restricted borrowing to the biggest 60 per cent of farmers (Naidu, 1975), and by the completion in 1977 surely to the bigger half. Yet we are told that 55 per cent of wells were completed by 'small farmers'.

In a third Bank-aided credit project, completed in the 1980s, again according to Naidu, the GoI's small/marginal farmer borderline (2.5 acres) placed 60 per cent of all farmers below it; yet, despite the use of this lower cut-off for lending the evaluators still claimed that '80 per cent of the lending went to small farmers'.

It is not clear that the smallest holdings cannot be made viable even with World Bank credit. The ratio of default to lending steadily increases with farm size (Lipton, 1976; Copestake, 1987). Nor is a tiny farm uneconomic or unviable merely because it suffices to meet only part of a family's needs. Donors and recipients often reduce the impact on poor farmers by defining the 'small farm' category to include the not-so-small. ARDC successfully modified the standard definitions of GoI (on which 'small' but non-marginal farmers operate 2.5 to 5 acres, modified to allow for irrigation, land quality, etc.) as 'too restrictive' and has edged the upper borderline of 'small farmers' higher. In one IDA project, eligible 'small farmers' could cultivate up to 14 acres, so that, by project completion in 1977, only the top 10 to 15 per cent can have been excluded from the 'small' group (while the smallest half of farmers could not qualify for credit). In another state, the upper limit of 'small farm' for project purposes is set so high that 91 per cent of cultivators in the state are 'small' – while the smallest 65 to 75 per cent of cultivators were too small to be eligible for credits.[14]

The donors are, of course, fully aware of such problems. They affect not only rural credit projects, but most rural and some urban projects, since these contain large credit components (to help beneficiaries acquire inputs before outputs are bringing in income). The *de facto* exclusion of the poorest springs largely from the concern of Indian intermediaries to keep administrative costs down, and to secure good collateral.[15] Overall, despite the clear intentions of the Bank group, the facts cast some doubt on its claim (in one impact study) that 'the main effect of IDA participation was on the qualitative side, i.e. increased targeting of credit to small farmers'. The lending conditions excluded the smallest. Meanwhile Indian intermediaries have edged up the limit that defines 'smallness'. Indeed, in the late 1970s an evaluation complained that 'there seems to be little incentive at present for lending agencies to assist small farmers'. This is reinforced by the high-tech, labour-displacing emphasis of much investment linked to these credits. It might appear that the large anti-poverty outlays under the Sixth and Seventh Plans, especially via IRDP (Chapter 2), would redirect NABARD, as the apex of credit intermediation, towards the poorest farmers; but the great bulk of such programmes, and associated credit, support the acquisition of non-farm assets. In India's large semi-arid areas, where (as in most of Africa) the very poor are still mainly smallholders, a credit gap can emerge, especially after a new form of technology has been introduced (e.g. some HYVs permit such people to get less poor if, say, fertilizer credit is available).

It is especially unfortunate – since smaller borrowers are normally the most intensive users of land, loans and water (Berry and Cline, 1979; Booth and Sundrum, 1984) – that definitional laxity at the upper end, and credit exclusion at the lower, direct so little Bank-assisted 'small farm credit' to the poorest 50 to 60 per cent of Indian farmers. Of course, though not the poorest, a farmer with 3 to 5 acres is in most of India far from adequately housed, clothed, or educated. But farmers with 0.5 to 3 acres need working capital even more. They are probably better at using it and at repaying the loan. They need all the help they can get – from GoI, NGOs, and donors – in combating the strong local forces that tend to exclude them from formal credit.

The regional direction of aided projects also greatly affects their poverty-focus. This applies internationally: probably the best single thing that donors could do for poverty-focus is to shift bilateral aid away from some of the heavily over-aided middle-income countries towards the really poor countries in South Asia and in Africa. Bank Group aid, especially through IDA, expressly aims to offset some of this huge imbalance of bilateral aid against large, poor LDCs. To help to offset similar imbalances within India, IDA support of ARDC was used in the late 1970s to open a dialogue to determine where aid for rural credit could contribute most to the less developed states. A major Bank-aided project was intended to direct one-quarter of the funds to nine such states, but in fact forty-two per cent was spent there. If – as the evaluation of this project suggests – ERORs on such credit projects are about as high as on others, such regional focus improves poverty impact, not only because average income of beneficiaries is less in poor regions, but because distribution within backward rural areas is less unequal (Dasgupta, 1977). For both reasons, the bias of many aided projects against the poorest farmers (p. 184) may have less impact in these regions. Also, the proportion of landless labourers – missed out, of course, from farm credits – is smaller there than elsewhere in India.

Cash aid to poor states, however, is not a simple way for donors' projects to benefit poor people. Some poor regions are associated with systematically bad project performance, (see p. 161). The evaluation mentioned on pp. 184–5 points out that remote areas may feature 'physical inaccessibility of a large number of target group farmers' or other poor people. Conversely, some sorts of project location, while efficient, provide poor people with special difficulties of access. Two evaluations of marketing projects pointed out that markets selected for aid appear to be the central or intermediary rather than the primary or farmer market type, so that only farmers living close to the market or larger farmers with adequate transport and other incentives would be expected to bring their produce to them. As in most of Africa, so in these more backward, dispersed parts of India: high ratios of very bad land to people require a new approach to infrastructure if the remote poor are to be reached at acceptable unit cost. Development of transport types and organizations less subject to economies of scale and of agglomeration could be relevant here. Analogously, Bank and USAID experience with rural electrification shows that forced-draft dispersion of grid-style projects – power lines, major transport, and market links – to remote areas can be an inefficient, and ineffective, way to relieve poverty there. More imaginative research and development of local non-grid systems may be more promising, especially in view of the very strong (albeit not causally simple) association between poverty incidence and access to key infrastructural items (Wanamali, 1986).

These PPAs exemplify three types of approach to 'including the poor' at appraisal and evaluation: technical, institutional, and market. The accepted long-term remedy to the issue of technical choice, more research into poor people's technologies, is exemplified by the Indo-UK Dryland Farming Project, but has often been hampered – e.g. in the cases of improved animal implements, and of some bio-gas technologies – by lack of early integration between technical and economic analysis, and of timely field-testing for robustness and profitability at small-unit level.

Market approaches to 'reaching the poor' are exemplified by water sale from big to small farmers. This has partly corrected for the initial bias, from location of wells on better-endowed, less risk-averse larger farms, and from restrictions placed upon subsequent small-farm well development by well-spacing rules aimed at groundwater conservation. In some cases, water sales were not considered at appraisal; two OED evaluations state that, if they had been, their redistributive effects could probably have been increased by appropriate design decisions.

Similarly, the World Bank and Canadian site-and-service and slum-upgrading schemes initially sought to forbid renting-out, so as to avoid the emotive accusation of diverting poverty-focused aid to slum landlords; but the prohibition was dropped after evidence accumulated that rentals of rooms permitted both fuller use of capital and, via increased supply and hence lower prices of rented property, some sharing in benefits by the very poorest urban dwellers.

Market approaches in the other direction – enabling the poorest to own groundwater and pumping rights co-operatively, for sale to better-off farmers (as with *Proshika* in Bangladesh; see Wood, 1984), or to develop artisan assets at household level through IRDP in India's Sixth and Seventh Plans – can also offer promising levers upon poverty alleviation in the context of aid projects.

However, a crucial weakness of this approach – in the hands of most official donors, including the Bank group – is their scant interest in specifically 'pro-poor' market actions, as opposed to less directional types of marketing projects and market improvement. Yet the widespread fear that undirected markets harm the poor is not as absurd as is sometimes claimed. Participation in most markets requires a threshold endowment – an ox cart, numeracy, knowledge – which the poor are especially likely to lack. Especially in remote areas; or where there is great initial inequality; or where the providers of some commodities (e.g. transport to market) can apply pressure by using their control of others (e.g. credit); or where big operators can affect licences (e.g. of urban retailing) or price policies – in such cases market development, if it is to benefit the poor, must be supplemented by direct Government provision or competition, or indirect government actions to secure these. Unregulated market development may well pull key inputs away from pro-poor providers. A Bank study in one Indian state of private and public tubewells installed up to mid-1986 (many of which were backed by Bank-funded credit or equipment) concluded that 'without public-sector development, the weaker elements of the farming population may be permanently excluded from irrigated agriculture'. If prices in other markets are set to meet overall policy requirements – which in every country include the placating of the powerful – 'improvement' of a specific market may be inefficient by the same process that renders it inequitable; in the above case, private tubewells used twice as much (heavily subsidized) electric power per acre served (four times as much at peak periods), thereby bleeding the rural grid in general, and the more poverty-oriented public-sector tubewells in particular.[16]

Institutional approaches towards 'reaching the poor' are also exemplified in Bank Group aid projects. However, several of these, even in India, have shown insufficient regard for the role of existing institutions in concentrating benefits upon the already wealthy. At least one evaluation points out that, in pre-appraisal, the likely distribution of gains from new irrigation devices was ignored – and farm models were developed simply assuming scale-neutrality – despite clear evidence of great initial inequality. We have already highlighted lending rules, and even definitions of smallness, excluding small farmers and perhaps tenants. Smallness of plots on small farms is a further barrier to irrigation. One irrigation project performance audit recognizes the obstacles posed by fragmentation – both because small farms mean small plots, and because of wastage of land in bunds – but appears to dismiss the remedy of consolidation because 'Bank land consolidation programmes in other projects have been unsuccessful' and because farmers expressed 'widespread opposition' on grounds of soil heterogeneity. Time is certainly needed to win farmers' confidence, and to test out farming systems that will replace the real risk of fragmentation to small farmers. However, the Bank's absolute objections appear to ignore the long history – and considerable achievements – of official consolidation programmes in some Indian states, and its prospects to help very small farmers in the context of water resource development (Minhas, 1970).

Efficient growth

Our review of Bank aid projects in India should close by reiterating their generally high real EROR. We have pointed to some possibly overestimated ERORs, notably on projects linked to provision of tractors, but this is not a general feature. Nor is it plausible to dismiss most Bank-aided projects as largely fungible. GoI would not, in the absence of Bank Group aid, have proceeded nearly as far, as fast, or in the chosen direction, with rural credit, urban drinking-water and sewage improvement, the reform of agricultural water management, reorganized agricultural extension, or the shift of urban development away from subsidized formal-sector housing for not-so-poor civil servants, towards slum upgrading and site-and-service. These were largely efficient projects and they produced substantial extra real GNP.

However, almost all evaluations assume that a project's contribution to real GNP per person depends entirely on its economic rate of return. In fact, the rate of saving out of extra income is also important.[17] Even with projects loosely in the banking sector, such as aid to LDBs and

ARDC/NABARD, the question of savings mobilization is seldom adequately addressed. It is not just a question of gross savings flows out of extra project income, or through new project institutions. The extent to which such flows are additional – as opposed to diversions from other savings, or from earlier savings channels – also matters. So does the efficiency with which extra savings are channelled into high-yielding and/or poverty-reducing investments. What is more, the important question about savings is, 'What difference does the project make to the total uses of income?' And 'total uses of income' include possible contributions to public savings via increased tax payments – just as hidden project returns may include the reduction of real claims on health outlays, as beneficiaries become less poor and ill-nourished. Such savings effects can be important, especially with big area-based projects.

A final consideration, co-determining the impact of a project upon efficient growth of income-per-person, is its population effect. Widely-spread growth is known to lead to reduced fertility (World Bank, 1984). With a large localized project in irrigation or urban development, this can be an important hidden benefit – and its scale can be affected by choices at the design and implementation stage. Savings and population considerations in large projects should be allowed for throughout the project cycle, in assessing the choices likeliest to generate efficient growth. At present only the rate of return on capital is considered.

Some projects from other donors

No other donor has either such a large number of projects as the Bank Group, nor such a systematic evaluation procedure. We were able to obtain evaluation documents only from the Federal Republic of Germany (BWZ), the European Community (EC), the UK (ODM/ODA), and the USA (USAID). Few of these documents contained formal EROR estimates, and many were subjective, relying on project officers, or on beneficiary or implementing organizations. Baseline studies and control groups were even rarer than in Bank Group projects. Nevertheless, the evaluations have three advantages. They confirm that both the generally good performance of aid projects, and their major weaknesses (e.g. in respect of intermediation and of employment analysis), are not confined to the Bank Group. Second, because these non-Bank evaluations are attributable to outside consultants, we are permitted to identify specific projects and places. Finally, these evaluations cast light on types of aid not given by the Bank group, notably on food aid (from USAID and EEC) and on technical assistance (from West Germany and the UK). Although these two types no longer loom large in the total Indian aid programme, they may have lessons for Africa, where their role is much bigger.

Aid from USAID

The USA suspended project aid to India in 1972, before the development of its current evaluation procedures, and resumed it only in 1978. Therefore, few recent US aid projects in India have been completed and can be evaluated. Employment and income-distribution effects of projects could not be discussed, nor ERORs re-estimated in a major review of two ongoing and five planned USAID irrigation projects (Keller *et al.*, 1981).[18]

The substantial sums spent in evaluating the oilseed growers' cooperative project (NDDB *et al.*, 1983), which was funded from counterpart funds to GoI sales of US soybean oil aid under PL 480 Title II, appear to have been wasted. This highly favourable review was executed by the two agencies which received jobs and cash from implementing the project, plus the two financing agencies. The implementing agencies did their proper job, showing their results in a good light to their visitors.

The most useful USAID project review concerns food aid: in particular the US food aid being used in school feeding (SF) programmes. In FY 1984, this cost US$27.5m and reached 6.7 million beneficiaries, as against US$54.7m (six million beneficiaries) for Maternal and Child Health, and US$34.8m for food-for-work (USAID, 1984, 4). Conventional wisdom is that SF programmes have little nutritional impact on schoolchildren (and/or do not reach the hungriest, who do not attend school) and should give place to other uses for food aid. This study (pp.ii–iii, 25–31), however, shows that school enrolment, especially of girls and in backward districts, is in India increased substantially by SF projects.[19]

The balance between the three main types of food aid projects – food-for-work, school feeding and maternal and child health – may therefore need reassessment in India. Certainly it cannot now be assumed that food aid, whatever the projects supported, must self-destruct by depressing producer prices, with consequent disincentives to domestic food production. Moreover, with India no longer a net importer of grain, food aid should be seen mainly as a form of balance of payments support (Maxwell and Singer, 1979) – normally from donors whose food surpluses are by-products of their farm support policies, would glut grain markets if not given as aid, and are not, if cut, likely to be replaced by other and theoretically 'better' forms of aid. Unlike most forms of balance of payments support, food aid can to some extent be targeted upon needy groups, or can indeed be self-targeting. Further – though a ton of food aid increases food availability by only 0.8

189

tons (Blanford and Plocki, 1977) – this can be concentrated on increasing food entitlements for those at greatest risk (Sen, 1981).

EEC, WFP and 'Operation Flood'

In view of the difficulty of directly targeting food on the needy (Beaton and Ghasseimi, 1982), food aid should ideally consist mainly of 'self-targeting' foods – and/or should be sold by recipient governments to finance self-targeting projects. Cereals, especially cheap foods, would seem likeliest – both as aid to be eaten by the poor, and as extra project output – to enhance income of small farmers, and employment of rural labourers. However, for several years Operation Flood (OF) has provided most of food aid to an India now a net exporter of cereals via OF, the EEC/WFP provides India with milk powder and butteroil – foods that loom much larger in rich people's budgets than in poor people's. GoI sales of these products are then used by NDDB for projects to raise dairy output and processing. These are seen as good ways to help poor producers, because in some parts of India considerable numbers of the landless poor either own one or two animals each or are being, or could be, helped to own them via IRDP loans. Is OF a sensible use of aid? Does poor people's actual or potential producer benefit outweigh the facts that cattle use land in ways requiring more capital and less labour (per acre and per unit of output) than crop production, and produce foods consumed mainly by the better-off?

One would expect objective evaluation of OF, given the importance of the flows. In 1970–81, Rs.1.5 billion of aid went to the first phase, OF I, Rs.1.2 bn as counterpart funds from GoI sales of WFP/EEC dairy products – comprising US$150m from the EEC alone. A further Rs.2.3bn ($275m) from EEC counterpart funds, and Rs.1.7bn from IDA, were projected for OF II, which began in 1978. In 1981 alone, and from EEC alone, Rs.448m of OF aid (48m European Units of Account) were transferred (Zurek, 1982, 4, 16, and 25). A UN Inter- Agency Mission visited India for a month to evalute OF I and produced a lengthy terminal evaluation (Jasiorowski *et al.*, 1981), and – in effect – a one-man mission later evaluated EEC food aid to OF I and OF II on the basis of three weeks in Delhi and Gujarat (Zurek, 1982). There has also been a great mass of interim evaluations, and of papers by representatives, supporters, and critics of NDDB – an excellent bibliography appears at the close of a highly critical and rather polemical review (by S. George, 1984). However, the central questions remain: have OF operations achieved an adequate EROR? Have benefits from OF gone mainly to poor people?

Neither of the evaluation missions was asked in its terms of reference to produce an EROR or any other overall benefit/cost analysis

(Jasiorowski *et al.*, 1981, Annex III). Indeed, neither the WFP evaluation of OF I, nor the EEC evaluation of its food aid to India (entirely to OF in respect of counterpart funds), assessed even cost-effectiveness in regard to OF I or its components. Yet a standard EROR on OF I is feasible and most desirable in view not only of the large sums spent on OF I, but also of their even larger expansion, which is replic-ating elsewhere the central features of OF I: a rather high-tech approach, based on exotic crossbred cattle, greater dependence on purchased feed, and state-of-the-art milk processing technology; plus apparently co-operative, but in fact centralized, management institutions. Plainly, the Bank Group estimated an EROR on OF II at appraisal, before committing US \$150m of IDA aid to it (Zurek, 1982, 15); but a basis in objective economic evaluation of OF I is not reported by the WFP or EEC teams, and no OED documents on OF are yet available.

The WFP evaluation confirms that 'by far the greatest part of milk is used by the medium and high income groups' (Jasiorowski *et al.*, 1981, 77), and that 'milk would be too expensive a food, even at the sale price from village co-operatives ... for promoting increased consumption [by the poor] in preference to other nutritious, cheaper foods' (p.69). The claims that OF aid benefits the poor, therefore, rest upon production of OF outputs. There are two problems of consistency. First, suppose that poor rural producers and employees, engaged in dairy production in OF areas, gain substantially from OF. This must be set against the loss by poor people, on a national scale, from the diversion of resources towards increasing the output (and cutting the price) of costly dairy calories for the better-off, and away from doing so in respect of cheap cereal calories for the poor. This diversion is especially serious because marginal land which NDDB seeks to divert towards green fodder on private and common lands (George, 1984, ch. 7) is likely to be diverted from poor people's activities.

Second, even assuming that NDDB's activities unambiguously, even cost-effectively, help the poor dairy producer, such benefit is nevertheless undermined by the financing of NDDB through 'free' aid in the form of milk products, which when marketed must reduce producer prices. With butteroil, dairy aid is about 2 to 3 per cent of domestic dairy production (Zurek, 1982, 25), and much milk production is consumed by the producing family. So this 2 to 3 per cent ratio of dairy aid to dairy output could well mean a 4 to 7 per cent ratio of dairy aid, by value, to marketed dairy products in India. On reasonable assumptions about price-elasticity of demand, that could reduce producer prices by anything from 8 per cent to 21 per cent.

OF 'seeks to help ten million rural families'. Yet OF I reaches only 1.33 million, and scheduled-caste and landless households are badly under-represented (*ibid.*, 4, 42; Jasiorowski *et al.*, 1981, 63–5).

Even if OF/NDDB benefits only 10 to 15 per cent of the landless poor, this is better than most government production-oriented activities, aided or not. Even if the poorest 76 per cent of farmers provide 23 per cent of NDDB milk, that is a creditable outreach. It is wrong to attack NDDB/OF, on these data, for not reaching the poor. The true criticism is that neither NDDB/OF nor their evaluators have estimated the net benefits to poor people (or others), or the costs of achieving such benefits, in an objective way. Also, we do not know if some districts, sub-projects, times of year, or activities – in this large project, now being replicated with massive EEC/WFP/IDA involvement in OF II – are better or worse than others at benefiting the poor.

If poor milk sellers do benefit, by how much? 'A family's herd average is 1.3 cows and/or she-buffaloes, each producing 1 to 2 litres daily'.[20] Obviously, so little milk cannot support a very significant proportion of income for typical rural families of five to seven persons; a person-day of cattle work normally produces about 10 litres of milk (Jasiorowski *et al.*, 1981, 65).

Although 'the poorest 20 per cent [of Indian villagers] own less than 5 per cent of the milch stock' (George, 1984, ch 7), these poorest 20 per cent own far below 5 per cent, closer to 1 per cent, of farmland, and enjoy only some 5 per cent of total village income. Some evidence has been produced to indicate that the increases in income were generally accompanied by widening income disparities (George, 1984, ch 7) but this in no way rules out major, NDDB-related income gain for poor milk- producers. Perhaps most worrying is the fact that – despite evidence (Moore, 1978) that the mini-herds of small and landless milk sellers make more cost-effective use of scarce land and capital than bigger herds – NDDB/OF technology may greatly and artificially raise unit costs and risks in cattle production, so that it may well redirect advantages (and perhaps also hidden subsidies) towards larger farmers (George, 1984, ch 7; Jasiorowski *et al.*, 1981, 63).

Such technology may displace unskilled labour. The estimate of one extra person-day of work per ten daily litres of extra milk must be set against the fact that 'the new [NDDB] system has replaced to some extent the old methods, [so that] certain employment opportunities have been reduced' (Jasiorowski *et al.*, 1981, 65). Also, to the extent that extra milk is procured from small family herds, owners will tend to supply their own extra labour – especially if landless, and above all in the slack season. As in other cases (see p.181), so with milk production: proper analysis of a project's effectiveness in raising employment cannot be based on partial-equilibrium comparisons of labour requirements from 'before' and 'after' new milk technology alone.

Objective evaluation of EROR, poverty, non-owner employment effects, and replicability of this large, expanding and heavily aided scheme is now essential. We hope that ongoing research at the World Bank may provide the necessary information. At present OF is a costly, promising initiative – probably with a satisfactory EROR, moderate poverty impact, and limited replicability – damaged by the confusion of public relations with evaluation, so that learning effects are lost. The story of OF suggests that both the EEC and (with the striking exceptions of IBRD/IDA and IFAD) the UN system may well, in their world-wide as well as Indian operations, damage the prospects of their aid projects by the imperfections of their evaluation processes.

UK aid projects in India

Around 1983, the UK was spending about £0.5m on evaluation (commissioned and in-house) – well below 0.05 per cent of UK aid – and produced only twenty or so evaluations yearly worldwide, of which about a tenth remain confidential (Cracknell, 1984, v, 3, 29). India now receives 35 to 45 per cent of UK gross bilateral aid. Already in 1976–80, UK gross bilateral project aid to India averaged over £40m a year (ODA, 1981, 46; 1982, 46; 1983, 34–5). For 1981–5, the average rose to over £103m yearly, plus £8m under the aid and trade provision (ODA, 1986, 40).[21]

We saw thirteen evaluation documents published since 1974 (covering completions from 1973 to 1985) but totalling only £21m. Of these documents, two (Wilmshurst and Stevens, 1975; Henderson, 1974) covered ongoing programmes with a British aid input, rather than aid projects. The other eleven evaluation documents (published from February 1974 to September 1986) are summarized in Table 5.4. One was really a pre-appraisal. Five were of small research-cum-training TC operations, totalling only £831,000 of aid. Two covered small 'appropriate technology' projects, absorbing £118,000 of aid.

Therefore, we could review only three evaluations of substantial UK-aided capital projects in India. ERORs had been calculated by ODA's evaluators only for these, a decision discussed below. ERORs at evaluation were estimated at 12 per cent on the totally aid-financed £4.5m tractor project (*EV 36*, and see below), probably an overstatement; at 5 per cent on the £52m pair of fertilizer projects (£7m being UK aid; see discussion of *EV 4* below); and at 18 per cent on the fertilizer manufacturing project, *EV 308*, also costing £52m (of which £8.5m was UK aid).

Except for the Dryland Farming project (*EV 282*) and the appropriate technology projects (*EV 325*), poverty impact was not assessed at evaluation, nor does it appear to have been formally considered elsewhere in the project cycle.

Table 5.4 Some UK-aided projects in India

Project and date of evaluation	Main objectives	Executing agency	Opening date	Duration of the project (years)	Amount of credit (£'000)	Total project cost (£'000)	Credit as proportion of total (%)	Evaluation remarks
1 Birkbeck/Bangalore chemistry link (EV 231) 1982	The training of young Indian scientific workers: 5 PhD's plus 6 under way	Indian University Grants Commission	April 1971	10	167	207	80.7	The fact that four out of five students who have completed their studies are no longer in India militates against the success of the project.
2 Indian manpower project (EV 9) 1977	Training programmes for about 60 middle and senior level officials at GoI in the UK, designed to improve the management and administrative skills of the participants.	GoI	1975–6	<3	126	126	100	Satisfactory. Some of the resources used could also be effectively used to strengthen training capacity within India.
3 British aid tractors in India (EV 36) 1976	3,850 tractors exported from the UK to India, under a UK/India loan agreement. Repayments made by the GoI over a period of 25 years with no repayments during the first 7 years.	GoI	1971	3	4,500	4,500	100	The tractors are likely to cover their social costs. Estimated EROR: 12%. The tractors are owned mainly by large farmers. They allegedly did not displace human labour.
4 Indian Farmers' Fertilizer Co. Ltd (IFFCO) (EV 148) 1980	Providing foreign exchange for licensing of processes, purchase of equipment and for services of foreign experts and contractors.	Indian Farmers Fertilizer Co-operative (IFFCO) Gujarat	1971	4	7,000	52,700	13.5	'Satisfactory' internal rate of return for overall project of about 5%. Cost overrun 6.5% No significant employment generated. Co-financed by USAID: £7m; and Holland: £0.3m.

Table 5.4 Some UK-aided projects in India (continued)

Project and date of evaluation	Main objectives	Executing agency	Opening date	Duration of the project (years)	Amount of credit (£'000)	Total project cost (£'000)	Credit as proportion of total (%)	Evaluation remarks
5 Co-operation with Indian Bureau of Public Enterprises (EV 10) 1977	Training programme. Designed to improve management in priority public sector industries, and assistance with the introduction to India of the Action Learning approach. 22 awards.	GoI	1975	5	44	44	100	The course has been a success. Although it is recommended that the course be repeated in the UK, consideration should be given to ways of transferring the programme to India.
6 Indian Institute of Technology (IIT)Delhi/ British Universities research collaboration (EV 265) 1982	Finance for up to 15 collaborative research programmes between British universities and IIT by providing funds for equipment, books and two-way exchange visits.	IIT/Delhi	1976	6	318	1,243.1	25.6	Although 12 collaborations benefited the Indian economy, only two have immediate practical value for industry, with 4 more offering probable short-term gains.
7 Evaluation study of fertilizer bagging in India (EV 273/282) 1982	To undertake a technical and economic review of the bagging options of fertilizer with particular reference to the Kalol/ Kandla plant in India.	ODA	n.a.	–	n.s.	–	n.s.	The report evaluates five different options, all of which have some merit. It is stressed that a visit to the Plant would have been of much value.

Table 5.4 Some UK-aided projects in India (continued)

Project and date of evaluation	Main objectives	Executing agency	Opening date	Duration of the project (years)	Amount of credit (£'000)	Total project cost (£'000)	Credit as proportion of total (%)	Evaluation remarks
8 Indo-UK dry-land farming operational research project in Indore (MP) (EV 282) 1982	On-farm extension, soil and water management and data collection on a 'micro-watershed' of 2,300 hectares and involving 3 villages.	Madhya Pradesh State Agricultural University; Indian Council of Agricultural Research.	1975	4	176.7	429.4	41.4	Because of the innovative character, higher costs including staffing and supervision were accepted; formal cost/benefit analysis is not appropriate. Socioeconomic impact: land productivity changes which brought about significant increases in agricultural incomes: net farm revenue rose by 65% from 1974 to 1979.
9 Indian Explosives Limited – expansion of fertilizer production at Kanpur (UP) (EV 308) 1986	Expansion of existing urea manufacturing plant by 50% to 450,000 t/yr. plus 12MW captive power plant.	Indian Explosives Limited Uttar Pradesh	1979	2(urea) 6(power)	8,500	52,000	16.2	12% appraised EROR, 18% evaluated EROR; 'outstanding success', but 51% equity owned in UK. Urea technology good, power technology inappropriate – many problems. Aid to private sector recommended. Poor records of aid flows kept.
10 Decentralized cotton spinning in India – Khalidabad (EV 325) 1984	Establishment of experimental cotton pre-processing centre.	Intermediate Technology Industrial Services (ITIS)	1978	5	86	382	22.5	Technical objectives largely attained but more ITIS input needed to achieve desired dissemination to women and poorer communities.

Table 5.4 Some UK-aided projects in India (concluded)

Project and date of evaluation	Main objectives	Executing agency	Opening date	Duration of the project (years)	Amount of credit (£'000)	Total project cost (£'000)	Credit as proportion of total (%)	Evaluation remarks
11 Fishing boats in South-west India (EV 325) 1984	To use a stitch and glue technique to build a strong boat to be landed even in monsoon surf.	Intermediate Technology Industrial Services (ITIS)	–	Ongoing	32	–	–	More testing of boats needed; project has contributed significantly to increased living standards. Economic rate of return similar to financial rate of return 26.4%.

Note n.s.: not specified

Table 5.5 UK gross bilateral aid to India (£m)

Year	INDIA Project aid (excludes ATP)	ATP	TC	ALL LDCs Project aid (excludes ATP)	ATP	TC	Of which not allocable by country Project aid (excludes ATP)	ATP	TC
1981	161.3	–	7.2	323.8	33.3	216.4	0.2	–	70.5
1982	46.2	–	7.7	194.2	62.6	211.4	0.6	–	69.8
1983	110.7	6.7	10.3	236.9	32.6	231.6	0.3	–	80.5
1984	108.6	24.4	13.4	239.4	51.5	240.0	0.1	–	82.4
1985	80.8	8.9	16.6	236.1	42.4	278.1	0.4	–	100.2

Source ODA (1986), Table 18. CDC gives a further sum as project support to LDCs: 1981, £68.0m; 1982, £71.4m; 1983, £51.0m; 1984, £37.0m; 1985, £48.7m. Of this, India received respectively £0.1m, £0.3m, £0.2m. However, only a small proportion of CDC's receipts are from ODA; most are from equity earnings.

The IFFCO fertilizer project consisted of plants at Kalol and at Kandla (Snowdon and Stafford, 1980). It was a two-donor project, with US$20m (£8.4m) from the USA and £7.0m from the UK. Indian sources met the rest of the £49.5m planned (£52.7m actual) capital cost. Kalol produced an EROR just over 12 per cent but Kandla produced a negative EROR. This 'unpacking' of project components at evaluation, so that separate ERORs can be estimated and explained, is valuable and should be commoner. Kalol was on time, due to competitive tenders confined to 'pre-qualified' bidders. Kandla – which would have been stopped by correct appraisal arithmetic – involved risky, interdependent high-tech, in process and scale. Further delay in operation, until a period of low demand, was due to a switch from US to UK aid (*ibid.*, sections 3.2–3.7).

Responding to the House of Commons Select Committee (HOC, 1979) which criticized non-evaluation of large capital aid in India, ODA in late 1986 published an evaluation of a major fertilizer expansion project (no. 9 in Table 5.4). It clearly showed good economic and financial returns, and was sustainable and environmentally careful. However, there are several disturbing features, of which the evaluators (Haley and Hesling, 1986, 9, 12) point out only the first two: the captive power plant combined high-tech with GoI insistence on domestic origin, leading to major delays, cost escalation, and hence bad returns; and a wide range of estimates for actual aid disbursed. Capital aid is £6.3m by ODA expenditure records, but only £4.3m on project files (Haley and Hesling, 1986, para. 5.2).

Most seriously, though just over half the equity in Indian Explosives Limited (IEL) was (and is) held by ICI (UK), the terms on which the aid money was loaned forward by GoI to IEL – and thus, indirectly, by the UK aid programme to British shareholders – are not specified. Of the project's costs *not* covered by aid, part was met by a debenture issue (Haley and Hesling, 1986, para 1.3); in the absence of clear information about on-lending terms for the UK aid, it must be inferred that it was used, at the margin, as a cheaper source of money, enabling ICI and/or IEL to reduce their debenture borrowings.

The two fertilizer projects and the tractor project comprised £20m of the £21.2m UK aid credits in the evaluations of Table 4. The fertilizer projects were adequately evaluated. However, seriously inadequate resources for evaluation of employment, and indeed of efficiency, mark the 1975 evaluation of aid-financed export of 3,850 British-made tractors to India in 1971–4. The method (Dalton, 1976, vii, 6–7) was a small survey in two months in 1975 in which 177 of these tractors were located. The tractor distributors provided transport, interpreters, and introductions to local dealers '[who often joined] our visit to the farmers... At the interview [,b]rief notes were made to be written up afterwards'. The possibility of statistical evaluation was thus precluded.

Not surprisingly, a favourable picture of tractorization emerges. Yet Binswanger, 1978; Farrington and Abeyratne, 1982 and Agrawal, 1980, 1984 all show that tractorization in South Asia has usually proved privately profitable only thanks to hidden subsidies upon foreign exchange, fuel or credit.

UK aid evaluation methods have greatly improved in the 1980s. It is quite unlikely that a 'rush job' such as Dr Dalton's on tractors would be done today. As a rule, it is quick-and-dirty or remote-control evaluations that have to rely on reports by implementers (or other beneficiaries), and thus under-estimate employment losses (or other costs to the poor) and negative off-project externalities. However, it is worrying to see Dalton's conclusions on tractor aid reiterated in a 1984 ODA assessment (Cracknell, 1984, 50).

The great emphasis of UK aid evaluation in India upon small training-cum-research projects creates a problem. It comes out most clearly with the largest such project listed in Table 5.4, Indo-UK Dryland Farming (no. 8). This excellent evaluation (Clark *et al.*, 1983, App D) in late 1982, cost at least £16,800 (fees, travel, subsistence, and administrative overheads cannot have been less than £150 per person-day (£150 x 28 days x 4 persons)). This is 9.5 per cent of total project costs. Good evaluation of small projects appears to be prohibitively expensive, unless more reliance is placed on local full-time aid personnel, and/or indigenous institutions, within India – and on smaller teams. (The alternatives – remote-control evaluations, very brief missions, or just one 'visiting fireman' – probably reduce the benefits from evaluation even more than its costs). Perhaps donor embassies, etc., might co-operate, so that each one need not appoint costly extra *ad hoc* personnel for these evaluations? There could well be all-round advantages if a resident economist at ODA, SIDA, USAID, etc. could each specialize in particular types of small projects and could evaluate appropriate projects for other missions.

What conclusions can be drawn from the UK training/research projects evaluated? There are three overlapping types of such technical co-operation (TC): training in India, training in the donor country, and research. All three types of UK training in India have sometimes suffered from lack of planning (Henderson, 1974, 3; Griffiths and Ackroyd, 1982, 12). Also, lack of benefit/cost evaluation may be justified, but steps to analyse cost-effectiveness are desirable, if donors are to improve on random responses to *ad hoc* recipient demands – or to donors' spare capacities.

Lack of planning for training in India leads to damaging delays because the correct experts cannot be recruited well ahead of time – as is essential to secure them.[22] In default of such experts, people with inappropriate skills are then sent, partly to end the delays. Because these projects are smaller than most aid projects, the most promising remedy – a long-stay donor official in India – is seldom feasible, though donor specialization and co-operation could make it so (Henderson, 1974, 4–5, 13–14).

Training in the donor country suffers from similar problems. Due to lack of planning, the precise requirements of recipients are seldom identified – and training seems to be much more successful when this is possible (Graham-Harrison *et al.*, May 1977, paras 17–18, 37; and June 1977, 13, 15). But the term 'requirements' suggests that the trainee's future, in the home country, is clear enough to be trained for. In fact, job shifts by trainees (Graham-Harrison *et al.*, May 1977, para 26) are a recognized problem. In the longer term 'brain drain' virtually destroyed the gains to India from doctoral training in the Birkbeck/Bangalore chemistry link (Griffiths and Ackroyd, 1982, Conclusion 7, and 11) and this echoes experience by many donors – much more seriously for other developing countries, with fewer facilities for post-doctoral work yet more acute research needs, than for India. If all the benefit goes to the migrant trainee or to the developed country to which he migrates, then an aid project is unjustified; it enriches only the rich, while depriving the 'recipient' country of a scarce human resource. In view of this, it is especially disappointing that the UK does not assess the poverty impact, or even ERORs, of these projects. Partly for these reasons, several reviews of training in the donor country recommend its transfer to the recipient country (eg Graham-Harrison *et al.*, May 1977 para 48; and June 1977, 14; Ball *et al.*, 1982, 17–20). However, this applies much less to shorter-term high-level training, in skills where donor resources, data pools, or contacts with other developing countries imply special advantages for developed-country training over in-country training.

The most serious problem about evaluation of training is the substitution of self-evaluation for objective assessment (Graham-Harrison *et al.*, June 1977, 14; Ball *et al.*, 1982, 17–20). In default of cost-effectiveness comparisons (with baselines) among training schemes, evaluators tend to ask trainees – or their employers, trainers, or administrators – what they believe. Obviously many respondents seek to justify past actions, and to put current realities in the best light. Failing proper cost-effectiveness comparisons, the next best procedure is for evaluators themselves to judge performance subjectively, preferably at the level of sub-projects, separately along a scale of, say, one to five; at least this avoids self-puffing, and permits sub-projects to be compared (Ball *et al.*, 1982, 17–20).[23]

The observation that pilots require baselines, control groups, and evaluation is as central to success in research and training projects as in capital aid – but more often neglected, due to the greater difficulty of suggesting clear-cut cost/benefit procedures. Another carry-over from capital to research/training projects is the danger that high-tech will prove too difficult and complex to manage, especially in interlocking bits. In the IIT Delhi/UK university link, 'equipment which has given most trouble has been prototype or advanced, still needing production development. [Such] equipment should be avoided in future' (Ball *et al.*, 1982, 27).

West German aid projects in India

The West German aid ministry (BMWZ) has made available seven evaluations of Indian aid projects, published in 1980–4. A heavy emphasis on technical co-operation (TC) projects, the scanty evaluations of the much bigger capital projects, and therefore the very low ratio by value of evaluated projects to aid flows to India in a typical year, are features of the West German (as of the UK) programme. This is particularly unfortunate because benefit-cost and even cost-effectiveness analyses are much harder to apply – and perhaps less appropriate – for TC than for capital aid. For flows in the 1970s from the two major bilateral donors to India, to the biggest single recipient of aid from each of them, project evaluations therefore cover only a small part of the programmes, and concentrate on projects where most of the assessment is inevitably non-quantitative and judgemental.

Nevertheless, at least five themes, recurrent in Bank Group, US, and UK aid, are also reflected in the BMWZ evaluations. First, as for the UK, reliance on assessments (self-evaluations) by TC recipients and administrators produces over-rosy views of TC (Fürstenberg and Zech, 1984, 44–5). Second, as with the World Bank, the balance of authority between centre and states proved a major problem. It led to serious excess capacity, and hence uneconomic results, in the schoolbooks project (Weber *et al.*, 1980, 11, 13, 40, 192–3); because the aided printing units were in the central sector, largely unsubsidized, the states (with responsibility for education) ordered mainly from their own or private suppliers. It also led to delays resulting from non-co-ordination of (central) infrastructure preparations and (state) plant materials delivery in a farm forestry project (BMWZ, 1983, A73).

Third, experimental high-tech, with project authorities in the field far less convinced than enthusiasts elsewhere, proved as dubious for West German aid and TC, (e.g. in a gas extraction and mining trial project) as with other donors (BMWZ, 1983, A68–69). Fourth, lack of good baseline data, even for 'key villages', once again impeded project evaluation in rural pilots. This was especially serious in integrated farm forestry (BMWZ, 1983, A74; Fürstenberg and Zech, 1984, 50). In such cases, therefore, replicability is proving very hard to estimate. Fifth, employment considerations, outside of 'poverty projects', once again get neglected in favour of evaluations that judge performance largely via labour-productivity (Weber *et al.*, 1980, 200–1). This defect would have been partly corrected had benefit/cost analyses (and therefore shadow wage rates, which for unskilled workers are normally below market rates) been used.

A new element is added by the West German evaluations of TC projects involving transfer of personnel to India for less than six months. Over 31 per cent of all West German TC time in India in the study period – 332 out of 734 expert-months, divided in 1980-1 among 16 projects – was in such short-run projects, 'the highest of all thirteen evaluated donor agencies, and perhaps of all donors' (BMWZ, 1982, 98, f-19). The appointment of a long-term, donor-financed, India-based person responsible for project co-ordination – not necessarily, of course, a different one for each project – would seem the key to successful avoidance of sequences of inadequately selected, briefed or motivated personnel (BMWZ, 1982, f-22). This once again suggests that donor co-ordination could bring major savings and gains from specialization.

The Indo-German approach is to use TC aid to support a series of 'short-term expert pools' (STEPs). These have been used mainly to co-ordinate consultancies, often for project maintenance or for improved capacity utilization. The unification of sub-project funds gives German TC in India the flexibility (BMWZ, 1982, f-25) provided in other donor agencies by other means: local-office discretion to spend small sums without reference to donor authorities at home (USAID); accelerated central procedures to appraise small proposed outlays (EEC/EDF). The negative evaluation of STEP results at one power plant – 'only 35 per cent of the 149 suggested improvements have been implemented [, and that often only] from a formal point of view....The STEP work has not achieved the objective of improving availability' (Hummen *et al*, 1981, 62, 67) – is explicitly not seen as a criticism of the STEP approach, but of the mistaken effort to use technical solutions in cases where they cannot solve the central problems are of administrative implementation (Hummen *et al.*, 1981, 67; BMWZ, 1982, f-27).

Health projects, SIDA, and voluntary agencies

A 1982 review of projects on health, nutrition and family planning in India (Faruqee and Johnson, 1982) produced interesting results. Cost-benefit analysis is not appropriate, but cost-effectiveness *can* be assessed, if one can see how much death and disease a project has prevented, per dollar, by comparing changes in death and disease in the project area with changes in a comparable population in otherwise similar areas. Once again, lack of baselines and controls impedes proper evaluation of pilots, and hence stops us from learning lessons about what can and cannot be replicated (Faruqee and Johnson, 1982, ix–x, 39–42). Nevertheless, some clear indications emerge.

First, 'integration of services for health, nutrition, and family planning is more cost-effective than delivering separate services, whether projects are multi-purpose or single-purpose'. This is confirmed by a careful study of the Narangwal rural health project in the Punjab, which showed that a given outlay produced a considerably larger health effect when divided between nutrition and primary health care, than when spent on one of these alone (Taylor, 1978). Second (despite a heading stating the contrary), most experience of 'participation' proved disappointing (Faruqee and Johnson, 1982, vi–vii). Third, partly due to intensive use of properly supervised and trained professionals (especially females), 'per capita expenditures in smaller projects that combine health, nutrition and population are fairly low – R3.70 to R21–30 (US$0.49–2.84) – and compare favourably with those by government' (Faruqee and Johnson, 1982, viii–ix, 31; see fn 19 to this chapter).

Sweden, which has concentrated in India on health-sector projects, in 1976 evaluated its monitoring as 'inadequate – notably as regards what goes on in the field' (SNAB, 1976, 32). However, its support to NGOs in Maharashtra appeared to have secured good results in exactly the problem areas of programme integration, smallness, supervision, and use of paraprofessionals spotlit by the World Bank. Penetration of health aid to disadvantaged groups, too, appears to work best with NGO management (SNAB, 1976, 33) – as USAID also found with food-for-work (USAID, 1984). Sweden has greatly strengthened evaluation since 1976, though the lack of formal cost-effectiveness or cost-benefit analysis remains a serious drawback. Nevertheless, indicators are often good (Macedo and Eduards, eds, 1987). SIDA's experiences in areas less familiar to it, however, appear less successful, although lack of ERORs makes this uncertain.

SIDA has pioneered attempts, currently being made by several other aid agencies, to operate with or through Indian NGOs. These, however, achieve their cost-effectiveness, overview, and concern for the disadvantaged largely by recruiting a few dedicated supervisory and professional staff, willing for the sake of their ideals to work at well below market rates. Such people are not 'replicable'. Hence such agencies' health-aid schemes, like the much costlier ones relying on fully salaried staff, each cover only a tiny part of the ground. Anyway, if beautiful is small, replication may destroy. Certainly, in health aid pilots as elsewhere, SIDA's lack of numerical estimates of ERORs or poverty impact in its evaluations is a major barrier to learning. Project aid has many successes to its credit in India, and few disasters; but, to do better, we must devote more resources to evaluative learning-from-doing.

Appendix: Does India's project aid matter?

A case can be made that it no longer does. In 1985–6, aid disbursements from all sources in India were US$2.2bn gross. But only a quarter came as grants, much less than for most LDCs. Of the US$2.2bn, US$0.5bn went back to donors to repay capital, and US$0.3bn interest, on past aid loans. (In 1985 only 6.7 per cent of the US$31.6bn of gross aid disbursements from the OECD to all LDCs went back to repay such capital, and 4.3 per cent as interest (*DC 1986*, 184). The remaining US$1.36bn of net aid transfers to India comprised only 0.8 per cent of GDP, 2.8 per cent of gross investment, or 3.3 per cent of Central Government expenditure. The proportions have fallen steadily, e.g. from 2.2 per cent of GDP in 1975-6, and further falls are projected (World Bank, 1987, vol. 3; *Financial Times*, 27 May 1987).

Yet these statistics understate the role of project aid in India. First, official aid excludes 'other official flows', with a grant element below 25 per cent; but such flows are also partly concessional. OOFs[1] disbursed over US$0.6bn gross in 1985–6 (offsetting about US$0.4bn of capital and interest on past OOFs). Second, partly to retain good access to commercial inflows, India gives priority to meeting past debts whatever the flow of new aid or OOFs. Hence repayments of such capital and interest would happen anyway, whatever the level of gross aid. Thus true aid inflows are best measured gross of repayments.

Third, these gross inflows are formally advanced to finance imports and public development investment. There is some element of fungibility, but not all that much; hence the nominally-financed totals are probably the most sensible comparators for gross aid. It comprised 11.8 per cent of imports of goods and factor services in 1985–6 (15.1 per cent if we add gross OOFs to it), and 21.2 per cent of public development investment (27.1 per cent). These are substantial numbers, though less so than in, say, 1977–8, when gross aid covered 21.2 per cent of imports (or, with OOFs, 23.7 per cent), and 33.5 per cent (37.4 per cent) of public development investment (World Bank, 1987, vol. 3) – and much less so than for low-income countries other than China and India. In these countries, net aid disbursed in 1985 (US$10.3bn) comprised over 40 per cent of merchandise imports (US$25.4bn) (World Bank, 1987a, 220, 244).

The statistical evidence that 'aid to India matters' is somewhat weakened – if the key sequence is supposed to run from aid, via *extra* capital, to growth – by the fact that, by 1980–1 to 1982–3, gross aid plus IBRD inflows financed barely 5 per cent of India's net fixed investment (*RCF 1984–5*, 6–7, 188–9). However, there are four substantive reasons why project aid remains important in India. First – in marked contrast to Africa, where much aid has shifted to balance-of-payments support for maintenance inflows, conditional upon 'structural adjustment' – Indian aid increasingly finances projects. Up to mid-1966, some 22 per cent of all utilizations had comprised US food aid alone. Already by 1974–8, all sources of food aid, oil credits, and debt relief comprised only 19 per cent of utilizations. By 1980–1, these forms of general balance-of-payments support loomed much less large. Oil credits and 'RTA debt relief' (under the 'retrospective terms adjustment') had ceased. Residual food aid was only 9.5 per cent of India's *net* aid receipts from OECD countries alone (*RCF 1981–2*, 6–7, 149, 151, 183, 185; *DC 1983*, 206–7; Zurek, 10), and by 1986 had declined further. Moreover, even such residual food aid was increasingly tied to projects, such as 'Operation Flood'.[2]

Project aid to India needs to 'earn its keep' perhaps even more than to other developing countries. There are two strands to this argument. First, India's aid is harder – more oriented towards loans (albeit soft ones) and more country-tied – than that of most recipients. In 1981–2, grants were only 18 per cent, and untied loans 29 per cent, of gross external assistance[3] to India (*ES 1982–3*, 151); comparable proportions for all DAC aid to poor countries in 1980–1 were 52 per cent and 31 per cent. Since even soft loans must be repaid, and since country-tying effectively reduces their worth – i.e. raises the true repayment burden – by about one-fifth (ul Haq, 1967; Bhagwati, 1970), it becomes especially important that the extra obligations (corresponding to the extra aid loans) are matched by extra Indian earning power, i.e. that aid projects create capacity to repay and still provide Indians with net benefits.[4] Second, until the 1980s, gross foreign savings inflows to India – either specific to projects, or as general transfers permitting expanded project finance – overwhelmingly comprised aid or IBRD loans. In the five fiscal years 1975–6 to 1979–80, they made up 87 per cent of all disbursements of non-IMF medium- and long-term debt (MLD). Only in the 1980s did commercial loans take off, approaching a fifth of such gross disbursements in 1980–1, a third in 1981–2 to 1983–4, and over half in 1984–5 to 1985–6 (World Bank, 1987, vol 3, 37). Even so, of India's outstanding MLD on 31 March 1986 – US$29.7bn – only 22 per cent was commercial (and barely half that was publicly guaranteed). India's repayment performance depends on her government's preferences, and on her overall economic performance. However, the economic performance of the assets built up with India's borrowings depends – much more than that of other comparably large

Third World borrowers – on projects corresponding to the US$20.3bn (March 1986) of outstanding aid loans and the further US$2.2bn, of IBRD loans. Even grant aid has often co-financed projects with aid loans. For India, cost-effective use of foreign savings, good aid project performance, and a satisfactory 'economic' balance sheet on foreign debt, all overlap – much more than for most other LDCs.

Although gross project aid covers barely 5 per cent of India's net fixed investment (i.e. of new projects), it looms larger in public investment. If we exclude the portions of aid flows that go directly to the private sector, or are on-lent to it (mostly as rural credit or via the Industrial Credit and Investment Corporation of India), about 80 per cent of aid inflows go to support public investment. Even the recent substantial expansion of public-sector activity, however, has left it in the mid-1980s supporting 'only' about half of investment. In 1980–1 gross aid utilizations appear to have financed rather over one-third of public sector investment projects.[5] By 1985–6, public capital expenditure (centre and states) at official exchange rates had reached US$16.2bn, of which US$10.4bn was 'developmental' (World Bank, 1987, vol. 3, 51); presumably about US$7bn of this was 'aidable', viz. public development investment net of depreciation. Compared to this, 80 per cent of gross aid inflows of US$2.2bn are a tidy contribution. Admittedly, debt service burdens upon central government, due to repayments of past aid loans, eat up 20 to 25 per cent of this gross aid. All the same, even net normal aid inflows financing 20 per cent of the cost of 'aidable' public-sector projects (i.e. developmental ones, generally not including depreciation) – and that is, we believe, a minimum estimate – are not negligible.

Finally, these inflows concentrate heavily upon a few sectors. In the Second and Third Plan periods, the base of India's massive expansion of the steel industry was largely financed by aid projects. More recently, as outlined in Chapter 3, aid projects (and associated policy dialogue and institution-building) have played a key role in other sectors, such as irrigation and agricultural extension. Hence there are substantive as well as statistical reasons for our emphasis on 'aided projects' as the key to assessment of aid performance in India.

References

Agarwal, B. (1980) 'Tractorization, productivity and employment: a reassessment', *Journal of Development Studies*, 16:3, April.
Agarwal, B. (1984) 'Tractors, tubewells and cropping intensity in the Indian Punjab', *Journal of Development Studies*, 20:4, July.
Ball, J. *et al.* (1982) *IIT Delhi/British Universities Research Collaboration*, London, Overseas Development Administration (EV 265).

Baum, W. (1978) 'The World Bank project cycle', *Finance and Development*, 15:4, December.

Baviskar, B. (1983) 'Operation Flood and Social Science Research', *Economic and Political Weekly*, XVIII:27.

Baviskar, B. (1984) 'Operation Flood and Social Science Research', *Economic and Political Weekly*, XIX:2.

Beaton, G. and Ghasseimi, H. (1982) 'Preschool feeding programs', *American Institute of Clinical Nutrition*, 35:4 (supplement), April.

Beckmann, D. (1986) 'The World Bank and poverty in the 1980s', *Finance and Development*, 23:3, September.

Berry, A. and Cline, W. (1979) *Agrarian Structure and Productivity in Developing Countries*, Baltimore, Johns Hopkins University Press for the ILO.

Bhagwati, J.N. (1985) 'The tying of aid' in *Dependence and Interdependence: Essays in Development Economics*, vol 2, Oxford, Basil Blackwell.

Binswanger, H. (1978) *The Economics of Tractors in South Asia: an Analytical Review*, New York, Agricultural Development Council.

Blandford, D. and Plocki, J. (1977) *Disincentive effect of PL 480 food aid to India*, Ithaca, Cornell.

BMWZ (Bundesministerium für Wirtschaftsliche Zusammenarbeit) (1982) *Der Einsatz von Kurzzeit-Fachkraften in der Entwicklungs Zusammenarbeit*, Band 2 (Anhang), 230-E7110-364/82, Bonn, June.

BMWZ (1983) *Querschnittsauswertung der im Jahre 1982 abgeschlossenen Inspektionen*, 230-E7110-380/83, Bonn, April.

Booth, A. and Sundrum, R. (1984) *Labour Absorption in Agriculture*, New Delhi, Oxford University Press.

Burch, D. (1980) *Overseas Aid and the Transfer of Technology*, Unpublished Ph.D thesis, University of Sussex.

Cassen, R. and Associates (1986) *Does Aid Work?*, Oxford, Clarendon Press.

Clark, N., Clay, E., Jackson, A., and Singh, R. (1983) *Evaluation of Indo-UK Dryland Farming Project, Indore, M.P.*, London, Overseas Development Administration (EV 273).

Copestake, J.G. (1987) *Loans for Livelihoods?*, Final Report on a Project entitled Credit for Rural Development in Southern Tamil Nadu, Madurai (India) and Reading (UK), Tamilnadu Agricultural University and the University of Reading.

Cracknell, B.E. (editor) (1984) *The Evaluation of Aid Projects and Programmes*, London, Overseas Development Administration.

Dalton, G. (1976) *British Aid Tractors in India: an Ex-post Evaluation*, London, Overseas Development Administration (EV 36).

Dasgupta, B. (1977) *Village Society and Labour Use*, New Delhi, Oxford University Press.

DC (annual) *Development Cooperation*, Paris, Organization of Economic Cooperation and Development (OECD).

ES (annual) *Economic Survey*, New Delhi, Government of India, Ministry of Finance.

Farrington, J. and Abeyratne, F. (1982) *Farm Power in Sri Lanka*, Reading, University of Reading.

Faruqee, R. and Johnson, E. (1982) Health, Nutrition and Family Planning in India: a Survey of Experiments and Special Projects, Washington D.C., World Bank Staff Working Paper, no 507.

Fürstenberg, P. von and Zech, W. (1984) *Hauptbericht zur Querschnittsevaluierung 'Schutz Natürlicher Ressourcen als Bestandteil fürstlicher Entwicklungvorhaben'*, Bonn, BMWZ, K8002-54/84.

George, S. (1984) *Operation Flood: an Appraisal of Current Indian Dairy Policy*, New Delhi, Oxford University Press.

Graham-Harrison, R. *et al.* (1977a) *Indian Manpower Project*, London, Overseas Development Administration (EV 9).

Graham-Harrison, R. *et al.* (1977b) *Cooperation with Indian Bureau of Public Enterprises*, London, Overseas Development Administration (EV 10).

Griffiths, I. and Ackroyd, P. (1982) *Birkbeck-Bangalore Chemistry Link*, London, Overseas Development Administration (EV 231).

Haley, G. and Hesling, S. (1986) *An Evaluation of Indian Explosives Ltd's Expansion of Fertilizer Production at Kanpur*, London Overseas Development Administration (EV 308).

Henderson, A. (1974) *UK Aid to Technical Teachers' Training Institute, Madras, 1964-73*, London, Overseas Development Administration (EV 184).

Hill, P. (1982) *Economic Assessment of Bagging Methods*, London, Overseas Development Administration (EV 282).

House of Commons (1979) *Select Committee on Overseas Development, Session 1978-79: the Pattern of UK Aid to India, H.C. 338*, London, HMSO.

Hummen, W., Baumgartner K., and Doka, W. (1981) *Evaluation – Power Station Badarpur: STEP – Missions II*, Bonn, BMWZ.

Jasiorowski, H. *et al.* (1981) *Terminal Evaluation Report on Project India 618 – 'Milk Marketing and Dairy Development' (OFI)*, Rome, WFP (UN/FAO), W/P4590 FAO, reproduced as Annex I in Zurek, 1982.

Keller, J., Clyma, W., Drosdorff, M., Lowdermilk, M. and Sedder, D. (1981) *Irrigation Development Options and Investment Strategies for the 1980s: India*, Washington, D.C., US Agency for International Development, WMS Report No 6.

Lipton, M. (1976) 'Agricultural finance and rural credit in developing countries', *World Development*, 4:7, July.

Lipton, M. (1983) *Labour and Poverty*, Washington DC, World Bank Staff Working Paper No 616.

Lipton, M. (1987) 'Improving the Impact of Aid for Rural Development', *IDS Discussion Paper No 233*, Brighton, Institute of Development Studies.

Little, I.M.D. and Mirrlees, J. (1974) *Project Appraisal and Planning for Developing Countries*, London, Heinemann.

Macedo, N. de and Eduards, K. (editors) (1987) *Project-Programme Follow-up 1987*, Stockholm, SIDA Planning Secretariat.

Maxwell, S. and Singer, H.W. (1979) 'Food Aid to Developing Countries: a Survey', *World Development*, 7.

Minhas, B.S. *et al.* (1987) 'On the Choice of Appropriate consumer price indices and data sets for estimating the incidence of poverty in India',

Indian Economic Review, 22.

Moore, M.P. (1978) 'Some microeconomic aspects of the Indian livestock economy', *Indian Journal of Agricultural Economics*, 33:1, January-March.

Mosley, P. (1987) *Overseas Aid: its Defence and Reform*, Brighton, Wheatsheaf.

Muscat, R.J. (1984) *Technical Cooperation Effectiveness: Determinants, Scores and Prescriptions*, Washington, D.C., US Agency for International Development.

Naidu, I. (1975) *All-India Report on Agricultural Census 1970-71*, New Delhi, Government of India, Ministry of Agriculture and Irrigation.

NDDB/CLUSA/GOI/USAID Project Evaluation Team (1983) *Report on the Evaluation of the Oilseed Growers' Cooperative Project*, Washington, D.C., US Agency for International Development.

ODA (UK Overseas Development Administration) (annual) *British Aid Statistics*.

Papanek, G. (1972) 'The Effects of Aid and Other Resources Transfers on Savings and Growth in Less Developed Countries', *Economic Journal*, vol 82.

Papanek, G. (1983) 'Aid, growth and equity in Southern Asia' in J.R. Parkinson (editor), 1983, *Aid and Poverty*, Oxford, Basil Blackwell.

RCF (annual) *Report on Currency and Finance*, Bombay, Reserve Bank of India.

Sen, A.K. (1981) *Poverty and Famines*, Oxford, Clarendon Press.

SNAB (Swedish National Audit Bureau) (1976) *SIDA in India*, Stockholm.

Snowdon, F. and Stafford, D. (1980) *'The 'Indian Farmers' Fertilizer Cooperative Ltd' Project at Kalol/Kandla: an Ex-post Evaluation*, London, Overseas Development Administration (EV 148).

Squire, L. and van der Tak, H. (1975) *Economic Analysis of Projects*, Baltimore, Johns Hopkins University Press.

Subbarao, K. (1987) 'Interventions to fill nutrition gaps at the household level: a review of India's experience', mimeo.

Taylor, C. *et al.* (1978) 'The Narangwal experiment on interactions of nutrition and infection', *Institute of Medical Research*, 68 (supplement).

ul Haq, M. (1981) 'Tied Credits – a quantitative analysis' in J. Adler (editor), 1981, *Capital Movements and Economic Development*, London, Macmillan for the International Economic Association.

USAID/New Delhi (1984) *Evaluation of PL 480 Title II School Feeding Programme in India*, New Delhi, US Agency for International Development.

van Arkadie, B. (1986) 'Aid Management and Coordination: Some Dilemmas', *IDS Bulletin*, 17, 2.

Wade, R. (1979) 'The Social Response to Irrigation: an Indian Case Study', *Journal of Development Studies*, 16:1, October.

Wanamali, S. (1985) *Rural Household Use of Services: a Study of Miryalgoda Taluka, India*, Washington, D.C., IFPRI Research Report, No 48.

Weber, U., Bleeck, J-J., Hacker, H., and Uhlig, C. (1980) *Hauptbericht zur Inspektion des Projektes der Technischen Zusammenarbeit mit Indien,*

'Schulbuchdruckereien in Chandigarh, Bhubaneshwar und Mysore', Bonn, BMWZ, 23-E7110-257/80.

Wilmshurst, J. and Stevens, J. (1975) *Evaluation of the Industrial Finance Corporation of India*, London, Overseas Development Administration, (EV 217).

Wood, G. (1984) 'Provision of Irrigation Services by the Landless: an approach to agrarian reform in Bangladesh', *Agricultural Administration*, 17:2.

World Bank (1983) *Focus on Poverty*, Washington, DC.

World Bank (1984) *World Development Report*, Washington, DC.

World Bank (1984a) *Tenth Annual Review of Project Performance Audit Results*, Washington, DC.

World Bank (1987) *World Development Report*, Washington, DC.

World Bank (1987a) *India: An Industrializing Economy in Transition*, Report No 6633-IN, vol 3, Washington DC.

Zurek, E. (1982) *Evaluation of the Efficiency and Impact of the EC Food Aid Programme – Country Report: India*, Cologne, Africa Bureau.

Chapter 6

Resource Management, Institution Building, and Technical Assistance

Aid's contribution to resource management and institution building: the organized sector

Since India had a history of the development of western-style secondary and higher education stretching back to the nineteenth century, her need to rely on foreign technical assistance has been very slight, compared with that of many other developing countries. Over the fifteen years of the first three Plans, fewer than 5,000 foreign experts of all kinds visited the country and fewer than 15,000 Indians travelled abroad for training financed by aid (Bhagwati and Desai, 1970, 213). This probably overstates the impact of technical assistance because some of the foreign experts' visits will have been brief and largely ceremonial, while, as will be explained later, the nature of some of the training abroad provided to Indians is general and diffuse. The years up to 1970 were mainly concerned with project-related aid, largely in the industrial sector and in the public sector, while in the years since 1970, more emphasis has come to be placed on aid to large-scale development programmes focused on aspects of agricultural extension, irrigation and credit, forestry, dairying, family planning and health.

In the first period, technical assistance in the form of foreign experts was very much part of a project package. It was part of the human input required to bring new projects up to their planned operational performance. Its cost was subsumed in the normal figures of aid authorization and utilizations and cannot readily be disentangled from them. The impact of these project-related foreign experts on institution-building and resource management is difficult to estimate because of its 'package' nature, but it is not likely to have been very powerful.

The corporate culture within which they worked was dominated by that of the public-sector bodies which commissioned their projects. At this time, the senior managements of these bodies saw themselves as an extension of the administrative service in the economic sphere. The top

211

managers were usually civil servants without industrial experience, often having been brought out of retirement to take up their jobs. Not surprisingly, they often did not stay long. In the three steel plants built with foreign aid, Rourkela in the 1960s had seven general managers; Bhilai and Durgapur each had four (Maddison, 1971, 117–18). At the middle level, plant officials were often anxious to move on as quickly as possible before they were seen to have blotted their copybook. The institutional ethos in which foreign experts worked would have been dominated by the weaknesses that could also be observed more generally in the Indian administration at this time. They were 'distrust of the man below, excessive zeal for collecting even faintly relevant opinions before reaching decisions, and a preference for co-ordinating and advising the actions of others rather than undertaking direct execution' (Morris-Jones, 1971, 138). A handful of foreign experts working on one project within this larger context would have found efforts at institution-building, other than of the most peripheral kind, very frustrating.

The same is true of efforts by foreign experts at improving resource management. Two areas of resource management were regarded at this time by foreign experts as being especially worthy of critical comment within new public-sector industrial projects. One was the tendency to hold excessively large stocks of raw materials. The other was a chronic neglect of routine maintenance tasks. Both implied a failure to observe due economy with scarce capital resources. However, it is very doubtful whether attempts to introduce foreign norms in these areas could possibly have succeeded for long given the wider economic context.

The wider context was what is called in Indian parlance the 'licence-permit Raj' or in western sociologese 'the control syndrome'. The attempt to control economic activity down to an inappropriate level of fine detail was built into the planning system, in the form of individual product quantity targets, from the Second Plan onwards. In the attempt to ensure that these targets were met, the economy was subjected to a very elaborate system of government regulation, including the licensing of imports and investment, and price and distribution controls on 'essential commodities'. Controls on imports, combined with the availability of aid, allowed the rupee to remain significantly over-valued for many years, with the effect that, to the Indian domestic user, imported capital goods and raw materials appeared cheap, but in erratic and unpredictable supply. In this context, abnormal forms of resource management became 'rational'. There was an incentive to buy well ahead of need, in case supply was interrupted in the future at some critical moment, and the full cost of doing so was never brought home to the project managers. Hence, the chronic tendency to overstock. There is also an incentive not to maintain equipment properly. Normal material for maintenance will have been given a low priority and so be difficult to obtain, while the deterioration of one new project can be apparently cheaply made good by the initiation of another new project. In any case, the time and attention of management was diverted into the search for new licences, and away from the routine tasks of stock control and maintenance. No wonder there is so little evidence of creative contributions to institution-building or resource management by foreign experts in public sector industrial projects.

In 1966, a moment came when the 'control syndrome' in India came under severe pressure from foreign aid donors. The World Bank, the IMF, and the Aid-India Consortium all took the view that, in the difficult economic circumstances of 1965–6, an appropriate policy would be to devalue the Indian rupee and to adopt a more liberal approach to the control of imports. The GoI concurred with this view and in June 1966 carried through a devaluation and import liberalization. But it obviously did so very reluctantly and did not disguise the fact that it had acted under pressure from foreign aid donors. The moves were very unpopular with nationalist political sentiment and, for a number of reasons, proved to be largely abortive. Chapter 3 provides a fuller discussion of this episode. In bare summary, GoI did not make a clean break with its former principle of 'indigenous availability', which forbade the import of anything that could be physically produced in India. The supporting aid package of US$900m, which was meant to underwrite the transition to a more liberal import regime by providing non-project aid for maintenance imports, was not drawn down very rapidly. Further, after a year, donors began to withdraw from their commitments and the World Bank's 'promise' of this aid was shown to be unfulfillable (Cassen, 1978, 213). At the same time, the response of exporters, who were in the middle of an agricultural and industrial recession, to the price advantage of devaluation was slow and undramatic. The political opprobrium of caving in to foreign pressure, plus the indifferent economic consequences of these moves together ensured that another big push towards economic liberalization was not attempted until recent years (Bhagwati and Srinivasan, 1975, 157–71). The unwisdom of donors in concentrating on macro economic policy changes, as a non-negotiated condition of continuing all forms of aid, could hardly have been demonstrated more clearly.

As explained further in Chapter 7 (p. 239), certain measures of economic liberalization have occurred since the mid-1970s. More categories of goods have been placed on open general licence for import. In 1978–9, a scheme of rationalization of Indian import policy was implemented. The 1985 Budget abolished or removed import duties on many capital and intermediate goods (Rosen, 1985). However, the basic approach of controlling imports by the use of quantitative restrictions rather than by a uniform tariff, has remained – along with an 'import replenishment scheme' whose structural features strongly resemble the import entitlement scheme that existed before 1966, even if its coverage is more restricted and its coherence improved. Furthermore, a battery of export incentives exists whose net value to exporters is R4.306m (World Bank, 1984: 2: 67; cf. Robinson *et al.*, 1983, 156–7). These are presumably intended to offset the bias against exporting arising from an overvalued exchange rate maintained by quantitative restrictions on imports. Thus, it is fair to say that the basic framework for administrative control over trade transactions is still maintained in India. On the industrial front, there has been no abandonment of government licensing of new industrial capacity – only a recent reduction in its coverage – and it can be argued that the nationalization in 1970 of domestically owned banks increased state control over the private business environment. All of these factors still severely inhibit the role which foreign technical experts are able to play in building up institutions in the corporate or organized sector of the Indian economy.

All this must suggest that the high hopes with which aid donors started their technical assistance programmes in the 1950s were, in the case of India, largely unfounded. The rationale for aid in the form of technical assistance was succinctly stated by President Truman when launching his Point IV Program in 1949:

> The material resources which we (the US) can afford for the assistance of other people are limited. But our imponderable resources in technical knowledge are constantly growing and are inexhaustible.
>
> (Kennedy and Ruttan, 1986, 297)

This sharp distinction between 'material resources' and 'resources of technical knowledge' quickly proved to be unsustainable in practice, leading to the attempt to transfer capital and knowledge together in large project packages. But, apart from this, considerable naivety is evident in the notion that it is the abundance of the supply of technical knowledge which determines the benefit to be derived from technical assistance, rather than the strength and structure of the recipient country's demand. This naivety was highlighted by John Kenneth Galbraith in 1979, when he wrote:

> There were, broadly speaking, only two things, that we could provide to lessen the deprivation (in India) ... capital and ... useful technical knowledge. The causes of poverty were then derived from these possibilities – poverty was seen as a result of a shortage

of capital, an absence of technical skills. The remedy included the diagnosis.

(Rosen, 1985, 229)

Experience of trying to administer this remedy in the 1950s and 1960s proved that matters were very much more complex. India has tended to take what she wanted, and could use within her self-imposed systemic constraints.

Where institution-building by means of foreign aid has been partially successful in the organized sector, it has been because the new institution has found an important niche *inside* the philosophy and practice of the Indian economic regime. One example is the creation of IITs – Indian Institutes of Technology – at New Delhi, Kanpur, and Ranchi. It has been a major aim of Indian policy to build up a strong indigenous technological capability, a human resources counterpart to the policy of capital accumulation, emphasizing heavy industry. The IITs, as producers of high-level skills in mechanical, electrical, chemical, and civil engineering (and many other forms of applied science) have filled an obvious complementary role in the overall economic strategy and have been subjected to relatively few restrictions as they did so. The restrictions have been directed instead towards the import of foreign technology. These tightened considerably after 1969, when the GoI insisted that imports of technology should be allowed only when no similar local technology existed; should be a once-off rather than a continuing process; and should permit only small rewards by way of royalties and fees (5 per cent of turnover, less tax). As the IITs grew in size and strength, they were brought into the official assessment of applications for foreign technical collaborations by means of a GoI Technical Evaluation Committee. Aid for institution-building was successful here because it assisted the GoI's policy of 'technological protectionism' (Cooper, 1984).

A second set of organized sector institutions which have been materially assisted in their growth by aid donors are the Indian development banks.[1] Since Independence, a number of such banks have been set up. All except ICICI are in the public sector, and so fit the GoI wish that the 'commanding heights' of the economy should be in public hands. They currently include the Industrial Credit and Investment Corporation of India, the National Industrial Development Corporation, the National Small Industries Corporation, the State Financial Corporation, the State Industrial Development Corporations, and the Industrial Development Bank of India. Their function is to provide the long and medium-term finance for private business development which the commercial banks are normally unwilling to provide, i.e. loans against the security of land or fixed durable assets, but not working capital. Both the World Bank and USAID have provided equity funds to these new financial intermediaries, which have then been on-lent to the Indian private sector, or used for buying into their equity when they make new issues on the local capital market.

Although the number and degree of specialization of development banks in India has markedly increased, thanks to major infusions of capital by the aid agencies, they have not fulfilled all the expectations of their founders. India still exhibits many of the signs of a financially repressed economy, and her capital market remains imperfectly integrated, somewhat thin organized sector markets coexisting with shroffs and rural money lenders. The paper issued by the development banks is often not very attractively priced and has to compete with other forms of asset-holding. The household sector often has the opportunity to buy assets which are less vulnerable to tax. The demand of the commercial banking sector is constrained because, since nationalization, the government can require it to hold large amounts of relatively unremunerative government debt. All of this restricts the size of the funds that can be transferred to the private sector. Of the funds that have been available, it is sometimes said that excessive caution leads the development banks to favour large, established enterprises. Some analysts (e.g. Professor J.S. Uppal of New York State University) believe that the activities of the development banks have helped to entrench the position of the so-called 'large industrial houses' in the structure of the Indian private sector, rather than encourage new entrants or add to the resources of small unincorporated enterprises which wish to develop as larger organized sector businesses. However, whatever the weight of these negative factors, there can be no dispute that foreign aid has promoted the growth of this new type of institution, or that their partial lack of success in achieving their initial aims is the result of the larger political/economic environment in which they have to operate.

Resource management and institution building: the rural sector

Aid agencies have also attempted to build up new institutions of rural credit in the agricultural sector. A number of these rural credit projects are reported on in detail in Chapters 3 and 5, particularly World Bank aid for the Agricultural Refinance Corporation and its successor NABARD and for state government rural credit programmes. The problem of institution-building here has centred on choice of the appropriate links in the long chain of lending and on-lending for the aid agencies to relate to for purposes of cash injection and policy dialogue. The Bank, for example, wants to withdraw from its initial practice of lending to non-apex institutions, and gradually to concentrate its lending through the apex rural credit agency. Its earlier relationships with the non-apex bodies has helped to strengthen them to the point where it appears that Bank influence can now operate at one or more removes.

However, in credit programmes fed by aid (rural as well as industrial), one has to distinguish the success or failure of new credit agencies from the impact of the wider context in which they operate. In the case of rural credit, the new agencies still face many serious developmental problems. Repayment rates are still poor, but this is by no means a consequence of success in directing funds to those in the rural sector with the lowest capacity for repayment. Cautious views on what constitutes adequate collateral have not succeeded in keeping overdues down to a reasonable level. One may be seeing the consequences of the better-off in the rural sector creaming off 'official' rural credit for 'traditional' money-lending purposes. The Bank's emphasis on financial return to credit agencies – perhaps at the costs of due attention to other matters – may not have been best suited to resolving this contextual problem (Chapter 3).

In the agricultural sector, where the apparatus of official regulation at Independence was much less elaborate and extensive, foreign involvement in institution-building and resource management has gradually become much more important. A major foreign contributor to the reshaping of Indian rural life was Dr Albert Mayer, who was deeply influenced by foreign research of the 1930s (e.g. Wiser and Wiser, 1971). Just after Independence, he established, with Pandit Nehru's active encouragement, a new type of community development project in sixty-four villages of the then United Provinces (the Etawah Project). In 1952, the GoI decided to build on apparent successes achieved at Etawah in crop yield per acre, improved technology, road construction, and the new institution of the 'village level worker'. Significantly, it decided to do so outside the existing channels of the Ministry of Agriculture and created for the purpose a supraministerial co-ordinating agency, the Community Projects Administration, which between 1956 and 1966 became a separate Ministry of Community Development. Expansion of coverage of community development and National Extension Service activities was deliberately designed to be dramatically rapid, with the goal of including the entire country by the end of the Second Five Year Plan. The availability of US foreign aid was the critical factor in facilitating this decision. As one commentator has expressed it: 'probably there was no more compelling reason for Community Development's activation than the availability of external funding and the knowledge that these funds would lapse if not used with a limited amount of time' (Sussman, 1982, 85). Between 1951–2 and 1960–1, the US Government and the Ford Foundation between them provided more than US$100m to finance the Community Development Programme (Brown, 1971, 5).

But the CDP programme showed many of the classic weaknesses of a foreign-funded development programme.[2] It was too grandiose. It was undertaken for essentially political reasons, without a proper appraisal of its long-term viability. It grossly under-estimated the problems of replicating *en masse* the successful features of its pilot project. Local-level participation was induced by the availability of foreign-financed equipment, rather than by much real sense of commitment to the development objectives of the scheme. Performance was judged in terms of intermediate objectives, such as the rate of expenditure of funds, rather than the final objectives of community development. Although over one hundred new training centres for VLWs were set up, only 15 per cent of training time was devoted to agricultural techniques.

This failed effort did, however, leave a legacy of new institutions. India was divided into 'development blocks' and at the village level, a new cadre of personnel was in place to carry out government-assigned tasks at the grass-roots. Admittedly, they were often poorly trained, weighed down by a multiplicity of tasks and used as a distribution mechanism for new agricultural inputs. But they were a necessary element in new and better initiatives on rural development. Unfortunately, and contrary to the original intention, the block development officers and their subordinates down to the village level workers remained a somewhat separate development cadre, not integrated with other administrative and infrastructural services. The block development officers (BDOs) were themselves subordinate to the district collectors, but the BDO's own officials reported to him rather than to the Collector's officials working in the same sphere. For example, the block health officers reported to the BDO and not to the Medical Officer of Health.

This separation was partly a matter of boundaries and partly a matter of finance. The CD movement was 'strong enough to divide the country into development blocks each with its assortment of officers and field workers, but not strong enough to re-align and match to these boundaries the administrative jurisdictions of the allied public agencies, such as the electricity boards, public works authorities, and irrigation offices' (Hopper, 1976, 4–5). Lack of co-ordination was as evident in finance. The central government intended that its funding for community development should merely be a nucleus and that the normal funds of departments would also flow into these projects. The state governments, on the other hand, saw community development blocks as separate entities that would be fed exclusively by central funds and concentrated their own funds on non-CD areas of spending. The institutional legacy of CD was thus some addition to the rural administrative infrastructure, combined with serious unresolved problems in the co-ordination of development action.

Apart from individual foreign experts, like Mayer, and donor country governments, foreign non-profit foundations were also involved at a high level in the formulation of development policy for agriculture. As early as 1951, the Ford Foundation was funding experimental work in fifteen area projects which were later taken over by the Ministry of Agriculture. It quickly identified the need for the training of VLWs and in 1952 funded twenty-five of the 100-odd new Extension Training Centres. With the limited success of the community development drive, the Ford Foundation began the exploration of alternative paths for India's agricultural development. As noted in Chapter 2, a diagnosis was offered in the Foundation's 1959 document, *India's Food Problem and Steps to Meet it* (1959).

In an attempt to learn from the unfortunate result of the over-rapid general expansion of the CD programme, the Foundation now emphasized selectivity, intensity, and complementarity. Certain districts were to be selected and agricultural inputs were to be concentrated there in sufficient quantities and in the correct proportions. This was done in 1961, with the launch of the Intensive Agricultural District Programme (IADP). Indifferent results were achieved with the existing traditional varieties of grain. It was only when the organizational changes of 1961 were combined with the adoption of new high-yielding varieties, especially of wheat, in 1967–8, that the 'green revolution' in wheat yields was achieved in Punjab, Haryana, and Western UP. Foreign-inspired institution-building of the CD and IADP kind was not sufficient to achieve the dramatic improvement in yields of the years 1968–74. But it was almost certainly necessary. It created the preconditions which, when combined with a technological breakthrough and strong economic incentives, did produce, for a six-year period, a very dramatic spurt of development.

The technological breakthrough in agriculture, when it came, also was influenced significantly by foreign aid. As early as 1955, certain US agricultural experts, acting jointly with Indian counterparts, had reported to the GoI that existing agricultural research and education were inadequate, and that the CD programme, which concentrated on the wider diffusion and application of existing knowledge of agricultural practices was lacking an important component for success. As a result of this report, five agricultural universities were established on the model of US land grant colleges in India. In addition, a number of aid-financed institutions for soil analysis and testing the response of crops to fertilizer application were set up.

But fertilizer research, or even increased fertilizer use, as promoted within IADP districts, had a small initial pay-off. Even when new high-yielding varieties were developed outside India, problems remained of adapting them to the varied set of agro-climatic environments within

India. This process of locational adaptation required an indigenous network of high-quality agricultural universities and research stations. Over the last twenty years, such a national network has been developed in India. Under the overall supervision of the Indian Council for Agricultural Research:

> There are (in 1983) 32 central research institutes and 7 soil conservation research and training institutes... (plus) 21 agricultural universities, 73 agricultural colleges (including those at the agricultural university campuses, and 21 veterinary colleges.
>
> (Krueger and Ruttan, 1983, 12–70)

In terms of resources employed and scientific activity, as measured by published work, the Indian agricultural research community has grown markedly in quantity, and quality. The contribution of foreign, particularly US agricultural experts to this institution-building process was a major one, both by helping to identify the need in the 1950s and by financing a set of institutional models in the 1960s.

Foreign influence was important again in one other aspect of the 'green revolution' episode. Once locationally-adapted high-yielding seeds became available, the productivity of a unit of fertilizer in producing grain greatly increased and demand for fertilizer accordingly soared in the middle 1960s. Fertilizer imports had to increase tenfold in 1968 to a value of US\$280m and most of this was supplied under foreign aid arrangements (Hopper, 1976, 11). Additionally, new indigenous capacity for fertilizer production had to be rapidly put in place and a considerable share of this was also financed by foreign aid.

The green-revolution decade of 1963–73 in the history of India's agricultural development carries an important lesson for the use of aid to build institutions and improve resource management. It is not the lesson that was derived at the time by, for example, Schultz (1964), and Rudolph and Rudolph (1967, 3–14). They inclined to the view that, once the technology of modern scientific agriculture was available in the international community, farmers would adopt it (though with inevitable learning difficulties) if it proved profitable. This willingness to adopt innovations would not be significantly determined by the institutional characteristics of the 'traditional society'. If this were so, then the use of aid for institution-building (other than that associated directly with the provision of modern agricultural inputs) would be largely redundant. But this seems too narrow and restrictive an interpretation of the Indian evidence.

The process of agricultural adaption in India was additive or cumulative, rather than one of total or selective substitution. A longish period of experiment and disappointment preceded the moment when *all* the required elements for dramatic change came together effectively

– at least in the most favoured agricultural areas. An intractable problem required a complex solution, involving administration, irrigation, new seeds, fertilizer, credit, insurance, economic incentives, and so on. No single factor solution was appropriate. A policy sequence of switching from, say, organizational change to price reform to new technical fixes would also probably have led nowhere. Techno-economic break throughs and institution-building are both needed for success. India's experience makes one doubt the nostrums of today's western governments that a food crisis can be solved by 'getting the prices right'. It is indeed important that input and output prices are such that producers are suitably rewarded. But this simple-minded approach neglects the problems of improving the elasticity of response of output to price change, which in a poor and primitive agriculture, means inducing massive technical changes in the face of ignorance and high risk (Lipton, 1985).

As the green revolution (in wheat, if not rice, and sorghum) ran out of steam in the early 1970s, agricultural progress had to be sought in new directions. Major avenues were irrigation and the quality of extension work. By this time, the lead was being taken, on the non-Indian side, not by the US Government (as with CD) or by the non-profit foundations (as with IADP) but by the World Bank from its position both as major lender and as convenor of the Aid-India Consortium. The cause of the additional salience of the World Bank at this juncture was the withdrawal of US aid to India to mark disapproval of India's policy during the Bangladesh War (1971). US withdrawal was also responsible for the marked decline of net aid to India in the early 1970s, (Cassen, 1978, 332–3). The World Bank, as indicated in Chapter 2, was, after 1973, switching an increasing proportion of its resources to agriculture and specifically cereal smallholder agriculture.

Recent World Bank initiatives both in the area of irrigation and extension have attracted criticism of their institutional aspects. In summary, the critics suggest that some of the faults of the CD programme in the 1950s are also evident in these initiatives. More specifically, it is suggested that the organizational imperatives of the World Bank, like those of other foreign aid agencies, continue to militate against sensible and sensitive rural institution-building in India. Since a major imperative is the rapid disbursement of large funds, there is pressure to identify quickly-replicable 'success stories' amongst experimental projects. It could be argued that the short time-frame of most World Bank projects necessarily precludes any serious institution-building work. But after allowing for the much greater actual duration of projects due to the delays noted in Chapter 5, this argument loses much of its force. The Bank could do more to understand fully the true determinants of its projects' experimental success and thus to avoid building either the wrong components, or inadequate components, into the process of long-term replication. Further, there must be considerable scepticism about whether the notion of a uniform set of components for widespread replication is sensible at all, given the very varied environmental conditions of Indian agriculture which, as has been pointed out above, had to be adapted to very carefully in the introduction of high-yielding seeds, and which make institution-building also location-specific to some degree.

For example, until fairly recently, the major effort in irrigation reform was focused on making improvements in water distribution below the main water outlet. Particular emphasis was then placed, by the Bank, on the encouragement of rotational irrigation (*warabandi*) outside the green-revolution areas where it already operates, in preference to the existing method of continuous flow. It was believed that where integrated water management had been practised, it showed high returns in terms of additional grain yield over cost. This made it an obvious candidate for replication. It was also believed that the formation of 'water users' associations' was a necessary institutional part of the adoption of integrated water management. Critics argue, however, that the link between *warabandi* and the existence of a 'water users' association' is a weak one. In the pilot areas of *warabandi*, no such associations exist and the system works because the vigilance of individual farmers is strongly backed up by a bureaucratic authority. The insistence on the formation of users' associations seems to derive from an assumption that 'poor water management is caused by the negligence and unco-operativeness of the farmers', plus a hope that 'government itself need not become involved in such messy problems' as enforcing a water rotation (Wade, 1982, 177).

It has also been claimed that in its funding reforms of agricultural extension in India, a similar conflict of objectives – between what is good for the Bank as a lending agency and what is good for India and its development – is at work. The suggestion is that projects 'supported through foreign aid are subject to pressures for uniformity, rapid spread and an appearance of achievement', pressures which 'militate against genuine institutional development, which requires time to adaptability' (Moore, 1984, 304). Currently, the World Bank has been supporting the 'Training and Visit' system of agricultural extensionism which was developed by a World Bank expert, Daniel Benor, from pilot projects in India and Turkey in the 1970s. T and V involves freeing the village level worker from non-extension duties, such as the supply and distribution of inputs: bringing him under the aegis of the Department of Agriculture (in non-IADP districts); and putting heavy emphasis on training him and channelling his newly acquired knowledge, as a sequence of simple weekly 'messages', through a minority of farmers who are contacted according to a strict schedule of visits.

Criticisms of the World Bank's support for the T and V system are, at first sight, somewhat contradictory. On the one hand, the Bank is criticized for evangelizing on behalf of the new system; on the other, it is criticized for not ensuring that it was adopted by all concerned in full and according to the original specification. But the thrust of the argument is really that the Bank was very slow to recognize that it was backing a system which cut against the existing system of incentives (given that input supply was a source of informal income to those concerned with it), and which could be embraced (as it has been, albeit partially) only because it provided material inducements - new vehicles, promotions, and larger budgets - for the senior cadres of the central and state departments of agriculture (Moore, 1984, 312). But this did nothing for the morale of the extension agent himself, who lost informal income, was forced to switch departments, and given a much tighter work schedule to maintain. Some agents were not able, because of age and low educational attainments, to take advantage of opportunities for further training and upward mobility that have been provided. However, other areas show evidence of agent mobility disrupting the routine of extension visits (Feder and Slade, 1986, 412).

Three lessons about the use of aid for institution-building emerge from India's T and V experience: first, successful pilot projects can be misleading. (This reinforces the experience of Etawah and *warabandi* and many other examples). One can be observing a pure 'pilot project effect', deriving from exceptional staff, close outside overview, or the excitement of being part of an experiment. There may also be special circumstances of time or place which are favourable but do not obtain at the times and places of replication. Second, rapid and uniform replication may be inappropriate, for example because it will draw resources out of the existing conventional system. But the funding agency has its own vested interest in not probing the question of appropriateness too closely. Third, outcomes will depend critically on the existing system of incentives plus the material effects of the new project. It is often cheaper and easier to win acceptance for a project at high levels of the bureaucracy and thus end up with a formalistic implementation which no-one except the person at the bottom of the pile has any interest in questioning. And that person may be too alienated to do so.

These lessons do not apply, of course, only to the World Bank and its projects, or only to those of multilateral agencies. Bank projects tend to be studied so carefully precisely because they are large, important, and innovative. Also, the procedures of project evaluation create prospects that critical insights may be incorporated into the Bank's planning at the next round of development effort.

Very similar criticisms can easily be found of bilateral aid to India. For example, a parliamentary review of the UK's bilateral programme contained the following observation:

> In the case of British aid and against the background of chronic underspending of the British aid budget, it is understandable that attempts should have been made to find projects which would disburse relatively large sums of money; and that deepening commitments are entered into to support these projects on the basis of inadequate appraisal.
>
> (House of Commons, 1979, xiii)

As evidence of this tendency, two projects are cited. The first was a fertilizer project of 1978–83, in which £30m worth of fertilizer was to be given to India, the proceeds of its sale within India being used to finance fertilizer extension activities and small capital developments in villages. At the time that the commitment to this project was made, no formal evaluation of the two pilot projects had been done and its potential contribution to social differentiation within affected villages had not been thoroughly investigated. The second project concerned a grant to the Agricultural Refinance and Development Corporation. Again, the disbursable sums were potentially large, the socio-economic effects were potentially significant and the UK Government had 'not been in a position to make a thorough appraisal of this problem' (House of Commons, 1979: xliii–xlv).

Thus, in both multilateral and bilateral programmes, one finds evidence of the phenomenon described by Tendler as that of 'meeting the target' (Tendler, 1975, 85–107). A shelf of projects which is too short leads aid agencies to act as if their capital is relatively abundant and must be committed quickly to justify further replenishment. Ill-prepared projects then inhibit successful institution-building twice over. In the first place, they overlook the need for institution-building, or meet it quite inadequately. In the second place, they produce unintended and undesired results. These results then lead many commentators to the erroneous conclusion that institution-building via foreign aid is inher- ently impossible, and that such efforts should be abandoned. It would be a great mistake to take that view. India over the years furnishes examples of success (development banking, agricultural research) as well as partial failure (community development) and work-in-progress (irrigation management, agricultural extension) where timely criticism can lead to successful modification of an initial flawed design.

Aid to remove administrative and manpower deficiencies

There has been some reluctance on the part of the GoI to acknowledge that India, in some sectors, may lack the capacity to absorb aid effectively. The tendency of the mid-1970s was to suggest that the problems of technology transfer and institution-building had been largely completed in the 1960s. The function of aid was seen as one of pure resources transfer. The concomitant of this was that foreign aid agencies were to be small and inconspicuous. This attitude was clearly in evidence in 1978, when the terms were agreed for the resumption of activity by USAID in India. It also seems to have affected the *modus operandi* of the aid section of the UK High Commission in New Delhi, which was described at this time as 'so understaffed that it cannot begin to contemplate conducting the thorough evaluations needed' (House of Commons, 1979: xlvi).[3]

Official Indian reluctance to acknowledge serious manpower deficiencies, at least in negotiations with foreign aid agencies, seems also to influence decisions on the use of foreign technical assistance awards. As an example, one might cite Indo-British technical co-operation, as highlighted in a recent joint evaluation study. The study found that: the majority of 'trainees' are government servants in mid-career. For IAS 'trainees', a minimum of nine years' service is required before selection for a single one-year overseas study visit. Second, study fellows 'often did not know the precise purpose of the course or scheme and their applications were not part of a considered training scheme drawn up by their organization highlighting overseas training needs' (ODA, 1982, para. 3.2). Third, 'many of the Indians coming for training already have a good grasp of the techniques in their field and are more interested in learning about applications' (ODA, 1982, para. 3.5). Finally, '97 per cent of Indian study fellows said that they were "satisfied" or "very satisfied" with the training that they had received' (ODA, 1982, para. 3.1)

This combination of features suggests a highly bureaucratic programme (both in terms of its subjects and its *modus operandi*), which has less to do with remedying manpower deficiencies inhibiting development than with rewarding loyal service to the Indian Government. At the same time, it is likely a programme of this type must have a considerable impact on improving Indo-British relations at governmental levels. This reminds us that political effectiveness of aid programmes may be quite different from their developmental effectiveness. Such a programme may also be commercially beneficial to the donor, if it strengthens trade and industry links.

If GoI chooses to send already well-qualified people for further training, the only way in which it can be highly relevant, applied, and useful is for it also to be highly specialized, almost to the extent of providing separate training packages for each individual's needs. This implication was drawn by the UK in the mid-1970s, with the initiation of the Indian Manpower Programme (IMDP). Under this programme, some 250 senior Indian officials from government departments and public enterprises undertook three-month visits, intended to be geared to the individual's specific training needs in his or her current position. The results were mixed. The main cause of failure was on the supply side, with approximately one-third of the placements not meeting the requirements that the training should be personally tailored to the visitor's situation. The programme was not renewed, because of doubts about the UK educational institutions' ability to continue to supply such a demanding and labour-intensive form of training. The numbers of Indians coming on regular or standardized forms of training has, however, increased in the 1980s.

As the number and quality of India's own manpower training institutions rises – particularly in development administration and management, agriculture, and agronomy – one has to question the need for continued flows of Indian personnel for standardized training in donor countries. After all, Indian institutions are beginning themselves to run training courses for nationals of other developing countries in project appraisal, development planning, and farm management. So the argument that training Indians abroad gave them an otherwise unattainable international perspective on these subjects is having some of its force eroded, and this trend will surely continue. This argument is, in any case, not advanced by Indian requests that their overseas training should increasingly take place in all-Indian study groups.

Part of the answer may lie in a move by donors to mount short courses on specialist topics where the donor countries have in-country expertise of international quality. This represents a compromise between standard nine month/one year courses and the bespoke-tailored three-month training visits for individuals exemplified by the IMDP. Another part may lie in expanding and rationalizing the secondment of donor country experts to more standard, longer-duration training organized by institutions like the Indian Institute of Public Administration (Delhi) or the Administrative Staff College of India (Hyderabad), if problems concerning the temporary employment of non-Indians within India on this kind of regular basis can be handled.

Unfortunately, experience to date with management of programmes sending technical experts to work in India has not been particularly encouraging. As noted in Chapter 5, evaluation of both UK and West German schemes for the sending of experts to work on training in India have shown marked deficiencies in advanced planning and timely recruitment and, in the West German case, in establishing a minimum period of stay if the visit is to be effective. We argued in Chapter 4 in favour of the idea of local missions organised jointly by aid donors. In Chapter 5, we pointed out that one of the uses of such joint missions would be to improve the organization and integration of short-term technical visits by donor country personnel.

An expanded and rationalized programme of technical assistance for in-country training seems to be highly desirable. At relatively low levels of responsibility, where very large numbers of people are involved, serious manpower training deficiencies do still prevail. Recent analysts have picked this up noticeably in relation to the rural sector, through criticisms of existing aid-funded programmes there. To return to irrigation management, no training was, in the early 1980s, being given to canal managers and this stood in the way of introducing 'flexible' main canal system operation:

> To implement such a rule (i.e. minimising fluctuations around full supply depth within each distributory) requires considerable know-ledge of operating techniques, which India's canal managers in general do not have because – remarkably – they are given no training in canal operation and – more remarkably – there is no body of systematised knowledge for them to be trained in.
>
> (Wade, 1982, 178)

As a key part of an alternative package of irrigation reforms to those currently espoused by the World Bank, Wade suggested that *all* canal staff, including field staff, should have training courses in canal operation. He noted that, 'none of the discussion of how to improve the training of professional engineers has recognized that there is an additional problem of massive proportions – the training of the 80 per cent of non-professional staff' (Wade, 1982, 181). This problem is now being tackled by the establishment of ten or so Water and Land Management Institutes, supported by Bank and USAID money.

In assessing the Training and Visit System of agricultural extension work, Moore noted that some of the elements of the pure T and V system were absent. One important example were the monthly training classes for extension staff by Master Trainers from universities and research stations, which had never been organized at all in some Command Areas in Andhra Pradesh. Another example were the field visits by Master Trainers, which had not been seriously practised anywhere: 'so far the training side of the T and V programme has been almost entirely neglected' (Moore, 1984: 8, 19, 24, note 33). Moore recommended special training courses in agriculture linked to promotion or salary increments, which might help to remove some of the empty formalism that has overtaken the training element in the programme and increase morale of field staff.

227

It is worth noting that neither Wade nor Moore was inclined to believe that lack of training at the operational level affected only the particular area which they were studying. The former suspects that lack of training in the management of complex systems relates to many other public-sector organizations as well as irrigation management. The latter sees neglect of training as 'but a symptom of the wider problem of lack of personnel planning which dogs the Indian public service in general' (Moore, 1984, 19). One can indeed find evidence of inadequate training in other sectors. Very similar problems to those in irrigation and extension exist in the rural health services. In the mid-1970s, some fairly modest targets were announced for the provision of rural health manpower: one male and one female multi-purpose health worker per 5,000 of rural population. This target implied a requirement for 73,000 extra personnel over the existing stock of 20,000 of auxiliary nurse midwives. But the existing rate of training was only 8,450 per annum. Thus, 'a considerable expansion of training facilities would be required to meet the target in any reasonable length of time (and) to allow both for further population growth and exits from posts' (Cassen, 1978, 195). This view that changes would be inordinately delayed unless the bottleneck in training rural health workers was broken was endorsed by the GoI itself (Cassen, 1978, 196). This situation has, in essence, altered little in the last ten years.

The requirement for large-scale, relatively low-level training, largely in the rural sector, is one that existing technical assistance programmes – foreign-focused, elitist, and urban-based – do very little to touch. This kind of training must be done in India, be tailored to the particularities of the local environment, and without foreigners playing too visible a part in the training process. However, this does not imply that aid can play no useful role. In fact, in the late 1980s, individual aid agencies are trying to find acceptable ways of responding to the need. USAID has adopted a strategy based on a sequence of resource transfer – identification of appropriate technology – suggestions for institutional change. Initially, resources have to be transferred in quantities that are significant within a central or state ministry's budget for the project or programme. Once the resources are accepted, help is offered, either directly or through the funding of consultancy studies, in identifying a set of measures likely to achieve the project/programme's objectives. Finally, where there are evidently institutional barriers to the adoption of required measures, suggestions for institutional changes may be seen as helpful, rather than as gratuitous interference. As a result of this sequence, the further development of Indian training and educational institutions has emerged as a point of emphasis in USAID's programmes for the irrigation, forestry, and health sectors.

In comparison, the UK bilateral efforts are extremely small (some thirteen technical co-operation officers (in man-years) working in India in 1986 (see ODA, 1987). In addition to involvement in planning low-cost housing, child welfare and community health care, a growing emphasis was evident on contributing expertise in the field of education. (House of Commons, 1979, xl). Institutionalizing expertise through strengthening Indian training institutes has still to figure prominently on the UK technical assistance agenda. It would appear that more could, and should be done here, on similar lines to USAID. An extension and redirection of British libraries and book presentations from urban to rural areas might be a modest first step.

One should not be tempted to get such suggestions out of perspective. Even if foreign aid for this kind of indigenous rural training were increased many times over, its contribution in a country the size of India would still remain marginal. At best, and if it showed good results, it would serve as a practical counterpart to the policy dialogue which aid sometimes permits, a highly selective joint demonstration that what had previously been taken to be impractical was not necessarily so.

References

Bhagwati, N.N. and Desai, P. (1970) *India: Planning for Industrialization*, London, Oxford University Press, for the OECD.

Bhagwati, J.N. and Srinivasan, T.N. (1975) *Foreign Trade Regimes and Economic Development*, India, New York, Columbia University Press.

Brown, D. (1971) *Agricultural Development in India's Districts*, Cambridge, Mass., Harvard University Press.

Cassen, R.H. (1978) *India: Population, Economy, Society*, London, Macmillan.

Cooper, C. (1984) 'Technical co-operation between South Asian and European industry: the case of India', Brussels, Centre for European Policy Studies.

Feder, G. and Slade, R. (1986) 'A comparative analysis of some aspects of the training and visit system of agricultural extension in India', *Journal of Development Studies*, 22: 2, January.

Ford Foundation (1959) *India's Food Problem and Steps to Meet It*, New Delhi.

Hopper, W.D. (1976) *Food Production in India*, Ottawa, International Development Research Centre.

House of Commons (1979) *The Pattern of United Kingdom Aid to India*, First Report from the Select Committee on Overseas Development, Session 1978–9, London, Her Majesty's Stationery Office.

Kennedy, J.V. and Ruttan, V.W. (1986) 'A re-examination of professional and popular thought on assistance for economic development: 1949–52', *The Journal of Developing Areas*, vol. 20, April.

Krueger, A.O. and Ruttan, V.W. (1983) *The Development Impact of Economic Assistance to LDCs*, vol. 2, ch. 12 (mimeo).

Lipton, M. (1985) 'Research and design of a policy frame for agriculture', in T. Rose, 1985 (ed), *Crisis and Recovery in sub-Saharan Africa*, Paris, OECD Development Centre.

Lipton, M. (1987) 'Improving the impact of aid for rural development', *IDS Discussion Paper 233*, Brighton.

Maddison, A. (1971) *Class structure and Economic Growth: India and Pakistan since the Moghuls*, London, Allen and Unwin.

Moore, M. (1984) 'Institutional development, the World Bank and India's new agricultural extension programme', *Journal of Development Studies*, 20: 4, July.

Morris-Jones, W.H. (1971) *The Government and Politics of India*, London, Hutchinson, third revised edition.

Overseas Development Administration (ODA) (1982) *Review of the Indo-British Technical Co-operation Training Programme*, London.

Overseas Development Administration (ODA) (1987) *British Overseas Aid 1986: Annual Review*, London.

Robinson, A., Brahmananda, P.R. and Deshpande, L.K. (eds) (1983), *Employment Policy in a Developing Country: the Case of India* (2 vols) London, Macmillan.

Rosen, G. (1985) *Western Economists and Eastern Societies: Agents of Change in South Asia, 1950-70*, Baltimore and London, Johns Hopkins University Press.

Rudolph, L.I. and Rudolph, S.H. (1967) *The Modernity of Tradition: Political Development in India*, Chicago and London, University of Chicago Press.

Schultz, T.W. (1964) *Transforming Traditional Agriculture*, New Haven, Yale University Press.

Sussman, G.E. (1982) *The Challenge of Integrated Rural Development in India: a Policy and Management Perspective*, Boulder, Colorado, Westview Press.

Tendler, J. (1975) *Inside Foreign Aid*, Baltimore, Johns Hopkins University Press.

Wade, R. (1982) 'The World Bank and India's irrigation reform', *Journal of Development Studies*, 18: 2, January.

Wiser, W.H. and C.V. Wiser (1971) *Behind Mud Walls 1930-60*, Berkeley, Los Angeles and London, University of California Press.

World Bank (1984) *Situation and Prospects of the Indian Economy: a Medium Term Perspective*, Report 4962 – IN, 3 vols., for official use only.

Chapter 7

Aid and Market Forces

The 'control syndrome' and the market critique

Ever since the Aid-India Consortium was formed in 1958, aid has been accused of helping to repress or distort market forces. In 1958–63, this market critique had little impact on either Indian policy or foreign aid. Indian consensus around the Nehru-Mahalanobis view (of social democracy spearheaded by forced savings via capital-intensive and state-owned industrialization) complemented the donors' neo-Keynesian consensus (around a 'big push', state-led even in a private enterprise economy, in which numerous expanding sectors would demand one another's extra products) (Mahalanobis, 1955; Nurkse, 1953). On such models, aid would help the GoI to set up an infrastructural and industrial base for steady private-sector growth in India, and to maintain balanced expansion of markets, not to undermine them.

The costs, inefficiencies, economic rents, and at times corruption, involved in this somewhat inward-looking and anti-rural set of perceptions – and its tendency to produce a control syndrome – have challenged Indian and donor faith in Nurkesean nostrums. For twenty-five years, the market critique has been regularly revived and reviled, rather than developed, proved or disproved. Not new knowledge or power, but fashions (in academic economics and US politics,[1] with the World Bank as honest but puzzled broker) have induced varying Indian and donor responses to the market critique. Therefore, the variations have been more rhetorical than real. Does aid help governments to support, correct, complement, or destroy markets? Has aid to India been sufficient (or consistent) enough to do any of these things?

The market critique of aid to India was first adumbrated by Professor Shenoy in a dissenting note to the background papers for the formulation of the Second Five Year Plan in 1955 (see also Shenoy, 1963, 1968). This theme was developed *con brio* by Lord (then Professor) Bauer. Having noted the extensive range of government controls over the activities of the private sector, Bauer continued:

> They necessarily retard the development of the controlled
> industries and the progress of the most efficient units and both in
> these industries and in the economy at large they inhibit the most
> efficient deployment of resources and also their growth. As they
> cannot take account of individual differences, specific controls also
> prevent people from making marginal decisions in accordance with
> their individual circumstances. In view of the diversity of social
> and economic conditions in India such measures are, therefore,
> especially likely to result in economic waste.
>
> (Bauer, 1959, 65)

Bauer's argument for the wasteful effect of government controls on the private sector was not an argument against 'big government'. He recognized that development required 'far-reaching and effective government action over a vast range' (Bauer, 1959, 114). Nor was it an argument against socialism as such: it was simply that 'Socialist policies based upon (false economic ideas) are likely to be wasteful in terms of their own objectives, which could be achieved at lower cost' (Bauer, 1959, 89). Indeed, Gunnar Myrdal developed a closely comparable critique of the control syndrome (and also parallelled Bauer's concern about discretionary controls as a cause of corruption) from a socialist standpoint, and long before he abandoned his then strong support for aid to India (Myrdal, 1968).

Subsequent discussion of this argument has tended to go in two rather different directions. The more fruitful has been the documentation and fuller analysis, in relation to industry and trade, of the claim that GoI controls have been perverse given the government's stated objectives (e.g. Bhagwati and Desai, 1970; Bhagwati and Srinivasan, 1975). Less useful has been discussion which overlooks Bauer's own clarification of his argument and extends it to an attack on widespread government activity as such or the pursuit of socialist goals (e.g. Roy, 1984, esp. 68–9). The Bhagwati-Desai-Srinivasan work concludes, surely correctly, that many regulations in the Indian economy have been excessive, inefficient, and counter-productive. For example, import restrictions – ostensibly designed to save foreign exchange – stimulated domestic production so inefficient as to *worsen* the balance of payments. As for domestic controls, Chapter 6 outlines some effects on industrial management in the public sector, which have inhibited institution-building (even despite appropriate foreign technical assistance).

It may be useful to try and understand why most senior, powerful, thoughtful and honourable Indian administrators, politicians, and advisers in 1948–63 so strongly favoured the adoption of economic controls that clearly risked proving restrictive, corruptible, or otherwise inefficient. In a newly independent country, GoI needed to show that its democratically based powers sufficed to give direction to India's economic future. That basic truth would have applied, even had Nehru and his colleagues been market liberals rather than (as they were) industrializing, nationalizing and welfarist Fabians. GoI feared two alternative sources of economic power, which were thought to be capable of preventing it from moving the economy in any desired direction: foreign private enterprises and domestic 'large industrial houses'. The GoI did not want foreign groups to control assets central to the industrialization drive; the support of indigenous capital for the independence movement, and its subsequent acceptance of planning,[2] made it natural for Nehru and his colleagues to see it as 'committed to India's national interests' as foreign capital could not be. Yet they also distrusted, as another major source of possible countervailing power, the 'large industrial houses'. They were highly diversified businesses usually under the control of a single family group; the Birlas, the Tatas, the Tandons, or Dalmia Sahu Jain. Both groups were also thought by the GoI to be capable of diverting or frustrating national economic plans.

In the early 1950s, the GoI took a dim view of any form of private enterprise that did not ally itself fully with the goals of the Five Year Plan. Explicitly responding to Mahatma Gandhi's notions of capitalist 'trusteeship', India's administrative and intellectual élite saw the economy, not as a conventional mix of private and public activity, but as a seamless unity in which the profit motive was partly diverted to, partly superseded for the public good:

> The concept of private enterprise, as, indeed, of private property, is undergoing rapid change and the view that private enterprise can function only on the basis of unregulated profits is already an anachronism.... The private and public sectors cannot be looked on as anything like two separate entities; they are and must function as parts of a single organism.
>
> (GoI, 1952)

Practice departed somewhat from this vision. In 1960, the Indian Government's attitude to the private sector was summed up, by a seasoned observer, in the words of Alexander Pope: the government was 'willing to wound, and yet afraid to strike' the private sector (Gregory, 1961, 145). Neither private enterprise nor private property had been seriously tampered with, apart from Zamindari abolition.[3] State industry and infrastructure were largely additional to – and less competitive, with them providing cheap inputs for – private business; only in 1969 did nationalization (of the banks) become briefly significant.

Yet private business had already, by 1961, been hemmed in by the control syndrome: a massive regulatory apparatus based on legislation covering foreign exchange allocation, industrial development, essential commodities, and the supply and prices of goods. A former economic adviser to the GoI (Little, 1982, 50, 33), speaks of 'the basic mistrust of the price mechanism that permeates Indian intellectual society to this day', but correctly noted:

> Even in India, however, the supply of, and demand for, the vast majority of things is a by-product of market forces and those particular controls that happen to impinge on them, rather than a matter of conscious planning.
>
> (Little, 1982)

The Indian Government's distrust of private enterprise, and high propensity to regulate it, have never amounted to a fundamental 'socialist' challenge. To the extent that a symbiosis has occurred between business and government, moreover, it is of a very different character from that envisaged in the First Plan. Rather, India's 'control syndrome' was a substitute for socialism. It satisfied some left-wing Indian intellectuals while creating spoils for, and increasingly, financing the Congress Party; and it created economic rents – status and influence for many honest bureaucrats and politicians, power and bribes for a few corrupt ones and huge extra profits for the 'large industrial houses' it was designed to control. All this is not meant to sound – as it so often does – like a condescending critique. History cannot be unpicked. India's federal and free democracy, fairly steady growth, and serious concern for the poor are part of the same picture as India's control syndrome; the same power balance sustains both.

Yet the results of the control syndrome were, and remain, inefficient and unjust. The fault lay in the deficiency of the type of planning that was pursued in the 1950s and 1960s. These plans comprised firm statements of intended levels and structures of activity for both public and private sectors – but no set of consistent means to obtain the private targets. Assorted incentives and controls, therefore, 'just growed', like Topsy. An enthusiastic advocate of development planning saw the defect clearly:

> The plans are silent on the crucial problem of how to achieve a rational co-ordination of controls so that *together* they direct development towards plan fulfilment. This means that the plans are not 'operational'. From another point of view, it indicates that implementing measures are not really planned in advance, but are improvised in an *ad hoc* fashion.
>
> (Myrdal, 1968, 902)

The same analyst neatly describes the paradoxical consequences of uncoordinated *ad hoc* controls:

> While everybody talks about the necessity of encouraging private enterprise, and while a great number of controls are instituted with this end in view, most officials have to devote most of their time and energy to limiting or stopping enterprise... With somewhat less encouragement, there would be less need for curtailment.
>
> (Myrdal, 1968, 925)

From the perspective of the late 1980s – where Indian private industry, protected and coddled as well as controlled, has for two decades responded sluggishly to an agricultural upsurge – it is even more relevant that with less curtailment there would be less need for encouragement. Also, avoiding curtailment wastes resources; businessmen in India had to spend an increasing share of their time in making and maintaining contacts with government agencies and officials. As in Pakistan, it paid businessmen better to finagle licences than to be good managers or entrepreneurs. The social cost of this time and effort never entered into the calculations of the planners: nor did the social costs of any corruption that might have ensued, as a result of the power over individual firms' profit prospects which controls conferred on officials. It was not until the mid-1970s that Indian experience was used to construct a theory of the costs of time spent in 'rent-seeking' to evade – or gain privileges from – economic controls (Krueger, 1974; cf. Toye, 1987; 117–27).

The effects on private foreign investment

It is difficult to say if either the 'control syndrome', or other Indian policies affecting private foreign investment (PFI) – even if either was affected by aid – in fact turned significant PFI away from India in the early years of planning. Below 5 per cent of Indian capital was foreign-owned at Independence. Most of this was British, and Britain's share in world PFI steadily dwindled in 1950–80. The USA was the main source PFI in the 1950s, but mostly directed towards Latin America. Formally, the GoI welcomed PFI. It promised in April 1949 to grant equal treatment of foreign and national firms in its industrial policy; 'reasonable facilities, consistent with the foreign exchange position' for profit remittances; and 'fair and equitable' compensation for nationalized assets. Although policy has changed somewhat in its degree of openness to PFI during the 1960s and 1970s (Lipton and Firn, 1975, 83–4), these three promises have been kept. But for foreign investors they did not go very far. There was considerable uncertainty, encouraged by the language of the Plans already quoted, about how far

India would go towards a 'socialistic pattern of society'. Equal treatment with national firms was hardly an attractive proposition given the shape of such treatment under the GoI's industrial policy. It was clear from 1957-8 that investors – private and Indian – would be chronically short of foreign exchange for some time. The only real incentive for PFI was the opportunity to benefit from the highly protected domestic market for consumer goods which the pursuit of import-substituting industrialization was creating.

The GoI has always been ambivalent about foreign savings; most Plan documents aimed at declining foreign inflows, even if in the form of aid, as a desirable route to self-reliance. Yet, within this ambiguously welcomed foreign savings, loans or grants to GoI (from international bodies or on a government-to-government basis) were more welcome than PFI. One obvious reason was that it increased the GoI's direct control over the disposition of such funds[4]. Another was the government's high priority for economic activities which were regarded as 'sensitive' because they had links with national military and economic security. Most in the GoI also believed that past PFI had neither promoted Indian exports nor transferred technology to Indian hands.

Indeed, Kidron (1965) documented four main failings of PFI in India; yet each of his criticisms can be traced, not to PFI alone, but to its interaction with the control syndrome. (i) Foreign investors' prices for their products were 50 to 100 per cent above those prevailing in their countries of origin, far more than can be explained by rupee over-valuation; yet this was not surprising, if foreign investors tolerated big set-up costs (imposed by GoI conditions) precisely in order to reap profits behind India's high protective barriers against imports (also imposed by GoI). (ii) Foreign investors were reluctant to earn foreign exchange by exporting— again, not surprising considering the anti-export bias of the GoI's foreign-exchange and foreign-trade regime (Bhagwati and Desai, 1970; Bhagwati and Srinivasan, 1975). (iii) Foreign investors' costs of production were high, with excessive patent fees, royalties, and management charges; but this was because licensing restricted competition, and was *required* by foreign investors because such charges 'invisibly' lifted their remittance profit ratios above legal, but uncompetitively low 'visible' levels. (iv) PFI brought in too many different types of equipment, yet they failed to transmit knowledge, skills, and processes to their Indian partners; but more open Indian competition would have frustrated such policies. All four failings, interpreted by the GoI as weaknesses of foreign investment, were in fact thus only as it operated in the controlled Indian environment. Unwilling to change that environment radically, the Indian Government was probably sensible in seeking to attract PFI only on a modest scale and only when the balance of payments has been weak and the aid prospects poor. PFI has been regarded only as a useful make-weight in a tight financial situation, but nothing more, given its weaknesses while the control syndrome prevailed. We later return to the very doubtful claims that aid increased the severity of the syndrome until the late 1970s; that aid (or anything else) has much reduced it in the 1980s; and that the (undesirable) syndrome can somehow be detached from other, more attractive, features of India's developing economy and polity. If such claims are, as we believe, unfounded, there is not a great chance for a major increase in PFI's role in India in the 1990s.

The control syndrome and domestic business

Rather different considerations prevailed in shaping the GoI's attitude to domestic private capital. The Plans' strategy of rapid industrialization based on indiscriminate, rather than selective, import substitution implied: (i) substantial capital formation in novel and defence-related areas of production; and (ii) high rates of effective protection across the full range of tradeable goods. As for (i), GoI saw the domestic private sector as too weak – too lacking in either capital or risk-taking entrepreneurship – to enter new fields, or to be appropriate owners of industries that would be critically related to national defence and security. Thus the new heavy industries of metal fabrication, engineering, and petrochemicals became largely the responsibility of the public sector. Yet GoI also saw the domestic private sector as so strong that unless heavily controlled, it would make excess profits from (ii). With protection, the 'large industrial houses' would enjoy lucrative domestic near-monopolies in certain commodities; hence their prices, imports and investment had to be strictly controlled. As Nehru put it to the Lok Sabha in 1956:

> Why should we fritter away our energies in pushing out somebody who is (building up industry) in the private sector? There is no reason *except that the private sector might build up monopoly*, might be building economic power to come in the way of our growth. *I can understand (the need to) prevent that, control that, plan for that.*
>
> (cited in Lewis, 1962, 207; his emphasis)

Political considerations also played their part. The large industrial houses include newspapers among their commercial interests. In the early 1970s, thirty-one of the forty-two top-circulation newspapers in India were owned by four major private companies: Express Newspapers, Hindustan Times, Bennett Coleman, and Statesman. Each of these four companies is part of a larger industrial conglomerate.

237

> The Goenkars, who control the Express Newspapers ... have interests in tea, chemicals, automobiles, cement, and sugar; the Birlas, who own the *Hindustan Times*, are in tea, jute, textiles, automobiles, aluminium, and consumer goods; Bennett Coleman's owners are in cement, coal, mining and paper; and the owners of the *Statesman* have interests in steel, heavy engineering, textiles, coal, mining, paper, chemicals, and consumer goods.
>
> (Hiro, 1976, 243)

In the 1950s there was a real fear that the economic power of the large industrial houses, if allowed to grow through unbridled monopoly, could be transformed into political power, by control over public opinion through newspaper ownership. This was especially worrying for a government committed to bringing about a 'socialistic pattern of society' and it strengthened its determination to control the large corporate sector. There are two alternatives: GoI control over the 'monopolists' press', as in the 1975–7 Emergency; or running battles between a Congress Government and courageous (but 'monopoly-linked') critics, as with the *Indian Express* in 1987. Most would agree that such alternatives are even less palatable in a free democracy than is the control syndrome for a 'free' economy.

Because economic controls were not rationally co-ordinated, and because private and public sectors developed personal interests in the economic rents created by both the controls and their irrationalities, controls have not had – some would say, could not have had – the results expected of them. Luxury import controls have not reduced luxury consumption, because rich people's incomes have grown faster than poor people's (i.e. the government's fiscal impact on the internal income distribution has been weak), so that luxury demand is now satisfied by domestic production, usually with higher unit costs. Protection, plus the restriction of entry via investment licences, means that profits in these luxury lines are high. So private enterprise has found ways of using licensed capacity for such purposes, and of adding unlicensed capacity undetected. However, such inward-looking bias against tradeable goods is least harmful in large developing economies, like India's, with very high ratios of domestic to foreign consumption. Despite import licensing, the almost continental scale of potential substitute products makes it more likely that a domestic producer will be low-cost. This might appear to justify its infant-industry protection, but only if such protection were necessary and sufficient for the internal Indian competition to emerge.

In fact, the original aim of curbing the large houses and bringing about a wider ownership of industrial assets has not been realised. As the Dutt Committee reported in 1969:

Not only was no attempt made to use licensing to prevent the further growth of the larger Industrial Houses, but the process actually worked in their favour, because they could better afford to maintain constant contact with the relevant officials.

(Nath, 1983, 45)

Thus they were the first to obtain relevant official information, and were well-drilled in satisfying all the bureaucratic requirements of an application. Some of them also discovered how to beat the system by making multiple applications ahead of need, so that officials concluded that there was adequate capacity in the product line, and rejected licence applications from potential competitors (Hazari, 1967, 8–9).

The attempt in 1970 to strengthen the anti-monopoly effect of industrial licensing by establishing a Monopolies Commission, under the Monopolies and Restrictive Trade Practices Act of 1969 (the MRTP) did not significantly change matters. It is an advisory body only, and has advised rejection of less than 5 per cent of the applications which it has been asked to consider. In one way, it has made matters worse: it has laid special requirements of registration (and extra stages of application processing) on 'large' firms, irrespective of whether they have a significant share of their markets. Large houses are regulated as such, rather than enterprises (whether small or large) which possess monopoly power. These new restrictions on large houses were counterbalanced in 1973 with measures which allowed them to invest in certain industries reserved since 1956 for the public or small-scale sectors, provided that more than half of the additional output was exported. However, during the 1970s, the size limits which triggered the MRTP procedures were never adjusted for inflation and more and more firms were being caught in the MRTP net. Despite being ineffective, the legislation became a major irritant to the private sector, until the 1985 'liberalization' Budget at last made a long-overdue adjustment upwards (Rubin, 1985).

Donors and the control syndrome

The failure of controls on Indian private enterprise to achieve their intended purposes of limiting luxury consumption and curbing the economic power of the large industrial houses has not led to a 'bonfire of controls'. Nor has the fact that controls over PFI plainly encourage it to behave exactly as the GoI does *not* want. Controls still in the 1980s remain on the statute book, although their administration has often been relaxed. The budgetary moves in 1985–6 to relax such controls further have clearly run into the sand (Harriss, 1987; Manor, 1987). The Indian private sector has long protested against controls, while declaring its loyalty to the goals of national planning. The aid agencies, as will be seen in the following sections, have become more articulate in recent years in arguing the case for liberalization of controls on the private sector. If such advocacy can be kept separate from instant conditionality and an arrogant pressure for smaller or weaker public sector activity, it may in time bear fruit. Yet the structure of economic power – and of support for political parties – in India remains favourable to the comparative alliance of senior officials, large houses, the ruling party, and 'controls' giving economic rents to them all. Nor is it clear that this alliance is politically separable from the delicate combination of democracy, control, and federalism on which India's stability is based.

This is not to say that vested interests (which the controls themselves have helped to create) will now prevent all change (e.g. Roy, 1984, 68–9). This view is much exaggerated. To the extent that controls have created vested interests in India, the process has gone less far than in many African countries. There is therefore ground for hope that, with vigorous policy dialogue with the aid agencies, the process is still reversible. But attempts to mitigate the control syndrome must be separated from dogmatic attempts to reduce the size of the state sector, or to abuse aid by renewing the macroeconomic arm-twisting that proved so self-defeating in the late 1960s (Chapter 3).

How much aid goes to the private sector?

One of the most persistent critics of the effects of overseas aid is Lord Bauer. This is his most relevant criticism for the discussion of aid and market forces:

> Official transfers have also often helped to bring to the fore governments' hostility to the market system and sympathy for the Soviet ideology. This is because aid goes directly to governments and ... tends to politicise life in the recipient countries. The effect is reinforced by the preference of many influential aid advocates and administrators for governments trying to run closely controlled economies.
>
> (Bauer, 1984, 56)

In India, with net aid (see Chapter 1) at less than 2 per cent of GNP, this attributes too much importance to aid donors. Also, we have seen above that India's 'control syndrome' had indigenous historical roots, largely independent of aid. The high water mark of hostility to an independent private sector, and of sympathy for certain aspects of the USSR's growth strategy pre-dated the large-scale influx of foreign aid, which began only after the foreign-exchange crisis of 1957–8. Hence the upsurge of aid did not bring to the fore a government with strong reservations about the market system. Such a government had been in place for ten years. At most, aid helped to sustain this government as its attitudes to the role of private enterprise in the mixed economy became increasingly pragmatic in the 1960s under Nehru's successors, Lal Bahadur Shastri and Indira Gandhi.

The other lesson is that 'a closely controlled economy' is not the same as an economy with many controls. India has always been an example of the latter; but its many controls are not rationally co-ordinated, and thus cannot be used for 'close control' of the trajectory of economic development. (Bauer made this very point in his 1959 observations with which this chapter begins.) Thus, if it were true that aid advocates and administrators as a group favoured governments running 'closely controlled' economies, this would hardly have led them to direct more aid to India. Its numerous controls certainly did not permit close control by government even compared with other mixed-economy developing countries, such as South Korea – partly because of the size, dispersion, and non-regulable *internal* competition of India's democratic, federal, vast, sprawling, dynamic, and deeply private economy.

Bauer attributes to aid India's (rather ineffective) hostility to the market system. This attribution rests on the statement that official development assistance 'goes directly to governments'. So it does by definition, but only in the first instance. At the second stage, the GoI transfers most resources received to other agencies. They may be in the private sector, the public sector or in a mixed or intermediate sector, containing joint ventures of public and private capital. Thus it is crucial to consider the distribution of ODA in its 'final uses' between these different sectors.

Up to the end of the Third Plan (1966), most aid was used in the public sector (Table 7.1). Taking loans and grants together, just over 57 per cent of aid was directed to the public sector up to 1966, while just over 12 per cent went to the private sector. The remaining 30 per cent went either to mixed public/private ventures or to unallocable items.

Within this overall picture, certain donors directed a larger proportion of their aid towards the private sector. The private sector received 38 per cent of World Bank loans. Of this, 17 per cent was allocated to steel plants of ISICO and TISCO, 14 per cent via the Industrial Credit and Investment Corporation of India (ICICI) and the remaining 7 per cent to coal and thermal power generation. The public-sector beneficiaries of World Bank loans were (in order of importance) the railways, electricity generation and transmission, ports, agriculture and civil aviation (Lok Sabha Secretariat, 1967, 78–9). Except perhaps for the last three sectors – totalling below 8 per cent of World Bank aid up to 1966 – its lending to India conformed to the line of division between public and private sectors which typifies western mixed economies. This trivial deviation from the presumed norm occurred when the government-led planned industrialization drive was at its height!

Table 7.1 Public/private-sector shares in foreign loans and grants to India up to 1966

Loans	Rupees (Crores)	%
Public sector	1,487.69	54
Private sector	338.83	12
Mixed	757.95	27
Cash credits/refinance credits	190.81	7
Total	2,775.28	100
Grants		
Public sector	295.78	88
Private sector	42.19	12
Total	337.97	100

Source Lok Sabha Secretariat (1967) 26.

Thus, although clearly the public sector was the dominant beneficiary of aid to India until the mid-1960s in terms of final uses, World Bank loans did not close off investment opportunities for the private sector by financing public activity in areas which on western norms are 'normally', or 'should be', the exclusive preserve of private capital. The record of the bilateral donors is different; they directed less than 12 per cent of their aid to the private sector. At this period, several bilateral donors – the UK, West Germany, and the USSR – were competing for international prestige and the Indian Government's gratitude by building huge showpiece steel mills in the public sector: respectively Durgapur, Rourkela and Bokaro. Meanwhile US bilateral aid increasingly came as PL 480 food aid, which – while arbitrarily assigned to the public sector (because foodgrains were released through publicly organized ration shops) generated resources mainly for private households – then mainly urban food consumers – who bought from the ration shops at administered prices below the free market price. The sales revenues of the ration shops were credited to the central government budget, and the profits of private foodgrain producers and traders were lowered by the competition of the ration shops. It was thus the activities of bilateral donors in the steel-making and foodgrain sectors which give most support to the argument that aid closed off opportunities that would otherwise be available to the private sector. Yet public-sector steel-making (while inefficient) probably benefited the private sector on balance; and food aid transferred resources largely to India private consumers, albeit partly at the cost of private farmers and traders.

Even where aid does 'crowd out' private investment, that is not the full story of its effect on the private sector. The interdependences between private-sector and public-sector activities are numerous. One convenient way to analyse many of them is through the price system:

> The transfer of aid money raises the price of some goods, depresses the price of some others, and hence has side-effects on the private sector of the recipient economy through the price system.
>
> (Mosley, Hudson and Horrell, 1987, 617)

The point applies *mutatis mutandis* to aid which goes to final uses in the private sector: as a result there will be side-effects through the price system on the public sector. Neither of these symmetrical indirect effects of aid has been much investigated, but in India one can make an educated guess.

Some 80 per cent of the cumulative investment in public enterprises producing goods and services was, until 1985, directed to four major industrial sectors: in order of importance, metals and minerals, steel, chemicals and pharmaceuticals, and petroleum. There has been chronic under-pricing of most products of the first three sectors, resulting in the chronic and continuing low profitability of many public enterprises (World Bank, 1986, 117–24). Thus public-sector production of steel and fertilizer facilitated by aid (mostly bilateral) has been sold by GoI, for policy reasons, well below the free market price; hence public-sector returns on assets at replacement cost has been low, or (with steel) negative. 'Aid to public-sector production' has been aid to transfer government resources to the private sector, not to diminish that sector.[5]

To deal with the resultant problem of excess demand, GoI has used various formal and informal methods of quantitative allocation. Private sector consumers, whether they are engineering or construction companies or individual farmers, have benefited from the depressed prices of steel and fertilizer when they have been able to secure an allocation. Yet such a system frustrates the demand of some potential private-sector users, and encourages wasteful use of the commodities (through excessive stockpiling and absence of cost pressures for economies) by those consumers who do secure access. Thus, at the sector level, the private sector benefits from the continuous transfer of resources implied by loss-making aided public enterprises – alleged 'socializing' aid raises the private corporate share of GNP. But the process is not efficient; the public enterprises are heavily protected and can thus persist in absorbing inputs (and raising their prices to private firms above world-market, albeit not Indian-market, levels) owing to a pricing system which is not aligned with microeconomic rationality.

It has often been remarked that the big Indian steel plants had negligible spread effects on economic activity in their vicinity: they failed to become growth centres. This implies that their impact on local input prices may have been quite severe. They provided an expensive output for which there was no local demand, and, in doing so, competed away local resources – building materials, skilled labour – which were scarce and becoming scarcer. Thus – although, even without aid, the GoI would probably have financed these steel mills (in the cause of long-term development, increased savings ratios, and national security) – 'steel aid' and its like did, in some respects, fit into a context of allocatively inefficient public policy. However, that is not because 'aid to public enterprises' raised the public sector's share of resources in India; most aid, by supporting public enterprises that made subnormal profits (or losses) through subsidizing the private sector, did the opposite, especially the 1970s and 1980s. Then, aid increasingly supported low-interest rural credit and industrial bank lending to private firms. This may well have raised public-sector patronage, but it raised the *private* sector's share of resources, though it was not big enough to make an enormous difference either way.

Aid and the private sector: recent policy changes

Since the early 1970s, many converging pressures have introduced significant changes in the relation between aid and the private sector in India. These pressures include the failure of aid to recover its Third Plan peak (in real dollar value) and thus the reduction of its macroeconomic effects on the Indian economy (see Chapter 1). In addition – within this smaller overall contribution – sector aid, aid for transfers to a wide range of recipients (via NABARD/ARDC and industrial banks), and programme aid have become a much larger element than in the 1950s and 1960s, when project aid (and food aid) were predominant. Such multi-purpose aid – especially programme aid (general budgetary support) – cannot, unlike project aid, be analysed for its final uses via indirect price effects. Also, this general support has been given to an economic strategy which changed somewhat in the late 1960s and 1970s. It became more pragmatic and more diversified. The initial strong concentration on industrialization, particularly in the heavy engineering and capital goods sectors, has been softened, with some rise in the shares of public-sector outlay going to agriculture and consumption goods. At the same time, the reservation of certain industries for the public sector has been abandoned. The result of all these changes has been that criticisms of aid for 'crowding out' private investment and raising key input prices for private sector enterprises have lost even the limited force which they had earlier.[6]

In the early 1980s, conservative administrations increasingly influenced aid policy in several major donor countries (USA, UK, West Germany) and through them in multilateral agencies such as the World Bank. Ironically, just when concern for the effects of aid on the private sector had a smaller objective basis in India than ever before, it received a strong ideological and political boost among major donors. Perhaps the clearest response is to be seen in the policies of USAID – just beginning in 1979–83 to re-expand aid to India after the long cut-off after the 1971 Indo-Pakistani hostilities. USAID – although concentrating on irrigation, health care, and social forestry (where public sector involvement seems more defensible than in, say, manufacturing) – has sought projects and programmes that permit private-sector participation when that appears to be appropriate or cost-effective. Also in 1982, USAID commissioned a special study of the possibilities of using aid for the development of the private sector *per se* (USAID, 1982). In the wake of its recommendations, USAID channelled funds into both agribusiness and small and medium scale private industry. This programme was intended to link back into USAID work in irrigation, health and forestry in a variety of ways. The agribusiness-forestry link was through the establishment of private firms to process forest products. The industry-health link was through the encouragement of a more favourable policy environment for contraceptives produced by private companies (USAID, 1983, 8–13).

These developments in India are in line with USAID's higher profile stance on the private sector's role in development worldwide (USAID, 1982). In 1985, USAID officials were told by the US Administration that developing countries' governments had to rely on the market mechanism as the principal determinant of their economic decisions 'to the maximum extent practical' (Toye 1987, 92). Apart from the choice of private enterprise as a major arena of effort in its own right,[7] USAID identified an important role for private initiatives in the field of technology creation, transfer and adaptation. It sought to facilitate these processes through the dissemination of information and the provision of seed money for associations of small enterprises which, because of their small resource bases cannot meet the threshold costs of engaging in technology transfer and which therefore tend to get excluded from it (Cooper, 1984, 22).

These policy concerns were seen also, though less starkly, in the thinking of the UK's ODA. A thoughtful contribution to its 1982 review identified five main 'current development issues', of which three bear directly on the public-private sector debate. Ireton (1982, 49) argued that the aims of checking population growth, reducing poverty and expanding employment

> can only be achieved by setting an environment in which market forces can operate effectively.... Much of this has to do with 'getting prices right', to encourage agricultural production, particularly of domestic foodstuffs, to develop industry more on the basis of a labour-intensive and export-oriented strategy and to generally stimulate domestic entrepreneurial activity and employment creation.

The UK approach to implementing this in India has been project-by-project, without major new initiatives in the bilateral programme. Its main recent structural re-orientation towards the private sector is via increased aid to finance rural credit - an interesting contrast to USAID, which has turned against aid for rural credit in the course of its re-orientation towards the private sector.[8] Apart from this shift to private-sector recipients, UK aid to India has increasingly been passed through non-governmental channels: private charities (through a joint funding scheme), volunteer agencies (through the British Volunteer programme) and appropriate technology groups (through its support of ITDG). These diversifications are welcome, not because public-sector channels or recipients generally use aid worse than their private-sector counterparts, but because mixed strategies are preferable to pure strategies (public or private). Risk to the total programme is less; competition among aid channels may improve performance; and, from the greater range of experience, better ways of solving particular problems should emerge. Unfortunately, this diversification of UK aid to India is accompanied by its increasing diversion through schemes like ATP, to benefit the UK private sector, especially capital-goods exporters, rather than Indians (see Chapter 4); this plainly penalizes the aid channels and recipients, public or private, from which such diversion exists, since it inevitably clouds both efficiency and equity goals of aid.

The World Bank is free from direct commercial objectives; one step removed from political and ideological shifts in donor countries; and more heavily and centrally involved in the Indian economy than the bilateral donors. Hence it has taken a lower-key approach in India (though not in Africa) to the shifting of aid towards the private sector. Having been less public-sector oriented than the bilateral donors (including earlier US Administrations, which financed Bokaro), the World Bank in India is now less inclined to bang the drum for private enterprise than some bilateral donors have become. The growing share of World Bank flows to India that are on 'hard' (IBRD) terms also reduces its leverage.

The Bank's view – with which we concur – is that (since India's economic prospects depend on speedy and effective relaxation of infrastructural and other supply constraints) it matters more to relieve the control syndrome, and to improve resource use within the public sector (even within parts of it that in other economies are privately operated), than to press for privatization, or even for private-sector competition. The Bank still accepts that in India, as in many other countries, infrastructure like ports, roads, railways, and electricity comprise natural monopolies that can well be provided by the public sector; that they need to be expanded rapidly even into activities and regions where costs are not fully recoverable; and that the private sector will benefit. This is not a shibboleth, but a judgement founded on a mature consideration of alternatives.

The Bank's position on public-sector manufacturing activities in India, on the other hand, is founded on a scepticism that there is much private-sector investment that is both eager to enter this field and frustrated from doing so by the existing public-sector presence. The proposition that public capital cannot be combined with efficient management is rejected, while much intellectual effort is devoted to whether particular projects or programmes correctly combine public and private involvement (World Bank, 1983).

One early (1983) example of the Bank with two bilateral donors promoting Indian private enterprise through aid concerned the training needs of programmes to develop social forestry. The GoI initially saw this need as requiring a doubling or tripling of the government cadres in the Indian Forestry Service. The Bank, with the two bilateral donors (the US and the UK), suggested that the Forestry Department should look again at whether, instead of public provision of services, existing cadres could catalyse private participation, through schools, agricultural universities, voluntary organizations, and local communities. In view of the heavy recurrent costs implied by the direct provision option, this suggestion was well received and a reappraisal has been undertaken.

It is easier for a donor long involved in a particular sector to pursue this approach at the margin, than for donors to seek to privatize historically established areas of public-sector activity. For these, there is little alternative to continuing sectoral dialogue designed to promote policies to improve resource use. To the Bank, this means the further dismantling of *ad hoc*, poorly co-ordinated administrative controls, and the progressive replacement of the 'control syndrome' with market pricing.

Some liberalization has occurred in India. Although the system of import control by quantitative restrictions is still in place, its use has been relaxed somewhat in the interest both of raising capacity utilization in the public sector and increasing the private sector's access to imports. Also, the industrial licensing system has been relaxed to permit private sector investors access to certain industrial sectors closed to them by the Industrial Policy Resolution of 1956. More recently, administrative pricing of public sector outputs has been ended either fully or partially for some key products – steel prices were decontrolled in April 1982 and cement prices have been partially decontrolled. Other administered prices, such as those of coal and oil products, have been adjusted to bring them fairly closely into line with free-market prices. The Bank can take some comfort from these events, which may be evidence that its advocacy of measures to improve microeconomic efficiency in the Indian economy has not been ignored in recent years, although – or, perhaps, because – that advocacy has been much gentler than in 1965–80.

However, the Bank Group (and other donors) need to recall the lessons from the 1966 episode of failed liberalization, discussed in Chapters 3 and 4. In this context, the significant lesson is that liberalization both stirs up considerable political turbulence among the supporters of Indian economic nationalism, and exposes policy-makers to uncertainties which they have little previous experience of handling. If, (as after 1966 and again after recent liberalizations) aid does not surge upwards, the liberalization measures will be at best halted – as has happened in the 1987 Budget (Harriss, 1987; Manor, 1987) – and quite possibly reversed.

The 1980s – taking recessions together with faltering recoveries – have featured slow world growth; declining capital flows from rich to poor countries; chronic agricultural dumping by rich countries; acute and widespread droughts; and many threats – and some realities – of nationalistic and 'beggar-my-neighbour' trade policies by leading developed countries. The big South Asian countries have survived this period – indeed the whole post-1973 oil shock period – with far less disruption than other LDCs. Indeed, India has accelerated her growth rate. This has been achieved partially by very rapid but perhaps parasitic 'growth', with outputs measured by inputs, in public administration and defence GNP – but partially, too, by a very gradual, cautious process of *internal* liberalization. 'Inward-looking' external economic policies have been liberalized even more slowly; but such policies, inefficient in normal times, may be associated with somewhat better short-term economic performance during recessions than are freer-trading policies (Kavoussi, 1985). Also, the size of government appears to be positively correlated with short-term growth (Ram, 1986). Thus, the encouragement of faster Indian liberalization could be irresponsible unless the Bank, as informal leader of the Aid-India Consortium, can promise *and deliver* the financial support that India may have to call on to see it right through a period of transition; that 'short-term' could hardly be shorter than five years. In theory, the advocates of trade liberalization are right that relaxation of import controls is necessary for an improved export performance. But it is not also a sufficient condition when world demand is depressed, trade barriers against India's exports are proliferating, and marketing has to be learned and financed. Such considerations must reinforce the scepticism expressed in Chapter 1 about the view that India can be switched rapidly and dramatically to non-concessional sources of finance.

Economic and social reasoning is most exciting when it shows that certain beliefs or actions, once believed unrelated, in fact hang together. In respect of aid and the private sector, we have the duller task of discriminating: of showing that it is perfectly respectable to believe some things without believing others, and without being committed to certain, allegedly implicit, pieces of advice or action. Consider the following propositions: (1) India's public sector is too big; (2) there are too many *ad hoc* controls over the Indian private sector; (3) more aid tends to make India's public sector undesirably bigger; (4) more aid tends to worsen the 'control syndrome'; (5) switching aid towards private-sector channels and recipients in India desirably shrinks the public sector; (6) this switch reduces the 'control syndrome'; and (7) aid to India is sufficient for major effects, upon the lines of propositions (3) through to (6), via changes in the volume or use. Our main intention in this chapter is not to pass judgement on these propositions, though we are quite prepared to do so on the limited evidence available. Our main intention is to assert that the seven propositions, when they are asserted and when they are denied, do not create a neat pair of packages: one set Manchester-liberal and free market, the other set radical-liberal and pro-planning. The reader should now feel free to assent to any of the seven above propositions, while accepting, or rejecting, any of the others. If that degree of intellectual flexibility can be achieved, the present authors will be well satisfied. They accept proposition (2) and perhaps (6), and reject the other five, although (7) was probably true in the early 1960s.

References

Bauer, P.T. (1959) *United States Aid and Indian Economic Development*, Washington DC, American Enterprise Association.

Bauer, P.T. (1984) *Reality and Rhetoric: Studies in the Economics of Development*, London, Weidenfeld/Nicolson

Bhagwati, J. and Desai, P. (1970) *India: Planning for Industrialization and Trade Policy Since 1951*, New York, Oxford University Press.

Bhagwati, J. and Srinivasan, T.N. (1975) *India*, New York, Columbia University Press.

Cooper, C. (1984) *Technical Co-operation between South Asian and European Industry: the Case of India*, Brussels, Centre for European Policy Studies.

Government of India (1952) *First Five Year Plan*, New Delhi, Planning Commission.

Gregory, T. (1961) *India on the Eve of the Third Five Year Plan*, Calcutta, Thacker, Spink and Co. for the Associated Chambers of Commerce of India.

Harriss, J. (1987) 'The state in retreat? Why has India experienced such half-hearted liberalization in the 1980s?', *IDS Bulletin* 18:4, October.

Hazari, R.K. (1967) *Industrial Planning and Licensing Policy: Final Report*, New Delhi, GoI, Planning Commission.

Hiro, D. (1976) *Inside India Today*, London and Henley, Routledge/Kegan Paul.

Ireton, B. (1982) 'A review of development theory and practice', *British Overseas Aid 1982*, London, Overseas Development Administration.

Kavoussi, R.M. (1985) 'International trade and economic development: the recent experience of developing countries', *Journal of Developing Areas*, 9: 3, April.

Kidron, M. (1965) *Foreign Investments in India*, Oxford, Oxford University Press.

Krueger, A.O. (1974) 'The political economy of the rent-seeking society', *American Economic Review*, 64:3, June.

Lewis, J.P. (1962) *Quiet Crisis in India*, Washington DC, Brookings Institution.

Lipton, M. and Fern, J. (1975) *The Erosion of a Relationship: India and Britain since 1960*, London, Oxford University Press for the Royal Institute of International Affairs.

Little, I.M.D. (1982) *Economic Development: Theory, Policy and International Relations*, New York, Basic Books Inc.

Lok Sabha Secretariat (1967) *Estimates Committee (1967-68) 11th Report (4th Lok Sabha): Ministry of Finance Utilization of External Assistance*, New Delhi, GoI Press.

Mahalanobis, P.C. (1955) 'The approach of operational research to planning in India', *Sankhya*, vol. 16, December.

Manor, J. (1987) 'Tried, then abandoned: economic liberalization in India', *IDS Bulletin*, 18: 4, October.

Mosley, P., Hudson, J. and Horrell, S. (1987) 'Aid, the public sector and the market in less developed countries', *Economic Journal*, 387: 97, September.

Myrdal, G. (1968) *Asian Drama: an Enquiry into the Poverty of Nations*, 3 vols, Harmondsworth, Pelican.

Nath, A. (1983) *'Evaluation of measures against industrial monopoly in India'*, University of Wales MSc dissertation (unpublished).

Nurkse, R. (1953) *Problems of Capital Formation in Underdeveloped Countries*, Oxford, Oxford University Press; (also published to include 'Patterns of Trade and Development in 1967', same publisher).

Ram, R. (1986) 'Government size and economic growth: a new framework and some evidence from time-series data', *American Economic Review*, 76: 1, March.

Riddell, R.C. (1987) *Foreign Aid Reconsidered*, Baltimore and London, Johns Hopkins University Press and James Currey for the Overseas Development Institute (London).

Roy, S. (1984) *Pricing, Planning and Politics: a Study of Economic Distortions in India*, London, Institute of Economic Affairs, Occasional Paper 69.

Rubin, B. (1985) 'Economic liberalization and the Indian state', *Third World Quarterly*, 17: 4.

Shenoy, B.R. (1963) *Indian Planning and Economic Development*, Bombay, Asia.

Shenoy, B.R. (1968) *Indian Economic Policy*, New York, Humanities Press.

Thornton, D. and Associates, (1987) *Credit for Rural Development in Southern Tamil Nadu*, (4 mimeo vols), Reading (UK) and Madurai (India).

Toye, J. (1987) *Dilemmas of Development*, Basil Blackwell, Oxford.

USAID (1982) *Private Enterprise Development*, Washington DC.

USAID (1983) *Country Development Strategy Statement: India FY 1985*, Washington DC.

World Bank (1983) *Economic Development and the Private Sector*, Washington DC.

World Bank (1984) *Situation and Prospects of the Indian Economy – a Medium Term Perspective* (3 vols), Report 4962-IN, Washington DC.

World Bank (1986) *India: Economic Situation and Development Prospects* (2 vols), Report 609U-N, Washington DC.

Appendix

Conclusions of the India Aid Effectiveness Study[+]

India's thirty-year encounter with aid and aid agencies makes her experience particularly rich for those in search of lessons on aid effectiveness. Although aid flows have always been small, measured per head of population and as a share in national income, they have made some clear positive contributions to India's economy and society. There have been also mistaken and even wasteful uses of aid; but a learning process in aid management has taken place, and many of the early errors are most unlikely ever to be repeated. India's aid performance is now significantly better than many other aid recipients, a fact which, ironically is now being used as an argument to support switching her away from concessional finance. Such a view is most questionable.

In recent years, aid has financed some 8 per cent of Indian investment (20 per cent of *public* investment) and about 15 per cent of imports. These figures fall well below those of the peak period of aid inflows (1955–65). As well as the levels of aid, its economic function has changed over time. In early years, its role was largely that of relaxing macroeconomic constraints – particularly the constraint on the domestic supply of wage goods imposed by bad weather in particular years. More recently, although the harvest cycle has continued, the foreign resources position has been eased by remittances and rising export receipts. Now aid is more concerned with easing sectoral bottlenecks and policy reform at the sectoral level.

Has aid reduced India's poverty? The aid (for agricultural research, fertilizer imports and production and input diffusion mechanisms) which supported the 'green revolution' in northern wheat-growing areas seems to have had the greatest impact on poverty. This impact, made by raising the level and stability of basic food supply, was marred in some areas by the accompanying dispossession of poor tenants and their conversion to landless labourers. Food aid itself had a similar overall positive impact, despite its early (but avoidable) adverse side-effects on domestic food prices. There is no doubt that, in the diffusion of key

[+] Extracted from Robert Cassen (1986) *Does Aid Work?*, 335–8

252

inputs (rural credit, irrigation water), better-off farmers have been successful in claiming the lion's share from aided schemes. They have tended to benefit most with regard to production, employment, and income. Recently, aid for irrigation has found ways of reaching the poor; but the gains to the rural poor generally have been mainly in terms of extra consumption, or prevention of consumption losses which would otherwise have occurred. But a number of poverty-oriented aid schemes have been implemented successfully, and more could be if the donors supported more actively the anti-poverty programmes mounted by the government.

Many aided schemes are for infrastructure, and the question of who benefits from them is rarely easy to answer but, sadly, even more rarely asked. The other main arena for aid is the 'human resources' sector. Here it is easier to identify success – urban slum upgrading, rural primary health care, and (at last, after many early disappointments) family planning and nutritional assistance. More aid should now be invested in these success areas, and in extending the scope of labour-intensive appropriate technology in both agriculture and industry. In agriculture, more donor support for integrated rural development programmes is recommended, subject to the lessons of past difficulties.

In developing a sensible donor-recipient policy dialogue, India underwent a long series of conflicts related to donors' attempts at macroeconomic aid leverage, especially in the period 1965–71. Since the mid-1970s, under the World Bank's leadership, policy discussions have focused on sectoral rather than macroeconomic issues, and the Indian Government has had no difficulty in making sectoral dialogue genuinely two-sided. But obviously its good effects – in supporting trade liberalization, for example – are conditional on continuing concessional flows.

The aid process in India is much more orderly than in other countries. Control of aid receipts is centralized in one department of government, investment planning takes account of anticipated aid receipts, and considerable experience has been built up in the field of international price comparisons. Procedural problems have been different for different types of aid. For multilateral aid, they have centred on international tendering, the payment of local costs, and long delays in the project cycle. For bilateral aid, tying has been the major issue. Discernible progress has, however, been made in ameliorating all of these problems, except project delays and bilateral tying, where 'invisible tying' and 'triple tying' have noticeably surfaced of late. Some further procedural benefits might result from a joint donors' mission to India, giving better co-ordination and better specialist input to sectoral policy dialogue.

Some sixty evaluations of project aid to India have been examined.

But many lack baseline data, calculated rates of return, and a focus on distribution. World Bank projects show good returns, which would have been much better had major delays not occurred. More recent Bank projects show better results than earlier ones, though more focus is still needed on employment/poverty aspects. In many evaluated projects, weaknesses were evident at the appraisal stage. Fuller consideration of alternative projects and alternative (less complex and capital-intensive) designs of the same project are needed. Specific faults can be identified in rural credit projects, especially in the use of such credit for tractor purchases. But more general lessons about the organizational form of successful projects are hard to come by, because some of the successes have used methods that may be unique to their circumstances and that have failed elsewhere. One clear lesson was the need for more and more rigorous project evaluations, especially those which make proper use of baseline data.

Aid to India for TC has been relatively modest (because of India's own very large stock of skilled and trained people), but highly significant in one sector – the development of agricultural research institutes (see above). Other aided TC initiatives in the areas of development, banking, fertilizer, irrigation management, agricultural extension, and the Indian Institutes of Technology have been more recent and varied in their results. Some anxiety has been expressed that donors have not looked sufficiently critically at the conditions for the replication of successful pilot projects, and that agencies' desires to disburse funds rapidly may be connected with this insufficiently critical approach.

TC for training of Indian personnel also has not undergone a sufficiently critical evaluation, and donors' comparative advantages in training, as well as the full range of India's training needs, have not been properly addressed. India still has large needs in low-level and particularly rural skills. TC for training should probably be tied much more closely to the development of sectoral aid programmes, which are themselves now much more rurally focused. USAID is moving in this direction, and other agencies might do well to emulate it.

India's is an economy with many government controls superimposed on the working of market forces. These controls largely pre-date the setting up of the Aid-India Consortium, and Consortium influence through the policy dialogue has consistently been in favour of greater liberalization. The Indian Government is now more willing to proceed with the relaxation of controls, many of which had, in any case, failed to serve the purpose for which they were originally intended. There is some evidence of possible 'crowding out' by aid of private investment in the 1960s. The effect from multilateral aid was certainly small, the effect from bilateral donors (particularly the classic cases of public sector steel mills) somewhat greater. The changing levels and composition of aid made these effects negligible in the 1970s. Nevertheless, bilateral donors particularly have taken a strong pro-private sector stance for aid in the 1980s; but this in turn brings new contradictions of policy that need resolution.

The multilateral agencies have followed a less fickle approach to the public/private sector question than the bilateral donors. They have maintained a consistent concern for the expansion of infrastructure through efficient forms of organization – regardless of the public/private division. They have coupled this with the view that any form of organization will perform better the more existing controls on trade, investment, and prices are relaxed. This pragmatic approach is hard to fault; but is should be remembered that, for liberalization to succeed, appropriate support through concessional flows must be given. And India, like many developing countries, would embrace trade liberalization more enthusiastically if it could count on liberalization in its industrial country markets.

India's experience of aid, stretching back three decades, is believed to contain useful lessons for aid to other countries today. Many problems now arising in aid to the poorest countries have already been met in India and India's aid history – in aid management, agricultural research, rural credit, sectoral policies, poverty-oriented schemes, and many other areas. Further study from this angle would no doubt prove fruitful.

Notes

Chapter 1
India's Aid Resources in Macroeconomic Context

1. 'Net' here means 'minus capital repayments of past aid loans' (if interest on such loans is also deducted, the term 'net transfers' is used). 'Aid' means disbursements of government-to-government grants, and concessional loans with a 'grant element', viz interest-rate concessions (with value discounted at 10 per cent) – of at least 25 per cent. Such aid can flow directly or via multilateral agencies, of which much the largest (especially for India) is the 'aid window' of the World Bank, the IDA; (the 'hard window' of the World Bank is IBRD whose loans have a grant element well below 25 per cent).

2. For example, in the 1950s and early 1960s half of South Korean government revenue came from the USA, while foreign capital (little of which was then direct investment) as a proportion of total investment varied between 42 and 65 per cent. In Taiwan US aid financed 34 per cent of gross investment between 1951 and 1965, and a much higher percentage of infrastructural investment (Hamilton, 1983, 53–4). In 1979 in sub-Saharan African countries, aid on average was 3.5 per cent of GNP and 20.7 per cent of gross domestic investment. While the latter ratio was attained by India in the late 1960s, the figures for low-income African countries around 1979 were 7.8 per cent of GNP and 50.0 per cent of gross domestic investment (World Bank, 1981a, table 22, 164).

3. These figures include a small, but unspecified, amount of assistance at grant levels below the 25 per cent limit.

4. The difficulties had several contributory causes. A major one was drought, leading to domestic production shortfalls in foodgrains. The making good of the shortfalls by grain imports was mistimed and India ended up buying dear. The 1971 Bangladesh refugees had to be financed from the government budget, leading to spiralling public expenditure and consequent monetary growth. Inflation was accelerating and the government's nationalization experiment with the foodgrain trade did not help matters (Joshi and Little, 1986, 13–14). Above all there was the first large increase in the price of imported oil, on which India depended quite heavily for her energy needs.

5. An exceptionally severe drought caused agricultural production to contract

by 15 per cent in a single year. The loss of domestic foodgrains output swelled the import bill and stoked up domestic inflation, despite the availability of substantial stocks. The balance of payments was thus doubly afflicted. Before it had begun to recover from the second substantial increase in the price of oil in 1979, the burden of drought-induced foodgrain imports was added to the deficit. The net deficit on current account was US$0.9bn in 1979–80, but trebled to US$2.8bn in 1980–1 and was projected to rise even higher in subsequent years.

6. These credits do not constitute aid and have therefore been excluded from the loan figures in Table 1.3.

7. If the composition and relative prices of Indian exports were both changing substantially, the choice of base year could greatly affect the apparent changes even in 'real' purchasing-power of aid: the so-called index-number problem.

8. In any year, on expenditure account, $Y = C + S + M$: national income is used up in : consumption of domestic products; savings; and imports. On output account, $Y = C + I + X$: national income is (paid out for) production of: consumption-goods for domestic use; investment-goods for domestic use; and exports. Therefore $I = S + (M - X)$.

9. Such data focus on breakdowns into the four broad divisions of the national accounts: households, the private corporate sector, the government/public sector, and the rest of the world. Moreover, figures of the contribution of saving from foreigners or the rest of the world do not include only net aid flows. They will also include net private investment, and official inflows that are non-concessional in character (or less concessional than aid; see fn.1).

10. ROW savings include net aid, net non-aid inflows, and net reduction in India's reserves of foreign exchange.

11. That is, on the part of private saving that comprised lending (to private-sector or public-sector borrowers), out of private disposable income neither consumed nor directly invested in the household's own enterprise (e.g. in the family firm).

12. Not all aid is directly used for public expenditure (e.g. aid to rural credit), nor for investment (e.g. food aid). However, it is useful to examine the ratios of aid to these items. It can contribute to them, not only directly, but by releasing government domestic resources for public investment (or public development outlays) that would otherwise have gone to procure food commercially, to lend to farmers.

13. Military and police, inventory-building, maintenance and replacement, etc. – all considerably larger proportions of public investment now than in the Third Plan period.

14. Assuming, for a moment, that 'growth', 'economic performance', and 'development' are co-terminous.

15. Thus Mosley (1987, 132–4), by holding the growth of adult literacy constant in his cross-section analysis of the impact on growth, would under-estimate that impact if aid increased literacy (e.g. by permitting more schoolbuilding) which in turn increased growth rates (for evidence that it does, see World Bank, 1980).

16. This acceleration was maintained in 1986, but badly dented by the 1987 drought.

17. Mosley (1987) makes a brave attempt to relate aid to lagged growth, following the assumptions of the World Bank about the speed with which typical aid-financed projects came onstream. However, there is no reason to assume that such assumptions correctly reflect the lag structure of Indian project aid in all periods; before the late 1970s, much aid to India was not in project form; and extra resources, made available (or freed) by aid, influence growth in other ways than by the yield of the investment in which they are embodied.

18. Agriculture-linked hired employment is thus increasingly the main income source for India's poorest. Growth apart, it is not easy to see how they can live unless agriculture expands. If so, poverty alleviation may require some sacrifice of comparative advantage – some 'over-expansion' of labour-intensive farming in India.

19. The rising ICOR – throughout the Indian economy and in most sub-sectors – may simply reflect the fact that easier investment chances are taken up first. But this is unlikely to be the whole story, since most LDCs have shown ICORs rising much more slowly, if at all. Does India's performance reflect the merits of public versus private ownership, the quality of management in Indian industry, or the effect of social and political pressure?

20. Latest data from the Sample Registration Survey confirm other evidence that total fertility has fallen from six to four children per woman in the past twenty years (T. Dyson, personal commentary 1987). The temporary upturn in population growth in 1976–85 (Table 1.12) was due entirely to the younger population (with greater population momentum produced by a larger proportion of women of childbearing age) in the wake of falling infant and child mortality in 1950–70.

21. For smooth flows of food aid – which increase government resources by their sale, and/or by reducing the need for commercial purchases to replenish stocks, by the Food Corporation of India – this exclusion is questionable. For extra food aid in droughts, it makes sense, but so would the exclusion of other emergency aid (correcting an exogenous reduction in public investment capacity, rather than increasing it), if it were identifiable.

22. For a detailed examination of the risks of commercial borrowing, see Anagol (1987).

23. Intelligent investment of short-term (e.g. seasonal) peaks in foreign-exchange reserves can, to some extent, offset these uncertainties.

24. This does not of course mean that a 100 per cent grant is infinitely more valuable than a loan; the value depends on the return to the asset which the moneys finance.

25. This could be termed the 'Zambia sequence'. in the light of that country's experiences from mid-1968 through mid-1987.

26. 1985 data (latest available year).

Chapter 2
Aid and Poverty in India

1. Aid for industry substantially financed extra output of fertilizers and other farm inputs; and of steel to make fertilizer equipment; and so on. These products do, of course, grow food in ways that employ many poor labourers. However, such products could be imported, and the aid channelled directly to poor rural people's activities directly. Aid to replace capital-intensive urea imports by domestic production urea *may* be efficient and good for growth – but it is not as a rule poverty-focused.

2. In the main food-aid period, most of this balance would probably not otherwise have been imported commercially, so that it represents genuine extra consumption.

3. The main source of EEC capital aid, the European Development Fund, is largely confined to asociates – ACP (African, Caribbean, and Pacific) LDCs, signatories to the Lomé Convention. Thanks to 'Operation Flood', however, India is now the biggest recipient of total EEC aid.

4. This may now be in process of remedy by a major study at the World Bank, directed by Dr Knudsen.

5. World Bank data during 1973–81 show a steady rise in the proportion of Bank and IDA flows only for (a) agriculture; (b) within agriculture, for cereal production; and (c) within cereals, for smallholders.

6. In India, itself supported by considerable aid, e.g. from USAID to agricultural universities.

7. Paddy intensification (at Indian yields) appears to show a 30 to 40 per cent rise in labour use for each 100 per cent rise in yield (Ishikawa, 1978, 70). Conversion from traditional to high-yielding varieties raised man-days per hectare by 32 per cent for wheat in Rajasthan, and 17 per cent for rice in Orissa (ADB, 1976, 60). These labour effects have fallen since the mid-1970s (Jayasuriya and Shand, 1986).

8. It has been claimed that, if the farmer is both to exploit double-cropping with short-duration varieties and to harvest their high yields, he must accelerate – and hence mechanize – ploughing, threshing, or both. Empirical work, however, suggests little or no relationship between such mechanization and double-cropping, given the degree and type of irrigation (Agarwal, 1980; IRRI/ADO, 1983).

9. However, a higher coefficient of variation does not mean greater risk if – thanks to higher yields – output improves even in bad years (though proportionately less than in good years). Also, appropriate trade and stock policies could transfer risks from Indian consumers to world markets to some extent.

10. A commentator (T.N. Srinivasan, the well-known Indian economist currently at Yale University) rightly remarks that this applies in general, not just to HYVs. Farm innovations that cut food prices (a) help poor consumers but (b) create disincentives to second-generation innovators. If prices are kept up, food buyers – and it is the poor who spend the biggest share of income – lose. If prices are allowed to fall, incentives to food production – which is the main employment source for the poor – decline. Only growth –

exceeding the increase in the poor population – in non-farm assets or jobs for the poor can resolve the dilemma.

11. Especially when governments (in effect) printed the money to allow central lending agencies to avoid bankruptcies, inflation was further increased by the process of default.

12. Even with no overt subsidy, a greater supply of rural production credit reduces farmers' interest rates – helping bigger farmers more, because they borrow a larger proportion of their total costs or incomes.

13. The extent to which this has happened in the case of World Bank-supported rural credit projects is revealed in OED (1981), which however does not assess the poverty impact of the credit support (or of tractors). It seems to accept the claims that tractors significantly raise output, are needed to make full use of 'green revolution' inputs, and show satisfactory economic rates of return. For convincing evidence against the latter claims, see Agarwal, 1980; IRRI/ADC, 1983; and Binswanger, 1978.

14. One can complain either that farm credit is fungible by farmers and thus need not be used as envisaged by planners; or that farm credit is tied to specific uses and thus impedes farmers' free choice of how to use their resources; but not both. Fungibility, where applicable, should be welcomed by supporters of private-enterprise routes to agricultural development.

15. Either as hired labour (to apply the fertilizers, well water, etc.), or because very small farmers divert time from the hired-labour market to managing the extra inputs on their own farms, and thereby free up casual farmwork for landless hired labourers.

16. Labour intensity is not now among the criteria for selecting extension priorities in India. As HYVs spread, selection and encouragement of profitable labour-using methods needs more extension emphasis with farmers wanting to save on all costs, including labour costs.

17. These have nothing to do with the GoI's 'integrated rural development programme' (IRDP), which seeks to get specific small assets to poor households.

18. The term is due to the EEC's former commissioner for aid and development, M. Pisani. The problems of specific 'island projects' are considered in Chapter 5.

19. Only since 1975, with hybrid sorghum, have cereal MVs raised yields significantly in rain-fed areas – although robustness has been significantly improved there, e.g. by IR-20 rice. Extra credit and extension are needed, unless the effect of MVs on profitability is unusually large and safe.

20. Seldom enough to keep up with the rate of growth of workforce, if the yield increase is achieved over a ten-year period (Jayasuriya and Shand, 1986).

21. 'Big' farmers overlap very badly with 'rich' farm households, because larger landholdings are associated with larger households, inferior land, and less off-farm income. Certainly the top quintile of households in a village, by area farmed per household, tends to be considerably better-off than the bottom quintile. But the tendency is weak and imperfect (Lipton with Longhurst, 1989), especially in badly-watered areas (Lipton, 1985).

22. Only the first-generation releases of HYV rice were objectively riskier than traditional varieties.

23. Partly because of concealed subsidy to such inputs (or credit or fuel to obtain them); partly because 'MV-enriched' middle farmers now have cash to afford the inputs, which were (or seemed) less attractive when obtainable only on credit.

24. Especially since farm products are probably 'worth' more, and other products less, at shadow prices than at market prices – i.e. the net effect of state and monopoly power is to raise non-farm prices relative to farm prices. Even despite this, investment on the farm is associated with more output (at distorted, market prices).

25. A careless reading of Hazell and Roell (1983) might suggest the contrary. What they really show is that the proportion of local extra spending on non-farm products is higher, if initial extra income accrues to big rather than small farmers. However, small farmers spend considerably higher proportions of extra income than do small farmers; and spend a much larger part of it on extra food, i.e. extra farm products, many non-local, and in India more labour-intensive than most non-farm production.

26. At least, until rising incomes greatly reduce the marginal propensity to consume cereals.

27. Recent evidence of low short-run wage elasticity of supply of total rural labour (summarized in Aldeman and Sahn, 1987) is perfectly consistent with a high long-run wage elasticity of labour supply to a sector such as agriculture (Lipton, 1983b).

28. Aid to SSA rose from 25 per cent of official development assistance receipts in 1978 to 30 per cent in 1984 (World Bank, 1986, 220–1).

29. This oversimplifies a complex reality, as Sen (1981) explains in his discussions of Ethiopia. For instance, if animals are drought-stricken, their impoverished owners, unable to sell much meat or milk, can lose income-based entitlements to the staple food (cereals or roots), although its availability in an area is increasing. However, extra food availability is more closely connected to extra entitlements for at-risk poor groups in most of SSA than in most of India.

30. We believe that these unconventional organizations, at national level, will continue to be born, to achieve very partial succes, and to be amalgamated, restructured, replaced, or ended every two to five years. This is because the reassertion of control by conventional line departments – a necessary outcome of their (desirable) strength – requires constant challenge by trans-departmental, problem-oriented approaches (e.g. to Marginal Farmers and Labourers, to Drought-prone Areas, to river watersheds or Command Areas, etc.) if poor people's multi-faceted problems are to be alleviated by state action. This, however, means that something wider than – and outlasting – 'scheme-specific' training is needed to staff anti-poverty programmes appropriately.

31. So why advocate foreign exchange to aid them? First, because they represent an injection of expenditure into the system of income generation, leading to extra imports. Second, because the programmes are constrained by tight budgets (savings, not just foreign exchange).

32. Yet the project will die, if the government cannot or will not pay recurrent costs, and the agency refuses to help. In some cases, the recipient might

agree to 'phase in' recurrent cost commitments as the project reaches fuller production levels; donors would meet some of the early recurrent costs, thus smoothing the transition.

Chapter 3
Policy Dialogue

1. For a flavour of just how easy they were, see Rao and Narain (1963) especially 36, 91–3.
2. Leverage seeking to 'help' a recipient to displace such inflows by export earnings – e.g., via threats to reduce aid even further unless a recipient devalues – can achieve its ostensible purpose, self-reliant foreign exchange management by the recipient, only if the donors' advice on how to raise export earnings is effective. This was not the case for India's 'levered' devaluation of 1966.
3. The World Bank alone hired 155 consultant-weeks of Indian institution-based expertise in its financial year 1983–4 for objective analysis of its Indian activities.
4. The ratio in 1980 was well over 50 per cent (World Bank, 1981, 164) and is today even higher.
5. Given public policy, each donor tends to 'improve' projects via project-specific conditions that divert the recipient government's skills and energy from other projects (Lipton, 1986).
6. To some extent, the need for some measure of policy agreement applies even to project aid. Good projects can be destroyed by a government policy that – good or bad – is inconsistent with their proper functioning, e.g. if low procurement prices by public-sector buying agencies deter farmers from using aid-financed agricultural investments such as tubewells. Also, if aid 'finances' a project that the recipient government would have undertaken even without aid, then the donor is in reality financing total public policy, not the stated project.
7. In Ghana in the early 1980s, agricultural price policy was so misaligned that the ratio of producers' prices of rice to cocoa was more than thirty times the ratio of world-market prices. In Zaire throughout the 1980s, government budget allocation to agriculture was well below 2 per cent of public outlays. However, in the vast majority of cases, progress in sectoral dialogue is possible because such huge distortions are absent, having proved unsustainable even without any outside leverage.
8. Based, we presume, on pre-1965 experience, and already somewhat frayed when published.
9. Another blow was dealt in 1983, when the Commission appeared to replace its former scholarly analyses of the rate of poverty alleviation by an unsustainably optimistic view (Krishna, 1983).
10. The heavy-industry priorities of the Second and Third Plans – then almost undisputed, except at the margin, either in India or by donors – required extra food sales by Indian farmers to feed urban workers. Lacking such extra sales, these workers' rising money-wages (needed to buy scarcer, dearer food) would: (i) leave their employers (including state-owned heavy

industry) with few or no reinvestible profits; and (ii) suck in food imports, denying foreign exchange to importers of industrial inputs.

11. Even if it were successful, and even if the donor's motive in giving aid were solely to revive its own depressed sectors, tied aid would be a doubtful procedure. If the donor government takes a given view of 'permissible' aggregate domestic demand (via money supply and/or fiscal policy), tied aid merely diverts such demand towards exporters not efficient enough to sell their products without it. This reduces the long-run efficiency of the donor economy.

12. It certainly reduces aid-effectiveness, but does create a lobby for aid from among its commercial beneficiaries. Thus it may be the only alternative to less bilateral aid.

13. The UK in 1969–73 ought certainly to have been conducting 'policy dialogue' with Sri Lanka on how to reduce capital intensity in new investment, and especially tractor imports, given: the surplus of tractors used in roadwork (or idle for lack of spare parts); severe and growing rural unemployment; and lack of spare cultivable land. Instead, due in part to commercial pressures, the UK sought to increase tractor aid to Sri Lanka. See Burch (1979), Farrington and Abeyratne (1982), ILO (1971).

14. Thereby reducing the likelihood that the recipient will be ready to accept conditions on aid later, because of past experience that such conditions reduce its value.

15. Furthermore, recipient political realities may rule out certain forms of donor pressure, even if they did not impinge on sovereignty. For example, one of the most careful and sensitive scholars of US aid to India has proposed that 'the US may be able to influence the Indian Government (towards) implementation and possible extension of land reforms to protect tenants'(Rosen, 1967, 263). A less promising area of bilateral intervention would be hard to imagine, because tenancy legislation, in the absence of land redistribution, is usually doomed politically (Lipton, 1974; Herring, 1983) and will be further hampered by 'foreign' advocacy. This is not at all to deny the usefulness of aid in support of well-considered land redistribution.

16. On the eve of his departure for Tashkent, USSR, to negotiate a settlement with President Ayub following the 1965 hostilities.

17. Patel (1986, 109) criticizes Indians for not seeing that the short-term failure of the 1966 devaluation did not rule out its possible long-term success.

18. IBRD funds also reach India from the World Bank group. These do not count as aid, but carry somewhat lower interest than loans from commercial banks, and thus increase the Bank group's 'leverage'.

19. The National Bank for Agriculture and Rural Development, which lends to Indian banks to support their on-lending to rural branches.

20. 'Policy dialogue' is increasingly represented to us, both by Indians and by donors, as 'leaning on an open door' – helping GoI to bear the transitional costs of generally-desired policy changes.

21. Such outcomes are discussed elsewhere. For sector-level issues (irrigation, agricultural extension), see Chapter 7; for project issues, see Chapter 5.

22. For example, some project staff, working in India, felt in 1983 that they had

to spend time and analysis to question or justify the placing of Indian electric power plant in the public sector. Yet the propriety of Bank Group support for this had never been questioned, even implicitly, by senior management.

23. One would not use such wording today; has India 'goals in the US'?

24. A leading Indian economic official, now with an international agency, told us in 1984: 'Strong ideological pressures are perceived *on* the Bank. They are beginning to affect what it says to India'. The Fund seems to be in better favour; its US$5bn standby, made available to India in 1982, was based almost entirely on the Plan and involved little or no new conditionality, in marked contrast to the experience of heavily indebted countries requiring urgent IMF relief.

25. A conspiracy-theorist might suspect that the 'up-front' statements and research positions of an extreme neo-classical, almost libertarian, nature – and the well-publicized resignations of dissident researchers, tightening of control of Bank research outlets, etc. – in 1983–6 were a deliberate camouflage, deflecting the attention of dogmatic opponents of state activity in the Reagan Administration from the rather small changes in Bank project cycles or advice.

26. In 1979–86 the IMF's *Occasional Papers* and *Staff Papers* have included sceptical, questioning analyses, from several positions, of both monetarism and the standard case-by-case approach to the management of Third World debt. In marked contrast, the 1986 *World Development Report*, on the impact of price and foreign-exchange policies on agriculture, included clear signs of dogmatism – e.g. the assertion that less interventionist farm price policies would be good for the environment! (Lipton, 1987).

27. In this context, India's unusually high incidence of distinguished academics in senior administration and government – and the familiarity of many Indian officials with an earlier, apparently more open and objective, Bank – increased the reaction against some of the styles of 1982–6.

28. Though we take the point, made to us by the chief of one donor aid agency, that 'what our elected legislators want to see is not a sophisticated discussion of fungibility (i.e. in this case, of possible reduced returns upon non-aided extension projects that shed good staff to the pilot), but a decent rate of return on the projects we pay for'.

29. For example, via the expenditures out of extra income created by the project: are they upon items produced by poor people (including employees) and in income-elastic supply? Also, does the project raise or lower output from *other* projects employing, or producing food for, the poor?

30. 'Self-help' – mainly high savings ratios – loomed large in US praise for, and aid to, India in the late 1960s (Singh, 1973, 43, 66). Now, such high ratios are seen as signs of over-high taxation and as causes of low returns to investment. In practice, of course, growth depends both on a high rate of savings and on their embodiment in efficient investment.

31. The National Bank for Agriculture and Rural Development – the 'apex agency' for lending to (state-owned) commercial banks, in support of rural and agricultural loans by their branches.

32. See the successive discussions in the Bank's *Annual Reviews of Project Performance Audits*.

33. Of course, persistently higher average repayment rates among small farmers: (i) partly represent fuller screening than for larger farmers, and may therefore not prevail at the margin when credit is expanded; (ii) reflect higher administrative costs per rupee loaned. However, we judge that expansion in share of loans to smaller farmers is usually consistent with reduction in proportion of money overdue, even given total administrative costs. Many overdues are incurred by powerful farmers who can, to some extent, evade or defy collection.

34. In the World Bank context this covers loans, with a major small-farm component, such that over half the benefits were expected to accrue to the absolute poor or to persons with income below 30 per cent of national GNP-per-head.

35. First, because India's output and net trade in several major farm products are so substantial as to affect world prices; second, because major shifts to non-farm exports by India would – apart from being so important as to effect world prices if freely permitted – incur protectionist responses; third, because the ratio of (internal and international) transport costs to production costs for farm products is high and rising; fourth and foremost, because with at least three-quarters of India's poor people involved in farming, SCBA of the sector-mix needs to include income-distribution weights.

36. They are made available to analysts in confidence, however. We have used them in this book, but have preserved confidence by concealing project-specific information.

Chapter 5
Project aid to India

1. Or all, or more than all: in some African countries, gross aid in many years exceeds gross public investment.

2. However, evaluation estimates are much better than either casual empiricism or estimates made earlier in the projects cycle. Sometimes, differences between these three assessments of how projects turned out are themselves important.

3. The widespread neglect applies *a fortiori* to the social rate, and often even to the financial rate. We use US terminology. 'Financial rate of return' (FROR) refers, in both US and UK 'language', to the return on project capital for the public or private agency operating the completed project. 'Economic rate' (EROR) in the USA also allows for external benefits (net of disbenefits) and external costs (net of external cost savings), and values commodities and inputs and shadow prices (e.g. importables and exportables at appropriately transport-adjusted border prices), sometimes with a savings premium (Little and Mirrlees, 1974); in the UK this is called the 'social rate' (SROR). In the USA, SROR means the number that is calculated by applying income-distribution weights to the internal and external costs and benefits used in calculating the EROR; this process in the UK produces what is called 'EROR with income-distribution weights'.

4. Recent rural-sector evaluations of IBRD/IDA projects do estimate numbers of beneficiaries, and occasionally the proportion who are smallholders (on

various definitions but normally below five acres) and the number of person-days of work generated. Even here, however, the proportion of project benefits accruing to the absolute poor is usually not evaluated. It is hard to see how any agency's estimates of the poverty impact of its total aid – for example those produced annually by the Bank group – are derived.

5. Thus by April 1979, 'only six [UK] projects, all relatively minor [spenders, had] been evaluated in the last four years, none a major item. The ODM and the High Commission [lack] staff to mount adequate evaluations [and] flying visits are no substitute' (*HOC*, 1979, paras 84–5). It is not only from the UK that the main evaluation effort was concentrated in 1960–80 on small and diffuse 'training' projects, to the neglect of capital projects 50–100 times as costly.

6. Since 1982, more UK resources have gone to evaluation. Most importantly, the World Bank (the most comprehensive and measurement-oriented evaluating agency), appears to have produced Indian evaluations independently of project and loan staff. Since 1982 it has increased resources for evaluation, and concentrated them on 30 to 40 per cent of projects (instead of 100 per cent as previously). This should make possible proper baseline studies, adequate control groups – and more impact studies, two to five years after project completion. Such impact studies are a strength of several recent US evaluations.

7. This could seem reasonable. Donors want aid money used to promote development and relieve need, not to pay evaluators, and EEC members such as the UK who have been highly critical of its weak evaluations have not been prepared to vote extra money to strengthen them.

8. It might be objected that SSA experience shows how often bad policy, e.g. on price incentives, can make even good projects fail, and bad ones appear better than they really are. However, the need for better policy analysis does not remove the need for project-level knowledge.

9. One of many examples is the role of these three issues in the causation of persistently unreliable and uneven water supplies which, in many Bank-aided and other irrigation projects, have reduced the area adequately served, and have led to considerable farmer reluctance to construct and maintain field channels.

10. For bilateral donors, their national self-interest – in placing personnel, selling exports, or advancing a political concern – make the task of raising such sensitive issues even harder than for the Bank. Offended local interest-groups can readily accuse the donor of modifying projects or policy conditions to support not 'rationality' but the CIA, KGB, ICI or whatever.

11. At least, the Bank Group is much less prone to commercial pressures towards undue capital-intensity than are bilateral donors, pressed for 'aid-trade links' by their under-employed domestic capital-goods sectors. Here the problem is certainly more severe, though not so fully documented (see, however, on UK tractor aid, Farrington and Abeyratne, 1982; Burch, 1980).

12. As with overuse of high-tech, this probably applies much more strongly to bilateral donors, which are under domestic pressure to use consultants in excess supply at home.

13. This is not said to attack the OED. It is courageous and highly competent. However, it must sometimes evaluate – and even do impact studies – too quickly and with too few resources for fieldwork. Also, too few studies of agricultural mechanization have absorbed the analytical lessons of Binswanger (1978), Agarwal (1980, 1984), or Farrington and Abeyratne (1982).

14. Data for distribution of operational holdings are from Naidu (1975). Of course, 'small farmer' is not co-extensive with 'poor farm-based person'. However, operated area per household may perhaps be just acceptable as a very rough-and-ready way to identify 'poor farmers' without costly and time-consuming surveys.

15. The latter need probably excludes most tenants from borrowing, in fact if not in form. This issue is not explored in the evaluation documents, but it also, on balance, reduces access to credit-linked projects for the poorest farmers in most areas.

16. These careful findings are in sharp contrast to a rather naively 'privatizing' Bank evaluation, made at about the same time, of public *vs* private groundwater development in Pakistan. Some might argue that in India the fault lay with power subsidy that encouraged private well-owners to overuse power (and groundwater). However, that policy is probably fixed – and there are also substantial subsidies in Pakistan to various private tubewell inputs, including power connections and tariffs.

17. Standard methods of calculating EROR (e.g. Little and Mirrlees, 1974) do include a 'savings premium' upon returns likelier to be saved. This is in principle incorporated in Bank ·guidelines for project appraisal and evaluation. In practice, we do not have evidence that this premium is often applied. Time and data shortages often prevent its estimation. Also, it would militate against 'poor people's projects', to the extent that richer and asset-owning beneficiaries have higher marginal propensities to save. In other words, failure to calculate 'savings premia' partly offsets the bias, in project selection, generated by failure to use income-distribution weights.

18. The review (pp. 33–6) follows the Bank in playing down consolidation and in (over-?) optimism about rotational irrigation.

19. (1) If schoolchildren who recieve school feeding (SF) thereby release food for other family members, infant nutrition or adult work capacity may benefit. (2) As primary school attendance increases, the danger of 'missing the poorest' in SF programmes decreases. Of course, it is more effective nutritionally to increase intake of the hungriest infants directly, but perhaps less cost-effective; such precise targeting may cost more than the value of the food 'saved' (i.e. not steered to the not-so-needy). The standard discussion remains Beaton and Ghasseimi, 1982. A comparison of poverty-focus and cost-effectiveness between IDA's highly targeted Tamil Nadu Integrated Nutrition project and the comprehensive, much larger and costlier, state-wide 'Chief Minister's Nutritious Meals Scheme' is very favourable to the former (Subbarao, 1987).

20. It is not clear whether this is averaged over all times, or applies only when the animal is in milk. If the latter, as seems likely, the average contribution to family income is even further below the estimated 40 to 70 per cent.

21. There is a major year-to-year fluctuation in UK gross bilateral aid to India, as Table 5.5 shows (p. 197).
22. Anybody who researches or administers any aspect of development is familiar with the recurring and longstanding problem that donor agencies seek to recruit at very short notice. This, of course, means that they tend to secure the services of experts for whose work the demand is relatively slack, and/or of consultancy firms geared to supplying apparently appropriate staff and outputs without advance planning.
23. Examples of relatively unsubjective evaluations of training from outside India appear in Robert Muscat's work, especially in Muscat (1984), and Cassen (1986).

Chapter 5
Appendix

1. IBRD, the main source of OOFs, normally lends to LDCs (and borrows) at 1 to 2 per cent less than commercial banks. Inter-governmental OOFs also often contain substantial concessional elements, though less than the very big proportions required for loans to count as official aid on OECD definitions.
2. This decline in the role of non-project aid can also be seen in the accounts of major bilateral donors. In 1970, some 30 per cent of UK bilateral aid to India (then £198m) comprised general import financing untied to sector –i.e. more or less, programme aid. By 1981 this had fallen to 13 per cent (of £143m) (Cracknell 1984, 84). By 1986, of £169m UK bilateral aid to India, £121m was programme aid (excluding a further £9m on the Aid and Trade provision) and £14m of TC (ODA, 1987, 40–1).
3. Unlike OECD's definition of aid, 'overseas development assistance', which is normally used in this report, the GoI's definition of 'external assistance' includes World Bank loans on IBRD terms. If these are excluded, the proportions change to 22 per cent and 13 per cent respectively (ES 1982–3, 144, 145) in 1982; all EEC aid counted as grants, all other multilateral aid as loans (*DC 1981, 199*).
4. Strictly speaking, it is the whole economy *with* the aid project that requires to enjoy net benefit after repaying the aid loan, as compared with the whole economy *without* the project (assuming the project is done if, and only if, the aid is advanced).
5. In 1980–1, gross domestic capital formation by central government alone (the recipient of aid) was 1.6 per cent of GDP, almost all fixed investment; government financial assistance for capital formation to the rest of the economy – almost all to state governments, local authorities, and nationalized industries – was 6.4 per cent; and other gross domestic capital formation (overwhelmingly private) was 16.0 per cent (*ES 1981–2*, 38, 73, 105). Thus, if gross project aid was financing about 6 per cent of gross investment in 1980–1, the four-fifths that stays with central government must then have been financing (4/5 of six) divided by ((6.6+1.6)/16) – or rather over one-third of public-sector project outlays. More recent comparisons are not feasible, but the proportion in 1985–6 cannot be below 20 per cent.

Chapter 6
Resource Management, Institution Building, and Technical Assistance

1. A third example of a set of institutions built up by the aid process would be elite institutes for research and training in economics and in management. As in the case of agricultural research discussed later in the text, the prime mover in this act of institution-building was the Ford foundation, rather than any official multilateral or bilateral aid agency. This is a somewhat academic distinction because the Ford Foundation activities were broadly agreed in advance with the US State Department (Rosen, 1965, 9). New economics institutions which India gained as a result included the Institute of Economic Growth in the University of Delhi and the National Council of Applied Economic Research. The Gokhale Institute of Economics and Politics in Pune, Maharashtra also benefited from a major expansion of its programmes, as did the Indian Statistical Institute, Calcutta and the Economics Department of Bombay University. In the area of management, Institutes of Management were established in Calcutta and Ahmedabad, with joint funding by the central and state governments and the Ford foundation. (For a fuller discussion, see Rosen, 1985, 88–97).
2. Nevertheless, it has been argued that the basic ideas (and faults) of the Community Development Programme of the 1950s reappeared on the policy scene in the 1970s in response to policies of redistribution with growth. (The Integrated Rural Development Programmes of the 1970s have been interpreted in this sense by Lipton, 1987).
3. In this quotation, the word 'evaluation' is probably not intended in its technical meaning in the aid lexicon as the final stage in the project cycle. It is more likely being used loosely to mean the pre-appraisal or appraisal stage of a project's life.

Chapter 7
Aid and Market Forces

1. As shown by Riddell (1987), the right-wing origins of the market critique – as of its manifestations during President Reagan's incumbency – are an intellectual accident. Many on the left, in India and the west, see aid as a source of strength for exploitative class élites. Such attacks, in their core if not in their detailed logic, come very close to the economic liberals' concern that aid may strengthen 'rent-seeking behaviour'. Krueger (1974), a leading analyst and critic of such behaviour, nevertheless sees aid as a way to help or persuade LDC governments to accept the market critique.
2. The 1945 'Bombay Plan', worked out mainly by businessmen around the Birla family and supportive of Congress's struggle for independence, exemplifies this approach. Cynics would add that larger businessmen correctly anticipated that: (a) the 'control syndrome' would be more readily manipulated by them than by their smaller rivals; and (b) they could effectively oppose unwanted legislation, partly by using their lobbying and financial power on the Congress Party.

3. This was the legislation that, in 1950–7, abolished the rights of 'intermediaries' (tax farmers) to own or control agricultural land.
4. The third option, commercial-bank borrowing by GoI, did not become important until the 1980s (see Chapter 1, pp. 20–1).
5. True, in some sectors this is an accident of the foreign-trade regime. Publicly produced urea, although sold to farmers below the equilibrium price, would have to be cheaper still (i.e. to fall even more below normal profit rates) with no restrictions on imports. But (i) this in no way refutes our statement that aid to public-sector fertilizer production raised the *private* sector's share in Indian GNP; (ii) in any case India's foreign trade regime is probably a 'given', whether it is public or large private corporate (fertilizer) production that is being protected.
6. This statement would have to be qualified if the reductions in aid somehow induced the changes in public policy. there is no evidence for this whatever. If true, it would support the Bauer school ('less aid as leverage'), against the Krueger school ('more aid as leverage'), of critics of India's control syndrome.
7. Reliance on private-enterprise production is neither necessary nor sufficient for reliance on the market mechanism, though across countries a strong correlation exists. Empirical work to associate either with better (or worse) economic development performance, especially via comparison across countries, has not so far been successful.
8. The US re-orientation is based on dislike of public-sector credit as a subsidy to not-so-poor private farmers – in marked contrast to US domestic policy. The UK view lacks clear appreciation of how the Indian rural credit chain works in practice, though ODA has sponsored research in progress (Thornton and Associates, 1987) which gives a much more favourable view of rural credit, at least in Tamil Nadu.

Index

Index

Index